The Spirituality of the Religious Educator

The Spirituality of the Religious Educator

edited by
JAMES MICHAEL LEE

Contributors

James Michael Lee
Leon McKenzie
Randolph Crump Miller
Joanmarie Smith
M. Basil Pennington
William E. Reiser
Andrew J. Sopko
Justin O'Brien

REP

Religious Education Press
Birmingham, Alabama

Library of Congress Cataloging in Publication Data
Main entry under title:

The Spirituality of the religious educator.

Includes bibliographies and index.
1. Spirituality—Addresses, essays, lectures.
2. Christian education—Addresses, essays, lectures.
I. Lee, James Michael.
BV4596.S9S68 1985   248.8'9   85-2250
ISBN 0-89135-045-4

Religious Education Press, Inc.
1531 Wellington Road
Birmingham, Alabama 35209
10 9 8 7 6 5 4 3 2

Religious Education Press publishes books exclusively in religious education and in areas closely related to religious education. It is committed to enhancing and professionalizing religious education through the publication of serious, significant, and scholarly works.

PUBLISHER TO THE PROFESSION

Contents

Introduction

When everything is said and done, the work of religious education is that of spirituality. The primary purpose of authentic religious education of every sort is to facilitate religious development in learners. This fact holds true whether religious education is done in school by a schoolteacher, on a couch or chair by a counselor, around the kitchen table by a parent, and so forth.

With all the rightful and deserved emphasis on religious education as facilitating spiritual growth in learners, what may be said about the spirituality of the religious educator during the facilitational process? How does the spirituality of the religious educator intersect religious education endeavor? What does concrete religious education activity do to the spirituality of the religious educator? What paths of spiritual growth are open to the religious educator not simply as a person but as a religious educator?

The purpose of *The Spirituality of the Religious Educator* is to focus on the religious educator's spirituality in terms of that educator's own religious education ministry rather than in terms of that individual's own personal spiritual development per se. In other words, this volume seeks to explore the ways in which religious education activity decisively affects the spiritual development of the religious educator as religious educator.

1

This volume is divided into two major parts. Each part contains four chapters. Part I examines the topic from an expressly religious education perspective. Part II treats the topic from the vantage points of major forms of spirituality. The chapters in Part I are written by religious educationists, while the chapters in Part II are authored by theologians whose specializations include one or another particular mode of spirituality.

In the opening chapter entitled "Lifework Spirituality and the Religious Educator," I situate the spiritual growth of the teacher squarely in religious education lifework itself. This chapter contends that the religious education lifework to a large extent forms the basic structure of much and in some cases of most of the religious educator's spiritual growth. Religious education activity does not only flow from the religious educator's spirituality; it also shapes and forges that individual's spirituality. Thus there is a distinctiveness in the concrete spirituality of the religious educator which makes that spirituality different from the spirituality of a person engaged in a different kind of lifework.

In the second chapter, "Developmental Spirituality and the Religious Educator," Leon McKenzie underscores the fact that spirituality takes place developmentally as a person attends to God's revelation, interprets that revelation, and responds to that revelation as God speaks in an individual's concrete existential situation. For the religious educator, such a concrete existential situation consists of the professional tasks in which the religious educator is involved. McKenzie and Lee thus agree that religious educators grow spiritually to the degree to which they fulfill their own roles as religious educators.

In the third chapter, "Process Spirituality and the Religious Educator," Randolph Crump Miller sees spirituality as basically a process, a process of coming to the full meaning of one's humanity as that humanity stands in the presence of God. Because a person works out his spirituality in processive encounters with others, the religious educator grows spiritually in the processive dialogical encounters he has with learners in religious education activity, as well as in the prayers and liturgical services which he participates in with learners directly or indirectly in the fellowship of believers. This chapter is written from a Protestant point of view.

In the fourth chapter, "Ecumenical Spirituality and the Religious Educator," Joanmarie Smith contends that by its very nature spirituality is necessarily ecumenical. Her line of argument is as follows. Faith is necessarily ecumenical because faith is nonspecific—there is no such thing, she claims, as Christian faith or Islamic faith or the like. Spirituality is faith in operation. Ergo, spirituality is perforce ecumenical; spirituality is not different from one confessional group to another. Seeking to sweep away dualism of every sort, Smith goes on to show how the everyday tasks in which religious educators engage are wonderful opportunities for spiritual growth.

There are many forms of spirituality which religious educators can use as the axis of their own spirituality as religious educators. Part II of this volume presents four of the most important, most influential, and most differentiated of these spiritual forms. Each chapter in this section highlights the major product and process contents of the form it treats, and then goes on to indicate what each form of spirituality means to the spiritual lives of religious educators as religious educators.

In the fifth chapter, "Western Contemplative Spirituality and the Religious Educator," M. Basil Pennington weaves his thesis around Thomas Merton, a liver and a doer of Western contemplative spirituality in the modern world. Using Merton as the figure and Western contemplative history as the ground, Pennington shows how Western contemplative spirituality is rooted in the deeply personal and abiding existential encounter with God which the individual has in awareness. Such an awared encounter is of practical import to religious educators since it indicates that Western contemplative spirituality is a delicious unity in oscillation between tradition and the prophetic. Pennington concludes his chapter by offering to religious educators three primary characteristics of Western contemplative spirituality, namely a spirituality which is rooted in the living bible, a spirituality which ascends from the cognitive to the existential, and a spirituality which makes heavy use of centering prayer.

In the sixth chapter, "Jesuit Spirituality and the Religious Educator," William E. Reiser highlights seven major characteristics of Jesuit spirituality and then directly interfaces these characteristics with the spirituality of the religious educator as religious educator. These seven characteristics are: the importance of critical thinking in the spiritual quest, the need to discern the movement of the Spirit in all aspects of one's daily life, a deep personal attachment to Jesus, loyalty and dedication to the church, experiencing the life of faith as companionate grace, a realization that the practice of faith includes the pursuit of justice, and the ability to find God readily in whatever circumstances one finds oneself.

In the seventh chapter, "Orthodox Spirituality and the Religious Educator," Andrew J. Sopko begins by offering some fundamental themes of Orthodox spirituality as a backdrop for exploring the spirituality of the religious educator as religious educator. These themes include the preservation of fundamental unity within the diversity of created reality, the integration of one's personal life with the person of Jesus, the replacement of the prayer of the mind with the prayer of the heart, the centrality of love, and others. Such central themes of Orthodox spirituality attain fruition in the spiritual life of the religious educator as religious educator through that educator's own faith commitment, through functioning as a spiritual director, through working in the eucharistic assembly, and in general through the ministry of service.

In the eighth and final chapter, "Eastern Spirituality and the Religious Educator," Justin O'Brien demonstrates that deep spiritual principles emanating from non-Christian quarters can significantly enrich the spiritual life of the religious educator as educator. In the Eastern perspective, spirituality is not just one dimension of life but the entire process through which a person attains the total realization of self. O'Brien shows that Eastern spirituality emphasizes the person-in-a-sacred-cosmos, the existential-in-the-essential. These are cardinal foci for the spirituality of the religious educator as educator. Through awakening self and learners to the spiritual nature and context of the universe by the practice of meditation, yoga, and harmonious living, the religious educator can achieve that transformation which is simultaneously the axis and the goal of the spiritual journey.

I would like to express my appreciation to the scholars who contributed chapters to this volume. It is our hope that this book will, in its own way, enhance the spirituality of every religious educator.

Rome, Italy   JAMES MICHAEL LEE

Part I

Religious Education Fonts

1

Lifework Spirituality and the Religious Educator

JAMES MICHAEL LEE

"We must learn to see the stars in the daytime."[1]
—Edward Lueders

The Existential Context

A person's spirituality does not take place in a vacuum independent of the individual's here-and-now life. Nor is a person's spirituality only mildly or tangentially affected by the individual's concrete life. Rather, a person's spirituality is suffusively part and parcel of the individual's here-and-now concrete life.

A person's spirituality is the way in which one mobilizes oneself religiously in the total and actual living out of one's daily activities. Spirituality is not something laminated on to one's here-and-now life. On the contrary, spirituality is organic to that here-and-now life. Psychologically and existentially, it cannot be otherwise.

Globally considered, there are two major complementary forms in which persons live out their lives. These complementary forms are lifeway and lifework. In order to understand the existential basis of

---

1. Edward Lueders, *The Clam Lake Papers* (Nashville, Tenn.: Abingdon Festival, 1977), p. 42.

7

the spirituality of the religious educator, it is necessary to understand first the nature of lifeway and lifework, and second the way in which these global patterns of human behavior dynamically intersect each other in the life of the religious educator.

Lifeway is a term designating a person's overall lifestyle pattern. For one person, lifeway might be that of a family man. For another person, lifeway might be that of an adolescent growing up and exploring the world. For a third person, lifeway might be that of a nun, and so on.

Lifework is a term designating a person's particular career or occupation. For one person, lifework might be that of a schoolteacher. For another person, lifework might be that of a politican. For a third person, lifework might be that of a medical missionary, and so on.

With the exception of the retired and the unemployed, each person is simultaneously engaged in a lifeway and a lifework. The person whose lifeway is that of a family man might be engaged in the lifework of a bookkeeper. The youth whose lifeway is adolescence is probably engaged in the lifework of a student.[2] A person whose lifeway is that of a nun might be engaged in the lifework of a medical missionary. And so on.

Most persons, including many religious educators, seem to equate their own personal spiritual development almost exclusively with their lifeway. A family man who toils as a bookkeeper typically regards his spiritual growth as residing almost totally in his life as a family man.[3]

---

2. Lifework may perdure for an entire career, such as that of a schoolteacher, or it might last less than a whole career, such as that of a student.

3. Many Christian groups add a juridical dimension to what most persons consider as lifeway. For example, the Catholic church, as well as certain other denominations, makes a major juridical distinction among the lifeway of a cleric, the lifeway of a person formally consecrated to religion by ecclesiastically sanctioned vows, and the lifeway of a layperson. It is probably safe to say that most Christian laypersons do not adequately recognize their layhood as itself constituting a very rich and precious lifeway. Largely accounting for this unfortunate state of affairs is the fact that for centuries the theologies of many of these church groups, especially the Catholic church, wantonly neglected and even denigrated the lay lifeway as a major and highly fruitful path of profound spiritual growth. In this view, layhood was regarded as a leftover, an intrinsically mediocre, low-level form of religious existence into which were placed by default those Christians who, it was claimed, were neither sufficiently generous nor divinely graced enough to be members of the clerical or vowed lifeways. I believe that this view, which has begun to change in theory (though often clung to in practice), is erroneous. See James Michael Lee, "Layhood as Vocation and Career," in *Evolving Religious Careers*, ed. Willis E. Bartlett (Washington, D.C.: Center for Applied Research in the Apostolate, 1970), pp. 144-166.

An adolescent attending secondary school generally regards his spirituality as residing almost exclusively in his personal life outside of school—in family life, church attendance, quality of relationships with other persons, and so forth. A nun tends to regard her spiritual growth as residing chiefly in her lifeway as a religious sister, namely in living a life faithful to her vows, in the communal activities of her religious congregation, in her frequent reception of the sacraments, in her cognitive prayer life, and so forth.

With the exception of the retired and the unemployed, there are two primary, indispensable, and co-central contextual sources of everyone's spiritual life. These two co-central contextual sources are lifeway and lifework.

Lifeway is not the sole source, or even the only major source, of a person's spiritual growth. This statement holds true for each and every lifeway, no matter how objectively exalted that lifeway might be. No person, except possibly for a retired or an unemployed individual, lives lifeway only. In the concrete existential order, everyone lives a combination of lifeway and lifework. Hence lifework is necessarily *co-primary* with lifeway as the major source and context of a person's spiritual living. It frequently happens, especially with individuals working in a profession, that one's lifework constitutes a more pervasive source and a more potent context for personal spiritual living than does lifeway.

As a general rule, the more a person's lifeway and lifework are congruent, the more that person's lifeway will tend to be fulfilling. Conversely, the less a person's lifeway and lifework are congruent, the less that person's lifeway will tend to be fulfilling. Conflicts between lifeway and lifework cause tension in the individual. Frequently the individual will resolve this tension in favor of lifework since lifework generally possesses more immediate salience and more felt relevance for a person than does lifeway. The more skilled and the more professional the lifework is, the greater will be the tendency for an individual to resolve lifeway-lifework conflicts in favor of lifework since skilled and professional lifeworks involve the participant at a deeper psychological level and for a longer portion of the day than is the case with unskilled and nonprofessional lifeworks.

The ideal situation for optimum spiritual development is for a person to select a lifeway and a lifework which are congruent. In this manner lifeway and lifework can reinforce and enrich each other, thus leading to a deeper all-around life. A family man or woman would be wise to choose a career which affords that individual with adequate time for family living and with many opportunities for personal enrichment within an interactive family context. For the professional person, the ideal career is one in which the person's lifeway directly enriches lifework and in which that individual's lifework directly enriches lifeway. A priest, for example, should select a career in direct sacerdotal ministry. Much of the decline in the quality and stability of family life can be traced to the husband and/or wife whose lifeworks lack felicitous congruence with family life, e.g., an on-the-road truck driver whose job takes him away from his family for extended periods of time. A great deal of the spiritual staleness of some priests probably flows from the fact that the lifeworks of these priests lie outside direct sacerdotal ministry.[4]

In this last-mentioned connection, I remember an incident which I witnessed in the days before the Second Vatican Council. A young priest whose lifework was that of diocesan fund raiser came to solicit financial contributions from a school group of which I was then a member. He was delayed and did not arrive at our meeting until

---

4. When the lifeworks of these clerics are professional, there occurs the phenomenon known as the hyphenated priest, such as the priest-professor, the priest-administrator, the priest-financier, and so on. Because the lifeworks of these clerics are professional ones, it is only natural that the hyphenated priest usually, though by no means always, becomes primarily or even totally immersed in the second part of the hyphen. Such primary or even total immersion in lifework tends to result in the priest neglecting or even occluding the first part of the hyphen. In such cases, lifework does not exist side-by-side with robust lifeway but instead debilitates it and sometimes chokes it. In these instances, the person either formally leaves the priesthood and becomes laicized, or informally leaves the priesthood by retaining the status and the trappings of a priest but living little if any of the priestly spirit and mission.

Of course it is quite possible for the hyphenated priest to structure his existence in a way that the basic incongruities between his lifeway and his lifework can be resolved. However, such a resolution usually takes the form of a compromise. By its very nature compromise is half-hearted because it is half-way. Compromise does not, and can not, go all the way in any direction. Because he is in a compromise situation at best, a hyphenated priest is intrinsically unable to participate as fully in his lifeway as he could if he were engaged in a different lifework. Conversely, in a compromise situation, a hyphenated priest is intrinsically unable to particpate as fully in his lifework as he could if he were in a different lifeway. A compromise is necessarily a limit imposed on all previously conflicting elements now resolved by the compromise. Consequently a hyphenated priest who has satisfactorily resolved his basic lifeway-lifework incongruities by skillful compromise has placed limits on his spiritual growth precisely because he has placed limits on the degree of his participation in lifeway and in lifework. Spirituality, after all, stems from and flows through lifeway and lifework. The full actualization of all the potentialities of one's spiritual growth can only occur in an open-ended situation which has no limits. Compromise is closed-ended with definite limits.

eleven o'clock at night. After delivering a skillful half-hour pitch for funds, he turned on the motion picture projector to reinforce his appeal with a splendid, emotionally charged film. Quite by chance I sat rather near the motion picture projector. There, by a small light coming from the side of the projector, the priest was reading his breviary, a book of set prayers which each and every priest in that era was required to finish before midnight of every day. This priest was obviously squeezing his priesthood into his fund raising activity. He was squeezing his lifeway into his lifework. Lifeway and lifework, in this case, were not congruent with one another. Lifeway and lifework operated at cross-purposes; they did not enrich and reinforce one another.

Was the spirituality of this priest weak? Was he not a holy man? Though there is no way for me to answer this question adequately, all the evidence at my disposal indicates that this priest was, in fact, leading a good spiritual life. The source—most probably the major source—of his spirituality was derived from and flowed through his lifework. But it seems to me that he would have enjoyed a deeper and more robust spiritual life if he were in a different lifeway, a lifeway which would complement, reinforce, and expand his lifework. He was, as far as I could tell, a fairly holy person but not a good priest.

A basic point I wish to make in the story of the young priest is that lifework is indisputably a potent and fertile source of personal spirituality. Therefore all persons, especially religious professionals, should consciously seek to maximize rather than neglect the life-giving spiritual character of their lifework. One important way to maximize the spiritual character of all lifeworks and especially overtly religious lifeworks is to choose a lifeway which complements and enriches one's lifework.

Lifework Spirituality

By and large, religious educators seem aware that their spirituality occurs in a lifeway context. But religious educators do not seem to be sufficiently aware that their spirituality also takes place in a lifework context.[5] Such a lack of awareness cuts off or at least seriously blunts

5. The truth of this statement is more than amply evident from listening to conversations of religious educators, from hearing convention talks or casette tapes on the spirituality of the religious educator, and from reading articles in professional journals on the religious educator's spiritual life. Seldom if ever is the great importance of lifework spirituality highlighted in the above-mentioned sources.

the possibility of the religious educator coming to that depth and breadth of spiritual living which is attainable in and through and because of the religious education lifework.

Whatever else it might be, a career in religious education is a lifework. Since lifework is so intimately bound up with a person's spirituality, it is vital that religious educators understand why lifework exerts such great power in the spirituality of all working persons, including themselves.

Of the many reasons which can be adduced to explain the enormous power and suffusiveness of lifework in the personal (and therefore spiritual) existence of each individual, two stand out as especially worthy of mention. These two are time and self.

Time

The quantity and the quality of time spent by an individual in lifework activities constitutes one major factor accounting for the remarkable power of lifework on personal/spiritual development.

In a normal nonprofessional career, the average person spends eight hours a day on the job. Other activities directly related to the person's lifework consume, on the average, another four hours.[6] Assuming that the average person sleeps for eight hours a night, the amount of time consumed by the average person who is not a member of a profession is as follows: lifework activities—eight hours; activities directly related to lifework tasks—four hours; sleep—eight hours; personal or non-lifework time—four hours. For the average person, much of the four personal hours not spent in lifework-related pursuits or sleep are eaten up by watching television, shopping, doing housework, cooking, and the like. Thus it is obvious that if a nonprofessional person is to grow spiritually, such an individual must grow in and through lifework activity and not rely exclusively on nonlifework pursuits.

Not only is the quantitative bulk of a person's waking day spent in lifework activities, but the finest portion of that individual's conscious existence is also consumed in pursuing lifework tasks. Most persons are at their highest levels of normal consciousness between 8 A.M. and 5 P.M.

For persons in professions—and this includes religious educators—lifework activities consume an even greater quantitative portion of the

---

6. The average person spends two hours getting ready for work (waking, washing and dressing, breakfasting, and traveling to the workplace), one hour for lunch, and another hour traveling from the workplace to home and relaxing from the rigors of the job.

day than is the case with individuals who are not working in a profession. A profession is a career which does not readily admit of time demarcations such as 8 A.M.—5 P.M. Persons in professions are never really off the job; professionals tend to take the job with them wherever they go, day or night, weekday or weekend. Overtime is a condition which exists only for persons who are not in a professional career. Professional persons in their private lives tend to make frequent connective relationships between what they are experiencing and their profession. Consequently, professional persons often use the experiences of their personal lives as one way of enriching the quality and effectiveness of their professional lifework. Over and above this, professional persons tend to reduce the time spent on their personal pursuits in order to devote more sustained effort to professional matters. Since the bulk of the religious educator's working day is spent in activities directly related to lifework, and since the level of the religious educator's conscious awarness is generally higher during lifework activities than during nonlifework activities in a typical workday, we can easily appreciate the fact that the religious educator's lifework represents an especially potent and suffusive factor in that individual's overall spirituality.

Let me etch this last-mentioned point ever more sharply. A person's lifework is not simply the medium or the context for that individual's spiritual growth or decline. A person's lifework to a large extent forms the basic structure and substance of much and in some cases of most of a person's spiritual growth.[7] This statement is preeminently applicable to persons engaged in professional lifeworks such as religious education.

Self

The intimate and thoroughly existential linkage of self with lifework constitutes a second major factor accounting for the remarkable power of lifework on personal/spiritual growth.

A goodly number of plausible, social-scientifically grounded theories have been advanced to explain the inextricable relationship between self and lifework. By and large, all these theories identify three

---

7. This fact explains why nonprofessional jobs which are routine or which require little or no involvement of the individual at the personal existential level tend to lead to a sort of spiritual numbness or even in some cases to spiritual erosion. Such jobs alienate the worker's lifework from his lifeway. Of course a person possessing strong will and spiritual mettle can overcome the deleterious effects of spiritually debilitating lifework.

key factors as essential dimensions of this dynamic relationship.[8] These factors are self-concept, personal needs, and human development.

Self-concept. A person's own set of perceptions about himself is called self-concept.[9] The self-concept includes all those realities of a person's perceptual field to which that individual refers when saying "I" or "me." It is the uniquely personal organization of thousands of perceptions of the self, an organization which appears to the individual as constituting what "I" or "me" really is.[10] Because of the great importance which the self-concept has for each person, the individual tends to act in ways which are consistent with the concept of self.[11] Self-concept thus forms a decisive frame of personal reference through which an individual perceives and responds to the elements of his experience.

A major factor explaining why a person initially selects and later lives out a particular lifework is that the person perceives that lifework as a fruitful means of implementing self-concept.[12] In addition to its function of operationalizing a person's self-concept, a lifework also expands and modifies that self-concept as that person engages in var-

---

8. What essentially differentiates these theories from one another is that each theory, while gladly admitting that all three factors are operative, nonetheless claims that one and only one of the three factors constitutes the primary basis of the relationship between self and lifework. For example, Donald Super proposes a form of self-concept theory as the primary and sufficient basis of the relationship between self and lifework. Anne Roe advocates a kind of need-oriented theory as the primary and sufficient basis. Robert Havighurst offers a type of developmental theory as the primary and sufficient basis.

9. Though the notion of self-concept has been important in the history of philosophy from Socrates down to the present day, current social-scientific investigation of the self-concept owes much of its impetus and flavor to psychological phenomenologists such as Arthur Combs. See, for example, Arthur W. Combs and Donald Snygg, *Individual Behavior*, 2d. ed. (New York: Harper & Row, 1959). For a so-called "second generation" treatment of self-concept in perceptual and phenomenological psychology, see Arthur W. Combs, Anne Cohen Richards, and Fred Richards, *Perceptual Psychology: A Humanistic Approach to the Study of Persons* (New York: Harper & Row, 1976), pp. 154-196.

10. Arthur W. Combs, Donald L. Avila, and William W. Purkey, *Helping Relationships*, 2d ed. (Boston: Allyn and Bacon, 1978), pp. 16-28.

11. James Michael Lee and Nathaniel J. Pallone, *Guidance and Counseling in Schools: Foundations and Processes* (New York: McGraw-Hill, 1966), pp. 36-39.

12. Donald E. Super, *Vocational Development* (New York: Teachers College Press, 1957), p. 196. Most of the seminal theoretical models of career-development psychology were originally elaborated in the 1950s and 1960s. This statement holds true for a large variety of theoretical models, including the personal needs model, the self-in-situation model, and so forth.

ious lifework tasks.[13] Consequently, when a person engages in a religious education lifework, such a person is working in a career which is a direct operationalization of that educator's self-concept. Because religious education is a professional lifework, at least in its optimal stage, it admits of a deeper and more inclusive implementation of the person's self-concept than is possible in nonprofessional lifeworks. In terms of self-concept, therefore, the religious educator identifies his very self with his lifework. Consequently, at the core of the self-concept of every religious educator exists not only the existential self awareness, "I am John Jones," but also and virtually as forcefully, "I am John Jones, religious educator." Furthermore, such an intimate and wholesale incorporation of a religious educator's lifework into his core self-concept means that: "My spirituality is not just the spirituality of John Jones, but concretely and realistically the spirituality of John Jones as religious educator." Lifework as an implementation of self-concept, then, means that a religious educator's spirituality at every dimension is tied up with that educator's lifework. Put even more strongly, the religious educator's ongoing lifework is, together with lifeway, one of the two primary elements in both the structure and the substance of that individual's entire spiritual life.

Personal Needs. Personal needs is a term which refers to that which a person must have in order to become fulfilled in some way. Needs differ from wishes (or wants) in that the former are necessary for personality fulfillment, while the latter are merely expressions of some nonessential item which an individual would like to have. Needs may be conscious or unconscious. Because needs are powerful forces pervasively influencing the entire personality structure, an individual's most fundamental and most global motivations in life are affected to a large but not total degree by that person's needs. A person will tend to live in a manner consistent with his needs.[14] Needs, then, operate as a powerful omnipresent motivational force in all a person's life activities, including the selection and living out of that individual's lifework.[15]

---

13. Donald E. Super et al., *Career Development: Self-Concept Theory* (New York: College Entrance Examination Board, 1963), pp. 17-32, 61-64; Donald E. Super and Martin J. Bohn Jr., *Occupational Psychology* (Belmont, Calif.: Wadsworth, 1970), pp. 147-152.

14. Needs, of course, are not lived out purely in themselves, but are given hue and direction by a complex of moral, socioeconomic, and situational factors.

15. A classic treatment of the pivotal role of personal needs in the choice and maintenance of lifework is Anne Roe, *The Psychology of Occupations* (New York: Wiley, 1956), especially pp. 23-132.

One of the most celebrated classifications of needs is that made by Abraham Maslow. The eight global needs in Maslow's hierarchy are, in ascending order, (1) physiological needs; (2) safety needs; (3) need for belongingness and love; (4) need for importance, respect, self-esteem, independence; (5) need for information; (6) need for understanding; (7) need for beauty; (8) need for self-actualization.[16] Maslow assigns needs to their designated places in the hierarchy on the basis of potency. The lower the basic need is situated in the hierarchy, the more potent (the more urgent and insistent) will that basic need be. A higher need can be adequately met only when a person satisfactorily meets all the needs which rank lower in the Maslow scale. While the general categories of needs are the same for all persons, the specific coloration and direction of any given global need will differ from person to person. A major factor explaining why a person first selects and later lives out a particular lifework is that the person is consciously or unconsciously motivated to fulfill his needs through a certain lifework. This fact holds especially true for professional lifeworks such as religious education.

There is, then, a decided interdependence between personality fulfillment and lifework activities.[17] Lifework is not only the objectification of one's overall need-structure; it is also the situational context wherein one's needs are met. When a person engages in a religious education lifework, such an individual is engaging in a career which directly advances (or thwarts) the fulfillment of one's basic needs and hence of a pivotal pervasive dimension of one's personality.[18] Consequently, both the quality of the religious educator's instructional activity and the quality of that person's spiritual life are strongly affected by the degree to which the whole symphony of the religious educator's needs are harmoniously met in the performance of lifestyle activities.

Spirituality can be holistically and authentically viewed as self-actualization. A person's highest need, a need which to a large extent encompasses all the other needs, cannot be satisfactorily met until the

---

16. Abraham Maslow, *Motivation and Personality,* 2d ed. (New York: Harper & Row, 1970), pp. 35-75.

17. For a frequently quoted elaboration of this thesis, see Anne Roe, "Personality Structure and Occupational Behavior," in *Man in a World of Work,* ed. Henry Borow (Boston: Houghton Mifflin, 1964), pp. 196-214.

18. One of the few serious books which pointedly and holistically interfaces the religious educator's needs with that person's growth as teacher and person is David Arthur Bickimer, *Christ the Placenta* (Birmingham, Ala.: Religious Education Press, 1983), especially pp. 22-39, 47-50, 62-63, 137-138. This engrossing book is one of the most refreshing and religiously expansive volumes to come along in years in the field of religious education.

lower needs have been adequately resolved. The term given to the blocking of one's needs is frustration. Frustration is an enemy both of effective teaching and of deep spiritual living. One of the greatest rewards of the religious education lifework is that this lifework in itself can be spiritual enrichment because it fulfills the highest need of those persons who are called to serve in this glorious lifework and who are truly competent to effectively discharge its responsibilities. Advancement in the spiritual life cannot be normally achieved through the thwarting of one's basic needs. Growth in the spiritual life comes about in large measure by placing one's lower-order needs at the dynamic and goal-directed disposal of higher-order needs. The religious education lifework is a career which itself forms the structure and the substance of this kind of spiritual growth.

Human Development. Human development is a term which refers to the personal growth which takes place in and through the dynamic interaction between one's organism and the environment. Developmentally considered, each human being is an interactive emergent, a self which arises as an existential consequence of the interaction between the growing organism and the impinging environment.[19] Development is an essential feature of human life and indeed of the world. From a Christian perspective, life is a progressive pilgrimage to Point Omega, namely the onward interactive development of the human being in Jesus and toward Jesus.[20] An axis of Christian hope is development, namely an individual's holistic interactive development in sanctity on this earth and in eternity.[21]

A major factor explaining why a person initially selects, changes (if necessary), and ultimately lives out a particular lifework is that the individual perceives the lifework to be a fruitful means of furthering

---

19. On this point, see James Michael Lee, "Christian Religious Education and Moral Development," in *Moral Development, Moral Education, and Kohlberg,* ed. Brenda Munsey (Birmingham, Ala.: Religious Education Press, 1980), pp. 327-329.

20. For some exquisite treatments of human *and* cosmic development toward convergence in Point Omega, see Pierre Teilhard de Chardin, *The Phenomenon of Man,* trans. Bernard Wall (New York: Harper & Row, 1959), pp. 257-272; Pierre Teilhard de Chardin, *The Divine Milieu,* trans. Bernard Wall (New York: Harper & Row, 1960), pp. 99-131; Pierre Teilhard de Chardin, *Hymn of the Universe,* trans. Simon Bartholomew (New York: Harper & Row, 1965), pp. 92-113.

21. Robert Kastenbaum is one of the rare psychologists writing for the "secular" market who even mentions immortality as a phase of the human developmental process. Robert Kastenbaum, *Human Development: A Lifespan Perspective* (Boston: Allyn and Bacon, 1979), pp. 15-19.

his own developmental process in a positive and fulfilling manner. Lifework plays a central role in a person's process of development because lifework is itself an essential molar aspect of one's own human development. After all, development is the dynamic process by which the self continuously emerges through the ongoing interaction between organism and environment. Lifework constitutes a major portion of a person's environment because lifework in itself is a set of conditions which initially are external to the organism.[22] Viewed from a developmental perspective, lifework does not just remain "out there" but rather, through the process of interacting with the organism, merges into the person's very self. Quite literally, then, my lifework becomes myself in the concrete developmental process. As a central feature of the self, lifework thus exerts enormous influence on the make-up of one's personal/spiritual life. This is especially true for persons in professions, including the religious education profession. Lifework not only orients and to a large extent controls the behavior of persons who participate in it; lifework also, and even more deeply, orients and even helps control the personal/spiritual development of those engaged in lifework. Thus lifework is *an* axis along which the individual's entire lifestyle or overall pattern of living is organized.[23]

The process of the positive development of the self is seen by some social scientists as presenting certain molar personal tasks to each individual.[24] These molar personal tasks are called developmental tasks because by psychobiological and psychosocial necessity each individual must successfully accomplish them in order to develop in a personally fulfilling manner.[25] One of the major developmental tasks each person faces in life is that of selecting, preparing for, and engaging in a lifework.[26] The religious educator's spiritual development is

22. For an illuminating treatment of environment as a co-central element of development, see John H. Peatling, *Religious Education in a Psychological Key* (Birmingham, Ala.: Religious Education Press, 1981), pp. 113-120.

23. On this last point, see Robert J. Havighurst, "The World of Work," in *Handbook of Developmental Psychology*, ed. Benjamin B. Wolman (Englewood Cliffs, N.J.: Prentice-Hall, 1982), p. 780.

24. Two classic statements of this position are Robert J. Havighurst, *Human Development and Education* (New York: McKay, 1953); Robert J. Havighurst, *Developmental Tasks in Education*, 3d ed. (New York: McKay, 1972).

25. Each developmental task rests on three bases, namely the biological basis, the psychological basis, and the cultural basis.

26. Other developmental tasks which each person must successfully negotiate in order to attain fulfillment of the self include the achievement of socially responsible conduct, the achievement of mature relations with persons of both sexes, and the attainment of a set of values and an ethical system which serve as a guide to conduct.

part and parcel of that individual's overall pattern of human development. Because lifework activity is so central in everyone's growth in personhood,[27] lifework activity is central to every religious educator's own spiritual journey. Together with the organism, the religious educator's lifework goes to form developmentally the substance and structure of that person's spiritual life. Since the religious educator's lifework activities are developmentally incorporated into the heart of that individual's spiritual life, then it indisputably follows that the quality of the religious educator's spiritual life is intimately bound up with the quality of that person's teaching ministry.

Religious Education Endeavor as the Confluence of Lifework Spirituality

The religious education lifework consists of three primary modes, namely, teaching, counseling, and the administration of religious education activities.[28] Each of these three major forms of religious education is extremely important. Indeed, well-rounded religious education endeavor necessarily includes all three. Since religious educators typically consider their primary function as that of teaching, my main focus is on the instructional process[29] as the concrete existential situation wherein the lifework spirituality of these persons actually takes place.

From the lifework perspective, the religious educator's spirituality is organically intertwined with that individual's participation in religious instruction endeavor. Put even more pointedly, the quality of the religious educator's lifework spirituality tends to vary directly with the quality of that person's performance in religious instruction endeavor.

By the term religious instruction endeavor I mean the religious instruction act itself, together with those essentially related functions leading up to, surrounding, and following the religious instruction act.

Religious instruction endeavor constitutes the here-and-now existential situation in which the religious educator's lifework spirituality is forged. The word *situation* is important because it denotes how and

---

27. A lifework is usually but not always financially rewarded. A homemaker, or in the case of the very affluent, a home manager, is an example of a lifework which is not rewarded in a direct financial manner.

28. This statement holds equally true for religious education in school as well as in nonschool settings.

29. Instruction is a term synonymous with teaching. Instruction is not a form of teaching (e.g., didactic teaching which takes place in a formal setting), but rather is coexistensive with teaching.

why religious instruction endeavor actually comprises the basic form and material of the religious educator's lifework spirituality. A situation is that set of definite concrete circumstances in which and through which a person works out his own particular form of existence. More than the word *state* and more than the word *condition*, the word *situation* lexically "implies an arrangement of circumstances not only with reference to each other but also with respect to the character or circumstances of the person involved" so as to intrinsically promote opportunity, difficulty, and the like.[30] A person is never situationless, but is always a self-in-situation. The power and importance of situation flow from the fact that the person is not only in a situation but indeed is existentially shaped formally and materially through that situation.

The gist of the previous paragraph is this: the religious educator grows in lifework spirituality because of here-and-now religious instruction endeavor and not despite this endeavor and not outside this endeavor.

The center of religious instruction endeavor is the religious instruction act. To be sure, everything in religious instruction endeavor flows from the religious instruction act and flows into the religious instruction act. It is the religious instruction act itself which gives meaning, relevance, and focus to all those essential functions which organically lead up to, surround, and follow this act. Therefore, the lifework spirituality of the religious educator is grounded in the way in which the religious educator prepares for the religious instruction act, performs this act, and follows up on this act.

The religious instruction act is a dynamic fusion of two global contents, namely, substantive content and structural content.[31] Consequently, the lifework spirituality of the religious educator is inherently connected to the form, the texture, and the quality of both the substantive and the structural contents of religious instruction.

Substantive Content

The substantive content of religious instruction is religion—not religion in itself but religion as it exists in the religious instruction act.

There is a vast difference between religion and theology. Religion is

---

30. *Webster's Dictionary of Synonyms* (Springfield, Mass.: Merriam, 1942), pp. 782-783.

31. My book, *The Content of Religious Instruction*, is devoted exclusively to the nature, kinds, and operations of substantive content. Another of my books, *The Flow of Religious Instruction*, deals solely with the nature, kinds, and operations of structural content.

a lifestyle. It is the way one lives one's life in existential relationship with God.[32] Religion is holistically experiential, concrete, flesh-and-blood. In sharp contrast, theology is exclusively cognitive, abstract, and scientific.[33] It is intellectual reflection from one and only one vantage point on God's workings in the world.[34]

Religion and theology have always existed side-by-side throughout the long history of Christianity. However, religion has always been primary and theology has always been secondary. Theology is incapable of directly generating religion; it simply is the cognitive reflection upon religion. Religion is holistic personal living while theology is nothing more than thinking.[35] Religion is a holistic personal operationalization of faith while theology is just an intellectual methodology attempting to offer one kind of plausible cognitive explanation of the contents of faith.[36] We live in grace and we attain salvation through religion and not through theology. In the practical order of the aver-

---

32. My formal and precise definition of religion is "that form of lifestyle which expresses and enfleshes that lived relationship a person enjoys with a transpersonal being as a consequence of the actualized fusion in his self-system of that knowledge, belief, feeling, experience, and practice that are in one way or another connected with that which the individual perceives to be divine." There are two major advantages of this definition. First, it is an operational definition rather than a notional one. Second, it takes into holistic account the person as *homo integer* rather than emphasizing any one human function such as cognition. See James Michael Lee, *The Content of Religious Instruction* (Birmingham, Ala.: Religious Education Press, 1985), p. 3.

33. By scientific is meant an activity which carefully proceeds from fact to law to theory in a logically coherent and systematic manner. When the average person theologizes, the quality and validity of this theologizing ultimately is judged on the basis of how well the person's thinking measures up to the substantive and especially to the procedural criteria proposed by the current state of theological science. Religion, on the other hand, is nonscientific. When a person engages in religious activity, the quality and validity of this activity is ultimately determined by the religious worth of his life, by the degree to which that individual concretely lives in existential relationship with God.

34. Other legitimate and highly illuminating vantage points for cognitively exploring God's workings in the world include the psychology of religion, the sociology of religion, religious literary activity, including fiction, and the like. Vantage points such as these are complementary to, and not subsidiaries of, theology in the human cognitive search for understanding God's workings in the world.

35. The source of the latter part of this statement is Karl Rahner, *Theological Investigations*, vol. 1, 2d ed., trans. Cornelius Ernst (Baltimore, Md.: Helicon, 1965), p. 14.

36. The source of the second part of this statement is Paul Tillich, *Systematic Theology*, vol. 1 (Chicago: University of Chicago Press, 1951), p. 28.

age Christian's daily life, the primary importance of theology resides in the degree to which it can be effectively integrated into that person's concrete Christian existence.[37] Both temporally and causally, then, religion is prior to theology.[38]

The distinguished theologian Helmut Thielicke makes a statement which is of supreme practical importance for the spiritual life of every religious educator (and for the substantive content of the religion lesson as well). Thielicke's statement is this: "In view of its structure, theological thinking is in some way an 'alien medium' into which statements of faith must be transposed."[39] As operationalized in personally lived religion, Christian faith is flesh and blood, here-and-now. Theology, on the other hand, is necessarily verbal, cognitive, propositional, and temporally/spatially independent of the here-and-now.[40] Thus theology will always remain in some way an alien medium for flesh-and-blood religion. There is a basic tension, and even a fundamental incongruity, between the inherently nameless God and theological attempts to cognitively identify him, between the daily life of a Christian living in faith and theological efforts to verbally circumscribe that life in intellectual propositional categories applicable over

---

37. Formally speaking, theology is targeted to itself and not to any area outside itself such as religion. By this I mean that theology attempts to devise theological explanations of religion and of other realities it might choose to cognitively investigate. Theology, then, does not seek to offer religious explanations, psychological explanations, literary explanations, and the like, of religious phenomena or of other realities. Consequently, theology is rendered religiously useful in a person's daily Christian life not in and through theology itself but rather to the extent to which that person appropriates theology into his own Christian life. Theology gains religious value only to the extent to which it is incorporated into religion on religion's own terms. *The fundamentally areligious nature of theology* explains why theology, unlike religion, can be and indeed is legally taught in public schools and universities in the United States.

38. For a further discussion of this important point, see James Michael Lee, "The Authentic Source of Religious Instruction," in *Religious Education and Theology*, ed. Norma H. Thompson (Birmingham, Ala.: Religious Education Press, 1982), pp. 100-197.

39. Helmut Thielicke, *The Evangelical Faith*, trans. and ed. Geoffrey W. Bromily (Grand Rapids, Mich.: Eerdmans, 1977), p. 3.

40. Though "story theologians" like John Shea and "developmental theologians" like John Dunne have attempted to make theology more personally living and more existentially real, nonetheless they must necessarily work within the parameters intrinsic to theological science. See John Shea, *Stories of God* (Chicago: Thomas More Press, 1979); John S. Dunne, *The Reasons of the Heart: A Journey into Solitude and Back Again into the Human Circle* (Notre Dame, Ind.: University of Notre Dame Press, 1979).

all time and space. Lao Tzu beautifully expresses the point I am making when he writes:

> The Tao that can be expressed
> Is not the eternal Tao.
> The name that can be defined
> Is not the unchanging name.[41]

The relative feebleness and inadequacy of theology as a suitable vessel for religion is graphically illustrated in the life of Thomas Aquinas, admittedly one of the greatest theologians in the history of the world. By the year 1271 Aquinas had written a prodigious number of top-quality scholarly works ranging from in-depth treatments of highly specialized topics to a major theological synthesis of the Christian religion. His brilliant books and articles still lie at or near the base of much of Christian theological reflection today, not just in official Catholic circles but to a certain less manifest extent in Protestant theology as well. While celebrating Mass on December 8, 1271, Aquinas had a major religious experience which profoundly altered his life. Speaking from the vantage point of this intense religious experience, Aquinas stated that after what he had encountered, all his voluminous theological writings were worth nothing more than straw. He never wrote a single line of formal theology again. As a matter of fact, he expressed the wish that he would soon die, presumably to join the God whom he had so deeply tasted in his religious vision. Three months later, at the age of forty-nine, Aquinas was dead.

The only medium which is not in any way alien to religion is religion itself. The more religious the substantive content of the religious instruction act is, the more potential will this act have for enhancing the spiritual lives of teachers as well as of learners.[42]

The fact that religion is the substantive content of religious instruction constitutes a direct advantage for the spirituality of the religious educator. As I observed a few pages ago in this chapter, the spirituality of the religious educator is inextricably bound up with the nature,

---

41. Lao Tzu, *Tao Te Ching*, Book I, 1-4.

42. The purpose of religious instruction is to enhance the religious lives of the learners. The purpose of theological instruction, on the other hand, is to enhance the cognitive theological understandings and skills of the learners. Consequently, the more religious the substantive content of the religious instruction act is, the richer and more authentic will that act tend to be. On this point, see James Michael Lee, *The Flow of Religious Instruction* (Birmingham, Ala.: Religious Education Press, 1973), pp. 14-15.

texture, and quality of that person's lifework. Since by definition the religious educator's spirituality is lived religion, and since the genuine substantive content of religious instruction is also lived religion, the religious educator is automatically in a uniquely favored position to significantly enhance his spiritual life through lifework activity. The religious educator's lifework lies in the same sphere of existence as his spirituality, namely, the religious sphere. Precisely because a religious educator teaches religion and not theology or biology, it is intrinsically easier for the religious educator to grow in spirituality through his lifework than it is for a theological educator or a biological educator to grow in spirituality through their respective lifework activities.[43] In other words, the religious instruction lifework is in itself inherently conducive to the educator's advancement in spiritual living.

The more religious the substantive content of religious instruction is, the more propitious will be the conditions for promoting the optimal spiritual growth of the religion teacher. In this case, as in so many instances throughout human life, virtue is its own reward. The religious educator who is truly faithful to the religious instruction lifework by bringing to heightened salience the full religious texture of substantive content in order that the learners might acquire religion is himself rewarded because it is this very heightened religious salience which does so much to contribute to that kind of enriched lifework situation in which the educator can optimally grow in spirituality. In this connection it is important to remember that the religious educator is personally and pedagogically affected by all the variables present in the religious instruction act, including substantive content.[44] When the religious educator heightens the religious salience of

---

43. This statement in no way implies that religious educators, because they are religious educators, are more holy than theological educators, biological educators, or anyone else. Rather, this statement indicates that the religious instruction lifework is a situation which in and of itself offers greater potential for the educator's spiritual enrichment than the theological instruction lifework or the biological instruction lifework. An enormous potential for the educator's spiritual growth is inherent in the religious instruction lifework. It all depends on the religious educator as to whether this person will capitalize on this potential. The religious instruction lifework does not function in *ex opere operato* fashion.

44. As teaching theory suggests and as empirical research indicates, any pedagogical act is a reciprocal endeavor in which the educators as well as the learners change and grow during the course of the instructional encounter. For a fuller discussion of this pivotal point, see James Michael Lee, *The Flow of Religious Instruction*, pp. 221-225.

substantive content, he is at the same time heightening the possibilities that he will grow spiritually as he interacts with and is changed by this substantive content during the course of the religious instruction dynamic.

The substantive content of religious instruction has many attributes which significantly affect the religious educator's lifework spirituality. I would like to briefly discuss three of these attributes, namely religion as experiential, religion as empirical, and religion as multicontent.

Religion as Experiential. Religious experience may be defined as an activity of the self in which a person existentially meets God by holistically encountering the divinity through some aspect of created reality.[45] The inestimable worth of religious experience as a necessary focal point and key attribute of substantive content lies in the fact that living faith is not just a thought or a concept or a feeling. Rather, the practice of faith, like that of any other religious act, is essentially a holistic experience in which the person existentially encounters in some way the actuality of God as God is manifested in some created reality.[46] No one can really know God, since God cannot be caught in conceptual nets. The best and the fullest a person can do is to experience God, however indirect and veiled this experience might be.[47] Since all experience is essentially communion, religious experience is communion with God. In its truest dimension, communion is the existential coming together and comingling of all the elements in-

---

45. Religious experience is thus considerably wider than any of its forms. Types or forms of religious experience include intense religious experience, mysticism, and so forth.

46. Faith is not a fixed entity or an immutable locus in our existence. Together with hope and love, faith constitutes the ongoing developmental matrix of our processive spiritual journey in life. Every spiritual journey requires a person "to be in the present," that is, to meet God existentially wherever and however God might be in the here-and-now. On this last point, see Jerome W. Berryman, "Introduction," in *Life Maps: Conversations on the Journey of Faith,* ed. Jerome W. Berryman (Minneapolis, Minn.: Winston, 1978), pp. 5-6. (By faith here I am referring to the set of behaviors which the construct called faith seeks to encapsulate. The same holds true for my use of the constructs hope and love.)

47. Though Christian religious educationists, psychologists of religion, and theologians generally agree *that* God does meet a person through religious experience, there is considerable disagreement about *how* this meeting occurs. Two helpful books on this very important and indeed seminal issue are Ian P. Knox, *Above or Within?* (Birmingham, Ala.: Religious Education Press, 1976); André Godin, *The Psychological Dynamics of Religious Experience,* trans. Mary Turton (Birmingham, Ala.: Religious Education Press, 1985).

volved in the communion, in this case the person, the experienced reality in and of itself, and the God who inhabits that reality. It is not wholly accurate to state that in religious experience the person has an experience of God. It is more accurate to assert that in a religious experience the person participates existentially with the realities which go to make up that experience—in other words, communion. It is in the communion of religious experience that the person partakes of the body of God.[48]

The quality and the frequency of one's religious experience is a prime factor in any Christian's spirituality. When the religious educator teaches religion as a personal experience rather than as simply a set of cognitive truths, that educator is directly promoting not only the learner's spiritual growth but his own spiritual growth as well. A particularly effective way of teaching religion as a personal experience is to so structure the pedagogical situation that it becomes a laboratory for Christian living. In a laboratory for Christian living, the learner experiences religion by performatively living one or another of its dimensions in a concrete, first-hand fashion.[49] Since the religious educator is a major interactive element in a laboratory for Christian living, it necessarily follows that the teacher will also tend to grow spiritually through the facilitation of those religious experiences and activities which comprise a laboratory for Christian living.[50] If, on the other hand, the religious educator constricts the range of substantive content to just the cognitive or the verbal and thus squeezes out the holistically experiential sweep of religion, the potential spiritual growth of the religious educators as well as of the learners will tend to suffer as a result.

Religion as Empirical. Because religion is experiential, it is also em-

---

48. This is a leitmotiv in the writings of Pierre Teilhard de Chardin. See, for example, Pierre Teilhard de Chardin, *Hymn of the Universe.*

49. For a fuller treatment of the nature, characteristics, and functions of a laboratory for Christian living, see James Michael Lee, *The Content of Religious Instruction* (Birmingham, Ala.: Religious Education Press, 1985), pp. 618-626.

50. The liturgy is a splendid example of one kind of laboratory for Christian living. (The liturgy has two co-primary functions, namely sacramental and religious instructional.) The liturgy is carefully structured so as to directly facilitate religious experience in all the participants and thus, from the standpoint of substantive content, to become one grand religious experience. In the liturgy, both the facilitator (celebrant) and the learners (the laity) grow in religious experiencing. On this point, see ibid., pp. 643-648. For a complementary perspective, see John H. Westerhoff III, "The Liturgical Imperative," in *The Religious Education We Need*, ed. James Michael Lee (Birmingham, Ala.: Religious Education Press, 1977), pp. 75-94.

pirical.[51] Though God, the ultimate ground of religion, is in himself nonempirical, nonetheless God's manifestations and effects as we experience them are empirical.[52] Because religion is empirical, its processes are not really hidden but can be directly or at least indirectly observed by others or at least by one's own self.[53] Religion is an empirical lifestyle lived in and through experience. Because it is an empirical lifestyle, religion is personal and social. As personal, religion is a primary way in which a person lives his own life. The personal dimension of religion endows each person's religious life with a certain individuality and singularity.[54] The social dimension of religion gives each person's religion a certain corporativeness[55]—a communal corporativeness, an institutional corporativeness, or a combination of both.

The empirical character of religion shines through virtually all of its forms and elements. Let me very briefly offer three examples to illustrate this point, namely liturgy, sacrament, and revelation. The liturgy is a highly empirical type of religious activity. Indeed, the liturgy really represents a form of enriched empiricalness because it endeavors to heighten, deepen, and make more evident the essential empirical na-

---

51. Etymologically, the word empirical derives from the ancient Greek word *empeiria*, which means experience.

52. Empirical in its proper and full sense encompasses the full range of human experience and so is not restricted to any one kind of experience.

53. My statement obviously includes observation which is private as well as observation which is public. (Of course to be rendered scientific, private observation must be rendered public in some satisfactory fashion. Empiric is not coextensive with scientific. Social- and natural-scientific method constitutes one way of studying and doing something with empirical phenomena.) My statement also includes indirect as well as direct observation. Some empirical phenomena are amenable to direct observation while other phenomena can be observed only through their discernable effects. On this last point, see C. Daniel Batson and W. Larry Ventis, *The Religious Experience* (New York: Oxford University Press, 1982), pp. 16-22. On the point discussed in the parenthesis, see James Michael Lee, *The Shape of Religious Instruction* (Birmingham, Ala.: Religious Education Press, 1971), pp. 134-142, and also John Macmurray, *The Structure of Religious Experience* (Hamden, Conn.: Archon, 1936), pp. ix-xi.

54. Each individual differs from other people physically, psychologically, and socially. Hence personal religion takes on the flavor and force of the individual's physical, psychological, and social characteristics and flow. It is in this vein that Alex Comfort writes: "Because religion is a human behavior it can be said to have a biology." Alex Comfort, *I and That: Notes on the Biology of Religion* (New York: Crown, 1979), p. 69.

55. Raymond F. Paloutzian, *Invitation to the Psychology of Religion* (Glenview, Ill.: Scott, Foresman, 1983), p. 11.

ture of the person-God encounter.[56] The liturgy is a particularly sensory form of empirical religion which is probably one reason why it is so powerful. The sacraments are unabashedly empirical. Composed as they are of material objects and accompanying words (both highly empirical realities), the sacraments represent empirical signs of what is construed by some theologians to be "invisible" grace.[57] What could be more empirical than an empirical sign which itself actually causes the grace which is brought about? Now this is precisely what sacraments do.[58] Revelation, whether general or special, is a disclosure of God to human beings. This disclosure is typically empirical, whether it occurs in the rolling of the waves, in the Zeitgeist,[59] or in the bible. Scripture is itself an empirical fact in at least four respects. First, the bible exists in empirical form, namely, as an empirical corpus of inspired words. Second, the bible was written in empirical fashion by persons who had empirically received messages from God and recorded their own experience of these messages empirically into written durable form.[60] Third, in both its historical and nonhistorical parts, the substantive content of the bible is empirical since it consists of an empirical account of empirical religious experiences.[61] The ministry of Jesus, surely a high point in the bible for Christians, is not presented as some sort of nonempirical otherworldly phenomenon, but rather as a series of empirical activities taking place in an empirical milieu and having empirical consequences. Fourth, the bible remains the

---

56. What I have just stated holds as true for liturgies in ancient primitive religions as in Christianity or Judaism. This is also a recurrent theme in the writings of Mircea Eliade. See, for example, Mircea Eliade, *The Sacred and the Profane: The Nature of Religion*, trans. Willard R. Trask (New York: Harper & Row Torchbook, 1959).

57. For an especially good treatment of the sacraments in religious education and liturgy, see Robert L. Browning and Roy A. Reed, *The Sacraments in Religious Education and Liturgy* (Birmingham, Ala.: Religious Education Press, 1985).

58. Thus Karl Rahner writes: "The sacrament effects grace *because* it is its sign. . . . In other words, it is not only true that sacraments are signs of grace because they are its cause, but essentially the converse is just as true: they are causes because they are signs." Karl Rahner, *Theological Investigations*, vol. II (Baltimore, Md.: Helicon, 1963), p. 123.

59. Hence the expression, *"Vox temporis, vox dei."*

60. It is important to remember that the inspired word of God (the bible) is not God's unmediated message but rather is the inspired writers' own empirical experiences of this message. On this point see John L. McKenzie, *A Theology of the Old Testament* (Garden City, N.Y.: Doubleday, 1974), p. 64.

61. For a fuller discussion of this point, see James Michael Lee, "Religious Education and the Bible: A Religious Educationist's View," in *Biblical Themes in Religious Education*, ed. Joseph S. Marino (Birmingham, Ala.: Religious Education Press, 1983), pp. 8-11.

living word of God; it is not a dead document.[62] However, the bible becomes living only when a person reads it or listens to it in such a way as to encounter it. This encounter is an empirical act and so is an empirical fact.

The more thoroughly empirical is the substantive content of religious instruction, the more potent will be this content for promoting the spiritual growth of learners as well as of the religious educator. Whether they realize it or not, learners and also the religious educator often ask themselves a crucial empirical question which gets to the very heart of religious instruction endeavor, namely, "Am I actually growing spiritually *in* the religious instruction act and *because* of the religious instruction act?" If the answer to this central question is no, maybe, or even a lukewarm yes, then part of the cause quite possibly lies in the nature and the texture of the substantive content being taught. Perhaps the religious educator is failing to bring to salience the deep and pervasive empirical character of religion. Perhaps the religious educator is trying to transmogrify substantive content into a highly abstract (and hence rationalistic and nonincarnational) affair in a foolish attempt to somehow make religion more intellectually and theologically respectable—as if religion in its empirical fullness needs any additional respectability. Perhaps the religious educator is striving to debase substantive content into an incomprehensibly ethereal (and hence spooky and amorphous) affair in a foolish attempt to somehow make religion more transcendently spiritual and reverentially sacred—as if religion in its empirical fullness needs any injection of special sacredness.[63]

Because the substantive content of religious instruction is empirical, then this substantive content should make a definite difference in the spiritual lives of the learners and of the religious educator during the religious instruction act and after it. The Christian religion is shot

---

62. For a lovely discussion of this point, see Luis Alonso Schökel, *The Inspired Word*, trans. Francis Martin (New York: Herder and Herder, 1965), pp. 361-362.

63. Throughout my career in the field of religious education I have frequently criticized the tendency on the part of religious educationists and educators to spookify the religious instruction act. By spookification I mean the unwarranted attempt to explain empirical phenomena in religious instruction by resorting to high-sounding but fundamentally meaningless spectral explanations of these phenomena (as, for example, calling these phenomena unfathomable activities of God) while at the same time rejecting as insufficiently religious and un-Godlike those empirical explanations which adequately and parsimoniously account for the nature and workings of these phenomena. For a fuller discussion of this point, see Lee, *The Flow of Religious Instruction*, pp. 202-204.

through and through with empiricalness. The religious educator and
the learners have every right to share in this heritage. For a straightforward and even hard-bitten statement about the centrality of empiricalness in the Christian religion, Jesus' line probably cannot be
surpassed: "You will know them by their fruits" (Mt. 7:16). Tertullian,
the great Church Father from Africa highlighted the empirical difference which Christianity makes in the lives of persons when he de-
clared: "Look how those Christians love one another."[64]

In their own spiritual lives as well as in their orchestration of the
religious instruction act, religion teachers should realize that empiricalness is the stuff of the human condition. Empiricalness is also part
and parcel of religion.[65] At bottom, the Incarnation is an empiricalization of God. Each person comes to the Godhead only through this
empiricalization of God, only through Jesus. We all affirm this fact
every day in the prayers we say. If the religious instruction act is not
empirical, then it is not incarnational, and if it is not incarnational
then it surely fails to partake adequately of the incarnate Jesus. If
Jesus is indeed the cosmic Christ, it is because he is physically incarnate in a certain but genuinely fulsome way throughout the universe.
If substantive content is to make a definite spiritual difference in the
lives of both learners and teacher, its empirical character must be
brought to salience so that everyone, learners and teachers alike, can
commune with the empiricalized God, with the incarnate Jesus as our
Lord empirically present in all things.

Among the innumerable blessings flowing from the Incarnation in
both the historical Jesus and the cosmic Jesus is that this empiricalization of God brings to holistic unity what otherwise would be an ontic
and operational dichotomy between sacred and profane, between God
and the world, between religion and the brass tacks of human existence. As a once-and-continuing empirical event, the Incarnation as an
empiricalization of God means that our spirituality rests upon and
flows through the natural world rather than emanating simply from a
supernatural world "out there."[66] The natural locus of spirituality
brought about by the once-and-continuing empirical events of the
Creation and the Incarnation shows from yet another perspective that

---

64. Tertullian, *Apologeticum*, XXXIX, 7.

65. In this vein Alan Coates Bouquet argues that Christianity is basically an
empirical experiment in coming closer to Jesus. A. C. Bouquet, *Religious
Experience*, 2d ed. (Westport, Conn.,: Greenwood, 1968), pp. 104-108.

66. In a particularly enlightening way, Abraham Maslow shows how the
false split between the "sacred" and the "natural" has resulted in all sorts of
essentially antireligious consequences. Abraham Maslow, *Religions, Values, and
Peak-Experiences* (New York: Penguin, 1964), pp. 11-18.

the spirituality of the religious educator organically stems in large measure from that person's religious instruction lifework, from that person's nitty-gritty involvement in everyday religion teaching.

Dermot Cox, the biblical scholar, underscores the fact that "the human environment is offered as a sacrament of Christ in the New Testament."[67] Consequently, Cox continues, the substantive content of religious instruction must be such as to constitute an arena in which the learner encounters God in his own experience of reality, at the empirical level.[68]

Edward Schillebeeckx contends that "the gulf between faith and experience is one of the fundamental reasons for the present-day crisis among Christians who are faithful to the church"[69]—and, I might add, among Christians who are not so faithful to the church. What Schillebeeckx is asserting is that modern Christians urgently wish to see and to feel a genuine synapsis between their religion and the real world, a world which they experience as empirical. If religion is not empirical, says today's Christian, then it is a sham and an illusion—or something to adhere to while suspending one's normal awareness of reality.

"Who is Jesus?" asks Schillebeeckx. Jesus is a new lifestyle, he responds.[70] A lifestyle is an eminently empirical reality. In a beautiful sentence summing up the incarnational Jesus as empirically present in the church today, Schillebeeckx writes: "The account of the life of Christians in the world in which they live is a fifth gospel; it also belongs at the heart of christology."[71] If substantive content is to enrich the spiritual life of each learner and the spiritual life of the religious educator as well, then substantive content must be revelatory, that is, empirically incarnational. "Revelation has everything to do with experience."[72] Experience is first and fully empirical.[73]

---

67. Dermot Cox, "The Discovery of God," in *Biblical Themes in Religious Education,* ed. Joseph S. Marino (Birmingham, Ala.: Religious Education Press, 1983), p. 113.

68. Ibid., p. 114.

69. Edward Schillebeeckx, *Christ: The Experiment of Jesus as Lord,* trans. John Bowden (New York: Crossroad, 1981), p. 29.

70. Ibid., p. 19.

71. Ibid., p. 18.

72. Ibid., p. 29.

73. It is in this vein that George Albert Coe states: "Every religious experience, without exception, is to me, a datum." By datum Coe means a living empirical fact. By religious experience he means religion as it is empirically experienced in the everyday lives of persons; he definitely does not restrict religious experience to mysticism or to any other kind of intense or "special" occurrence. George Albert Coe, *The Psychology of Religion* (Chicago: University of Chicago Press, 1916), p. xii.

If the religious educator is not growing spiritually through substantive content, then probably the learners are not growing spiritually through substantive content either.

Religion as Multicontent. Because religion is experiential and empirical, it is an amalgam of many contents. Religion does not exist in and of itself. Religion is not a separate entity somehow separated or disembodied from human existence. Religion exists only in personal or communal form. Consequently, religion as it is lived in concrete human existence is just as multicontent in character as concrete human existence itself.

There are nine molar formal contents which go to make up religion as religion is taught in the religion lesson. These molar formal contents are present in one way or another in every religion lesson. The molar formal contents are product content, process content, cognitive content, affective content, verbal content, nonverbal content, conscious content, unconscious content, and lifestyle content.[74]

Spirituality is another name for religion personally and/or communally lived. Therefore, if the spirituality of the religious educator is to be genuine and fulsome, it perforce must partake of the basic nature of religion as an inherently multicontent phenomenon.

The more the religion teacher during the religious instruction act brings to salience the full multicontent sweep of religion, the more the possibility exists for that teacher to grow spiritually during lifework activity. Conversely, the more the religion teacher during the religious instruction act constricts or diminishes the full multicontent range of religion, the more the possibility exists for that teacher to become spiritually lopsided and even spiritually crippled.

Let me give an example to illustrate the point I am making. Cognition is one major molar content of religion. But cognition is only one content—and not even the most important content at that. When the religious educator devotes most or even all of a religion course[75] to cognitive content, the result is a serious diminution of the full sweep of substantive religious content. Such a diminution of the full multicontent range of religion has at least two significant results which are quite deleterious to the spiritual lives of the educator and learners alike. First of all, a lopsided or even exclusive emphasis on cognitive content in the religious course purges from the spirituality of the

---

74. My book *The Content of Religious Instruction* is devoted entirely to a wide-ranging treatment of eight of these molar formal contents.

75. A course is an organized set of learning experiences which lasts several days, weeks, months, or years. A course need not be academic or occur in a formal setting such as a classroom.

religious educator and the learners that intrinsic multicontent richness which gives religion its spiritual power, its spiritual depth, its spiritual breadth, and its spiritual flavor. The part masquerades as the whole. Second, a lopsided or even exclusive emphasis on cognitive content in the religion course elevates this single content to a status and a power which it can never have in authentic religion.[76] In this severely skewed state of affairs, religion, and hence spirituality, becomes essentially a cognitive act executed within a cognitive matrix. Stripped of its multicontent sweep, religion is reduced to rationalism.

Rationalism is the attempt to assign to reason the first place and fundamental role in personal and social development. Rationalism seeks to validate human existence and human activity by cognition. Rationalism downplays and even negates the validity of experience, affect, or personal lifestyle as the ground, the axis, and the verification of human existence. Because rationalism stands opposed to the empirical stance toward reality[77] and toward justification of existence by faith or love, rationalism has always been a covert as well as overt enemy of religion and spirituality.[78]

Because its actuality occurs in the existential fabric and empirical flow of the concrete human person, religion is fundamentally a lifestyle. As a lifestyle, religion is the holistic operational integration of all the molar substantive contents of which it is composed. Lifestyle is the

---

76. In somewhat this same connection, Carl Jung writes that "in the course of the nineteenth century, when spirit began to degenerate into intellect, a reaction set in against the unbearable domination of intellectualism which led to the pardonable mistake of confusing intellect with spirit, and blaming the latter for the misdeeds of the former. Intellect does, in fact, violate the soul when it tries to possess itself of the heritage of the spirit. It is in no way fitted to do this, because spirit is something higher than intellect in that it includes not only the latter, but feelings as well. It is a line or principle of life that strives after superhuman, shining heights." C. G. Jung, *Psychological Reflections*, ed. Jolande Jacobi (New York: Harper & Row Torchbooks, 1953), p. 225.

77. The basis of rationalism is reason. The basis of empiricalism is experience.

78. One of the central struggles throughout the history of religion and religious education has pitted the rationalists against the empiricalists. Rationalist tendencies have more often than not manifested themselves in theology and among many so-called intelligentsia in religion. Religious educators have usually leaned in the direction of the empirical. Thomas Groome is a vigorous and thoroughgoing proponent of the rationalist position in religious instruction, while David Arthur Bickimer is a leading advocate of the empirical stance in the field. Religious counselors and guidance workers are almost always empirical in their orientation. See Thomas H. Groome, *Christian Religious Education* (San Francisco: Harper & Row, 1980); and Bickimer, *Christ the Placenta.*

concrete operational embodiment of multicontent. To educate others in religion, therefore, is first and foremost to educate them in a life-style, a lifestyle called religion. This cardinal fact suggests the axis of an authentic religion course. One kind of authentic religion course is what I have named elsewhere[79] a laboratory for Christian living, a set of conditions in which learners holistically engage in religious lifestyle pursuits. Because lifestyle is holistic, the power and place of each molar content such as cognition or affect is heightened rather than minimized.

A lifestyle-centered religion course such as the laboratory for Christian living helps empower the religious educator as well as the learners to attain optimum spiritual growth, namely, holistic Christian living. When the religion course is lifestyle-based and lifestyle-thrusted, all the molar contents of religion can achieve their proper role and function in the well-rounded spiritual life of the religious educator and the learners. Inasmuch as the spiritual growth of the religious educator is so deeply tied in with the level and intensity of that individual's participation in the religious instruction act, a lifestyle-oriented religion course will tend to color the religious educator's spirituality far more holistically and significantly than a religion course whose primary or even exclusive axis is anything less than lifestyle. By virtue of participating existentially in the religion course he teaches, the religious educator necessarily lives the substantive content which takes place in that course. Since the educator's spirituality is a personal lifestyle, the more lifestyle-based and lifestyle-thrusted is the substantive content of what is taught, the more that educator will be enabled through the course itself to grow spiritually.

The overall substantive content of a lifestyle-soaked religion course should be such that it admits of the entire range of religious experiences and activities.[80] To be sure, the substantive content of the course should be motile and wide enough not only to accomodate but also to empower in every sort of learner the entire gamut of religious experiences and activities. In this way, the spirituality of each learner

79. Lee, *The Content of Religious Instruction*, pp. 618-626.

80. When I write "the entire range" I mean the entire range all the way up to intense religious experiences including mystical experiences. For two strong advocacies of the role of mystical experience in religious instruction activity, see Lee, *The Content of Religious Instruction*, pp. 661-672 and Bickimer, *Christ the Placenta*, pp. 9-11. Indeed, the central thesis of Bickimer's book is that "the focus of religious education should be the facilitation of the acquisition of mystic states on the part of the religious learner" (p. 9, italics deleted). Bickimer's book is on its way to becoming a minor classic in the field of religious education.

as well as the spirituality of the religious educator can grow and flower in an optimal manner.

Structural Content

The structural content of religious instruction is pedagogical process—not pedagogical process in itself but pedagogical process as it occurs in the religious instruction act.

Pedagogical process is not the way in which content is taught. Rather, pedagogical process is full-fledged content in its own right. Pedagogical process is structural content and as such comprises, in fused union with substantive content, the religious instruction act itself.

To assert that pedagogical process is content is to assert that *how* a person teaches is a major part of *what* that person teaches. Let us say, for example, that two religious educators in a formal classroom setting are teaching the same basic substantive content, namely the Lord's Prayer. The first religious educator teaches the Lord's Prayer in a didactic, cognitive, verbal mode. He lectures on the historical background of the Lord's Prayer. He summarizes for the learners the current theology of the Lord's Prayer. He asks drill questions to see if the learners have adequately memorized the Lord's Prayer. The second religious educator teaches the Lord's Prayer from within the framework of a laboratory for Christian living. He structures a warm, acceptant, learner-active pedagogical climate. Some learners act out parts of the Lord's Prayer, such as asking classmates and the teacher for forgiveness, or bursting into song to praise the Lord. Other learners nonverbally express their feelings about the Lord's Prayer. Still other learners explore the theological and religious interpretations of the Lord's Prayer. Together with the teacher, the whole class plans and implements a class project[81] in which they live out the Lord's Prayer in a specified way during the next day's class, as well as in their wider family settings.

Was the total content of both of these religion lessons the same? Not really. What made the total content of these two lessons so very different is the fact that the pedagogical procedures used in each were different. These pedagogical procedures significantly altered not only how the student learned but what the student learned. The how was not only the how but even more importantly became the what.[82] Indeed, the structural content actually altered the substantive content

---

81. The project is a specific pedagogical technique. For a brief discussion of the project in itself and in its use in religious instruction, see Lee, *The Content of Religious Instruction*, pp. 699-700, 733-735.

82. In other words, pedagogical procedures are contents in their own right.

so that the substantive content of the lesson (the Lord's Prayer) was significantly changed by being combined with two different structural contents.[83] As George Coe observed many years ago, religion changes in the act of teaching it.[84]

Earlier in this chapter I stated that the spirituality of the religious educator is inextricably enmeshed with the texture and the quality of that person's lifework. Since the lifework of the religious educator is that of teaching religion, the texture and the quality of the pedagogical procedures which the religious educator uses are intimately tied in with that person's spiritual life. Pedagogical procedures are not disembodied processes. Pedagogical procedures are human activities enacted by human beings. Since what we do contributes in such large measure to what we are and indeed in some ways constitutes what we are,[85] it is obvious that the way in which a religious educator teaches is going to have a profound influence on that educator's personal life, including that educator's spiritual life. To enact a set of pedagogical procedures is necessarily to live out these procedures in that portion of one's life in which the religious educator is teaching. The religious educator is no less a person, no less a human being, during that portion of his life spent in lifework activities than during other times of the day or week. Since each person functions holistically and not compartmentally, the texture and quality of that portion of the religious educator's life spent in teaching becomes incorporated into and indeed shapes the educator's entire mode of living, including the educator's spirituality. In short, the pedagogical procedures which the religious educator uses in the religion lesson help to fashion the axis, direction, depth, breadth, and tint of that educator's spirituality.

The structural content of religious instruction has many attributes which significantly affect the religious educator's lifework spirituality. I would like to briefly discuss three of these attributes, namely pedagogical procedure as personal modification through interaction, pedagogical procedure as a set of specific behaviors, and pedagogical procedure as competent enactment.

---

83. My basic theory of teaching holds that the concrete religious instruction act is essentially a mediational one in which substantive content and structural content are so fused that each ceases to be what it was and takes on a new form, namely the religious instruction act. For a further development of this point, see Lee "The Authentic Source of Religious Instruction," pp. 165-172.

84. George A. Coe, *What Is Christian Education?* (New York: Scribner's, 1929), p. 23.

85. Randolph Crump Miller is fond of saying that what we do is what we are, and what God does is what God is. See, for example, Randolph Crump Miller, *The Theory of Christian Education Practice* (Birmingham, Ala.: Religious Education Press, 1980), pp. 7-21.

Pedagogical Procedure as Modification through Interaction. Religious instruction, like all other kinds of teaching, is an interactional process which takes place between or among persons. All teaching is an encounter of selves to one degree or another. It is a hallmark of human encounter that each person is changed by the encounter and through the encounter.[86] The teaching process, then, effects a change not only in the learners but in the teacher as well.

In the pedagogical act, the religious educator is not a catalyst.[87] The term catalyst derives from chemical usage. By definition a catalyst is a foreign substance which accelerates (and often initiates) a chemical reaction while itself remaining chemically unchanged. In the religious instruction act, the teacher is not alien or foreign to the learners. Furthermore, in the religious instruction act, the teacher necessarily changes in some measure by and through the act.

Two important consequences for the religious educator's spirituality flow from the fact that participation in the religious instruction act changes the teacher in some degree.

The first of these consequences is that pedagogical procedure in itself is crucial to the religious educator's spirituality. In other words, the religious educator's spirituality can never be separated from the pedagogical dynamics of the religious instruction act. The fact that the teaching process changes the educator as well as the learners accounts for the testimony frequently given by superior religious educators that they learn and grow so much during the course of their teaching. These religious educators painstakingly work to help facilitate learning in those whom they are teaching. In a word, these religious educators give a great deal of themselves during the pedagogical dynamic. It is in and through this process of giving that these educators receive so much and grow spiritually so much. It is both a great glory and an intrinsic reward for the religious educator's spirituality that pedagogical procedure effects a change in the religious educator. It is up to the educator to capitalize on this reality to the betterment of his own spiritual living.

There is a second important consequence emanating from the fact

---

86. Reviewing the pertinent research, David Hargreaves formulates the empirically derived "principle of reciprocally contingent communication," namely, that in every form of interaction the participants necessarily communicate in such a way that the behavior of each is in part a response to the behavior of the other. Interaction is a process of reciprocal influence and mutual dependence. David H. Hargreaves, *Interpersonal Relations and Education* (London: Routledge & Kegan Paul, 1975), p. 70.

87. For a discussion of this important point, see Lee, *The Flow of Religious Instruction,* pp. 221-225.

that participation in the religious instruction act changes the teacher in some degree. This consequence is that the change which the teacher undergoes during the religious instruction act is directly contingent upon the shape, texure, and flow of the pedagogical dynamic itself. As a general rule, the more interactive the teacher is during the pedagogical transaction, the more the teacher will be changed by the other three major variables dynamically present in every religious instruction act.[88] The degree to which the religious educator is interactive during the religious instruction event depends directly on the kind of pedagogical procedures which the teacher structures and enacts. For example, a transmissionist pedagogical strategy offers minimal and unidimensional teacher interaction during the lesson. A laboratory-for-Christian-living strategy, on the other hand, provides maximum and multidimensional teacher interaction during the lesson. The type of pedagogical procedure which facilitates a high degree of spiritual growth in learners is also the type of procedure which facilitates a high degree of spiritual growth in teachers. Religious educators who wish learners and themselves to grow spiritually through religious instruction should pay a great deal of high-level attention to the pedagogical procedures which they structure and enact.

Pedagogical Procedure as a Set of Specific Behaviors. Because it is a form of human interaction, religious instruction is composed of a network of specific behaviors.[89] At the most fundamental level, everything the religious educator and the learners do during the lesson is composed of specific behaviors—a smile, a word of praise, a touch on the shoulder, and so forth.

Teaching is the deliberate structuring of specific behaviors to facilitate desired learning outcomes.[90] The facilitation process itself is the purposive flow of a structured set of specific behaviors. The outcomes of this facilitation process are also behavioral in nature.[91] There is no "big picture" of the religious instruction act which is totally independent of the specific details comprising this act. Any "big picture" is composed of a host of specific details. Any "big picture" consists in the

---

88. Each religious instruction act is composed of four major variables, namely learner, teacher, subject matter, and environment.

89. A behavior is any performance of the organism and not simply overt activity. A thought is a cognitive behavior, a feeling an affective behavior, and so forth.

90. For an especially helpful discussion of this point, see Leon McKenzie, *The Religious Education of Adults* (Birmingham, Ala.: Religious Education Press, 1982), pp. 190-226.

91. For a classic treatment of this point, see Robert F. Mager, *Preparing Instructional Objectives* (Palo Alto, Calif.: Fearon, 1962).

relationship among the details and in the interaction which such a relationship either generates or flows from.

The more that religious educators pay careful attention to their own specific behaviors and to the specific behaviors of the learners during the religious instruction act, the greater is the possibility that their teaching and their lifework spirituality will be based on reality and will flourish. God lies in the details.

Almost every school of spirituality stresses the centrality of specific behaviors, for such is the kingdom of heaven. Contemplative spirituality both East and West places great store in specific behaviors of an ascetical sort. The spirituality of Ignatius of Loyola, especially in the practice of the examination of conscience, revolves around specific behaviors. Spiritual masters of every religion know full well that when persons fall away from sustained attention to specific behaviors in quest of so-called higher and more general pursuits, the result usually becomes amorphousness and vagueness, two of the most potent devils besetting the spiritual quest.

Specific behaviors form a central common ground for the intersection of the religious educator's lifework spirituality and that person's lifeway spirituality. The religious educator who disregards specific teacher behaviors and specific learner behaviors on the mistaken notion that teaching religion is a mysterious, unfathomable, spooky affair essentially uninfluenced by the specific behaviors which comprise it will likely be the same person who disregards the specific behaviors involved in lifeway spiritual activities on the erroneous presumption that lifeway spiritual activities are mysterious and unfathomable and spooky. Spookification of pedagogical procedure is detrimental to effective religion teaching and therefore to mature lifework spirituality. Spookification produces a magical mentality with respect to pedagogical procedure and to lifework spirituality, a mentality which falsely claims that God works in a magic fashion outside the laws of the creation which he has made and continues to make. Spookification of the religious instruction act is the last refuge of the teacher who does not care enough to give even the minimum. Spookification of the religious instruction act represents a pathetic attempt by the religious educator to evade the existence and functions of reality. Such an evasion of reality is no less harmful to lifework and lifeway spirituality than it is to effective religion teaching.

Unremitting attention to specific behaviors during the religious instruction act will enhance the teacher's effectiveness and the teacher's lifework spirituality. Such attention will also help improve the quality of the teacher's lifeway spirituality.

Pedagogical Procedure as Competent Enactment. It is a venerable maxim in Christianity that personal holiness does not dispense from skillful technique. The religious educator might be holy, but this fact is neither a substitute for nor a guarantee of effective pedagogical practice.

The venerable maxim mentioned in the previous paragraph looks at the relationship between the religious educator's spirituality and the religious educator's pedagogical practice from the perspective of the educator's personal qualities. Lifework spirituality, on the other hand, suggests that the relationship between the religious educator's spirituality and the religious educator's pedagogical practice be viewed from the vantage point of the religious instruction act. The concept of lifework spirituality implies that the quality and the texture of pedagogical practice itself contributes significantly to the shaping and the forming of the religious educator's spiritual life. Pedagogical practice poorly planned and ineptly executed has direct and far-reaching consequences for the lifework spirituality of the religious educator.

An example will illustrate the point I am making. The experience of many individuals as well as careful empirical research has shown that when a teacher cares about a learner, then that learner will tend to learn more than if he perceives that the teacher is indifferent or even hostile to him.[92] What is important here is not that the teacher cares for the learner but rather that the teacher effectively communicates this caring to the learner. Genuine caring is a pedagogical procedure. If the teacher fails to communicate caring, no significant learning will occur as a result of whatever care the teacher might have for the learner. Indeed, if the teacher fails to communicate caring to the learner, then in all probability the teacher does not really care for the learner since caring is a set of behaviors which connotes not just a personal concern for the other but more importantly doing all that is necessary to help the object of one's caring. Spiritually considered, caring ennobles the person who cares. But such spiritual ennoblement is impossible without the competent communication of one's care since caring itself necessitates competent communication of the care. In other words, a fundamental dimension of caring is the communication itself. To care for another is really just the prelude to real care. Authentic care is going out of our way to help the other person. Help is not help unless it is competently enacted. Incompetent enactment is bungling, and bungling is the opposite of help. The spiritual basis of care, then, lies in large measure in the competent enactment of care.

---

92. The bulk of the empirical research on this theme has been done with facilitation in the counseling process.

Care, spirituality, and competent enactment are all of a piece.

Competent pedagogical practice in religious instruction consists in two reciprocal, mutually interactive phases, namely, behavioral analysis and behavioral control. By carefully analyzing his own pedagogical behaviors and the behaviors of the learners, the religious educator is in a position to properly understand the communicative dynamics actually taking place in the religious instruction act. Armed with this necessary information, the religious educator is then in a position to effectively deploy his pedagogical skills in such a controlled manner that the learner acquires the desired outcomes.[93]

Since pedagogical competence is so important for lifework spirituality, religious educators would do well to improve the effectiveness of their teaching procedures as one major way of enhancing their spiritual lives. How can religious educators go about improving their pedagogical effectiveness? There are two primary avenues for accomplishing this goal, namely study and practice. These are the main avenues taken by all artists, be they musical artists, pictorial artists, literary artists, or pedagogical artists.[94] The religious educator ought to be a scholar-teacher. To be a scholar-teacher means to be a ceaseless student not only of religion (substantive content) but of the teaching process as well (structural content). One of the best ways to be a scholar-teacher is to frequently read serious, significant, and scholarly books in the field of religious instruction. Low-level books will tend to exert a stultifying and suffocating effect on religious educators who read such books. High-level books on religious instruction will help religious educators grow and stretch and avoid aridity.

In addition to studying seriously about religious instruction, the religious educator ought to strive to improve pedagogical performance through that kind of practice designed to improve teaching competence. Teaching, after all, is practice, namely the practice of facilitating learning outcomes in others. Probably the best medium for improving pedagogical practice in a sustained, deep, and lasting manner is the teacher performance center. The teacher performance center is a pedagogical laboratory in which (1) any aspect of pedagogical

93. For a further discussion of behavioral analysis and behavioral control as the basis of the teaching act, especially in terms of antecedent-consequent communicative chaining, see Lee, *The Flow of Religious Instruction*, pp. 277-284.

94. Teaching is simultaneously a science and an art. It is a science because the relationships among the interactive variables in the pedagogical dynamic can be explained by scientific laws and theory. It is an art because it is an enactment, an enactment done with purpose, effectiveness, and beauty. The science of teaching is acquired by relevant study. The art of teaching is acquired by relevant practice.

behavior such as caring or questioning or empathizing can be record-ed and analyzed through the use of currently available interaction devices, and (2) the teacher can practice and sharpen the control of this behavior through procedures such as microteaching, enactment of protocol materials, and the like. Dioceses and comparable denomi-national jurisdictions which are serious about improving the quality of religious instruction should establish and staff teacher performance centers.

The quality of the religious educator's lifework spirituality lies in doing religious instruction religiously and instructionally, that is to say competently.

Conclusion

The principal theme of this chapter is that the religious educator's spirituality is forged in large measure through the individual's lifework as a religion teacher. The quality and the texture of the religious educator's lifework spirituality is largely determined by the quality and texture of the religious instruction act, an act in which the religious educator is both facilitator and participant.

The leitmotiv of this chapter is beautifully and pointedly expressed in the closing lines of Irving Stone's magnificent biographical novel about Michelangelo Buonarroti.[95] Michelangelo is depicted in this stupendous novel as a man totally involved in and consumed by his lifework as an artist. At the end of the novel, Michelangelo lay dying. His final moments were consumed by thoughts and half-conscious reveries of his great lifework accomplishments—his superb sculptures of the Pietà and David, his wonderful architectural achievements like the Campidoglio and the Porta Pia, his exquisite paintings like the Genesis. And then, at the very end, his thoughts and his reveries stood still at St. Peter's, the Patriarchical Basilica whose dome he archi-tecturally designed and in which so much of his artistic energies were centered. St. Peter's, the crown and emblem of his lifework. "St. Peter's. . . . He entered the church through its front portal, walked in the strong Roman sunshine down the wide nave, stood below the center of the dome, just over the tomb of St. Peter. He felt his soul leave his body, rise upward into the dome, becoming part of it: part of space, of time, of heaven, and of God."

It is from within a lifework context that the religious educator ascends to God.

---

95. Irving Stone, *The Agony and the Ecstasy* (Garden City, N.Y.: Doubleday, 1961).

2

Developmental Spirituality and the Religious Educator

LEON McKENZIE

Lewis Mumford observed that the dominant themes of our culture are science, secular humanism, global industrialism, and social revolution. "But the emergent theme of the age," noted Theodore Roszak, "has been sounded . . . by those who begin to see themselves as unfinished animals summoned to unfold astonishing possibilities."[1] Despite the fascination with the dominant themes, the men and women who are at the frontiers of human progress are searching for lost meanings, and for meanings never before discovered. Science, secular humanism, industrialism, and sociopolitical movements of themselves cannot provide the impetus for authentic human growth.

The challenge of our era is clear to anyone who has not become befuddled by the ephemeral promises of the dominant cultural themes. We must, individually and collectively, develop ourselves spiritually. Those who are insightful recognize that it is necessary to begin a quest for meaning, a quest that is nothing less than a search for a way of being-in-the-world spiritually. Science, technology, economics, and politics are merely tools. The users of these tools must change fundamentally if humankind is to experience a worthwhile future.

---

1. Theodore Roszak, *Unfinished Animal* (New York: Harper & Row, 1975), p. 5.

43

This is to say that the most crucial issue that confronts us today is the issue of spirituality. To say that we must be concerned about spirituality is a notable imperative. If we are not concerned about spiritual development, it serves no good for us to be concerned about anything else.

The general framework for the chapters in this book includes: 1) a theoretical reflection on spirituality and 2) a discussion of the implications of this reflection for religious educators. This approach assumes that spiritual development must be grounded on sound theoretical foundations if it is to be fruitful and substantial. Prior to these considerations in this chapter, however, I feel compelled to comment on some pitfalls that lie in wait for those who undertake the journey toward spiritual meaning. The landscape is cluttered with questionable paths to meaning. To quote Roszak again, people often grope and stumble; "They follow false lights, they too easily mistake the theater for the temple, the circus for the sanctuary."[2] Contemporary enthusiasm for spirituality must be welcomed as a trend that holds promise for the field of religious education. But this enthusiasm can be misdirected and result in little more than involvement in endeavors that can actually impede spiritual growth. We turn first, then, to a critique of what I call the spirituality movement.

The Current Interest in Spirituality: A Critique

I confess to serious misgivings about offering an analysis of some of the dangers inherent in the spirituality movement. I have learned from experience that some religious educators are not receptive to remarks that do not celebrate unequivocally the glories of the spirituality movement. Gadflys are frequently appraised as malevolent pests who call into question the comforting conventional wisdom. To point out that enthusiasm for spirituality is sometimes associated with uncritical thinking or misplaced values often invites the wrath of some religious educators. "You are negative about things spiritual," some are wont to say, "because you are basically lacking in spirituality." This charge, of course, is merely a naive stratagem to block any criticism that calls into question some aspects of the spirituality movement.

Notwithstanding the fact that my criticisms may be dismissed, misinterpreted, or ignored, the commitments that constitute my personal spirituality urge me to speak with candor. Some religious educators who are deeply involved in the spirituality movement, it seems to me,

---

2. Ibid., p. 15.

are both superficial in their thinking and narcissistic in their pursuit of perfection. This needs to be stated regardless of the possibility that such an observation may be perceived as ill-intentioned carping. Before religious educators can reap the benefits of the spirituality movement, they must be alerted to potential pitfalls on the pilgrimage toward wholeness. These pitfalls are located in three areas: 1) the relentless passion for techniques of spiritual improvement; 2) the superficial level of thinking and discourse vis-à-vis spirituality; and 3) the tendency of some to become self-absorbed in the name of spiritual development.

The Search for Techniques

There is a pronounced inclination among human beings to focus attention on means instead of ends, on practical techniques instead of essential goals, and on solutions of problems without assessing the nature of problems. We tend to seek out a Yellow Brick Road, a Philosopher's Stone, a list of easy steps that lead ineluctably to desired results. This fascination with techniques is particularly strong in a technological-pragmatic culture, even among those who decry the values of a technological-pragmatic culture. Personal creativity is displaced by reliance on experts who map out procedures. Repetition of prescribed actions replaces reflection. Tactics are more important than strategic thinking.

The hunger for techniques is evident among religious educators who seek "things to do" and prepackaged instructional programs. This hunger for techniques is also evidenced in the area of spiritual development. Some religious educators, it seems, identify a particular tactic for spiritual development as the perfect recipe for personal growth. These techniques abound: Ignatian exercises, marriage encounter, yoga, the Jesus prayer, journal keeping, storytelling, Cursillo, directed retreats, biblical prayer, liturgical piety, centering prayer, breathing exercises, art as meditation, charismatic experiences, and so forth.

Nothing is wrong *per se* with tactical approaches to spiritual development. What is wrongheaded, however, is mistaking involvement in a tactical exercise as spiritual development. Techniques may be helpful for some, but ultimately the road to spiritual development is one that is traveled idiomatically. Spirituality is made of sterner stuff than the techniques that may lead to spiritual growth. And when a person enthrones a particular technique as the *via regia*, while at the same time disparaging other techniques, one can fairly assume that the individual knows dearly little about spirituality. Techniques may be useful for some at an early stage of spiritual development, but at a further stage techniques can actually get in the way of growth. This is particularly true of techniques that primarily emphasize psychological/emotional development.

The process of spiritual development is linked to the process of psychological development, but the processes are not isomorphic. While there may be an interpenetration of the dynamics involved in the two processes, spiritual development requires a commitment to values that are superordinate. Participation in activities that stress the mechanisms of psychological enrichment do not necessarily contribute to spiritual development. This observation is especially apt for those who confuse the paradigms of the human potential movement—many of which are highly valuable—with spiritual development. Participation in an Intensive Journal Workshop, for example, can be helpful psychologically but does not necessarily facilitate authentic spiritual maturity.

Human development, it is true, is all of one piece. Human development is one process. But there are distinct subprocesses enfolded within the overall process of human development. Not to recognize this is to place the doctrines of currently popular psychologists on the same plane with the teachings of Jesus. The doctrine of a currently celebrated psychological guru may be extremely worthwhile, but these teachings do not come to bear directly on issues of ultimate concern and faith commitment. This may seem to be an obvious statement. But even the obvious needs to be stated for those who are easily impressed by psychological novelties, esoterica, and/or the jargon of the therapy group. The point must be made forcefully for those who enjoy playing pop psychology games: Esalen is not Gethsemane, Big Sur is not Mt. Carmel.

Level of Discourse

The fascination with spiritual techniques is related to the tendency to speak about spirituality at a level of discourse that is often simplistic. I recall speaking with a clergyman after a workshop I conducted on adult education research. "The workshop was good," he stated. "It could have been excellent had you emphasized spirituality." I asked him what he meant by spirituality. "You could have at least mentioned God, Jesus, or the bible," was his rejoinder. "I had the feeling I was involved in a totally secular learning experience. After all, our goal is to bring people to Jesus. One can hardly be spiritual without talking about Jesus."

The incident is not atypical. Some religious educators are unable to discuss spirituality at a level that transcends churchy devotionalism. The language of discourse, in an apparent attempt to sound mystical, is frequently the language of obfuscation. Vagueness and conceptual fuzziness surround talk about spirituality. Anyone who does not use the language of conventional preaching or churchiness is judged by some to be inimical to spiritual concerns or, at least, secular.

There is a certain type of person who leads an inauthentic existence. These individuals, to adopt some notions of Martin Heidegger, are given to idle talk, curiosity, and ambiguity.[3] Idle talk trivializes that which is discussed while promoting the illusion that everything is understood. Curiosity constantly seeks novelty for the sake of novelty and inhibits an awe-full and critical appraisal of reality. Idle talk and curiosity combine to create an ambiguous language that clouds issues and fosters conceptual murkiness. It would be foolish to deny that such inauthenticity is never present when some religious educators attend to the topic of spirituality. But the ambiguous language of the religious educator, theologian, preacher, or spiritual master is well nigh unchallengeable because it is also a language that is pious. To challenge pious ambiguity or churchspeak lays one open to the charge of irreligion or impiety. Nonetheless it must be understood that spirituality does not consist simply of devotional discourse nor can it be inferred from the lack of pious language that a person is nonspiritual, aspiritual, or antispiritual.

The Peril of Narcissism

While the ardent search for techniques of spirituality and the tendency to equate pious language with spirituality deserve criticism, the strongest critique must be reserved for those whose interest in spirituality is rooted in a hidden narcissism. It is quite possible that some persons who have been swept along in the currents of the spirituality movement are victims of self-absorption.

In his analysis of the human potential movement or the "New Consciousness" movement of the 1970s, Christopher Lasch (among others) has pointed out that the political radicalism and concern for social causes that dominated the 1960s has given way to the origin of the therapeutic personality.[4] What is of primary concern today among those who formed the vanguard of the social activism of the 1960s is

---

3. For a more complete explanation of these notions see Martin Heidegger's *Being and Time*, trans. John Macquarrie and Edward Robinson (New York: Harper & Row, 1962), pp. 210-224.

4. Christopher Lasch, *The Culture of Narcissism* (New York: W. W. Norton, Warner Books Edition, 1979), pp. 33ff.

an exclusionary concern for self-fulfillment. Egoism, privatism, and self-absorption have triumphed over earlier concerns for the poor, the oppressed, and the victims of an imperfect society. The noble crusades for the welfare of others have been vacated by many; since the 1970s we have lived in the "Me" culture.

It is noteworthy, and not entirely coincidental, that recent interest in spiritual development is coterminous historically with the rise of the human potential movement. One wonders whether the various religious programs for spiritual development have their counterparts in the smorgasbord of self-awareness approaches offered in what Lasch calls "the spiritual supermarkets of the West Coast." Esalen, gestalt therapy, Transcendental Meditation, primal therapies, Silva Mind Control, and a host of other therapeutic products are not unsimilar to the various spiritual remedies offered by quasi-gurus who are institutionally affiliated with Christian churches.

What is at issue here is not, however, the similarity between the human potential movement and the spiritual development movement. Nor is the issue the similarity between techniques for self-improvement arising out of the human potential movement and the tactics that have been prescribed for spiritual growth. Both the human potential movement at large and the spirituality movement in the churches can help people grow; both movements possess some validity despite the flashy superficiality of gurus in both movements. The crucial issue is the intentionality of those who participate in these movements; the crucial issue is whether religious educators seek spiritual renewal out of a legitimate sense of Christian commitment or out of motives that are self-indulgent. Is the search for spiritual development rooted in the need to follow Jesus or is it the outgrowth of a need to follow this decade's trend?

Gordon Allport stated that ideal human maturation involves growth from egoism to altruism. Allport favorably regarded the law of affective evolution, first formulated by Auguste Comte. The law maintains that "with time there comes a diminution in the preponderance and intensity of personal inclinations, and a growth and extension of other-regarding sentiments."[5] Self-love remains a positive force in our lives, but it should not become so emphatic that it leads to narcissism.

Similarly, Abraham Maslow contended that self-actualization means "experiencing fully, vividly, selflessly, with full concentration and total absorption. It means experiencing without the self-consciousness of

---

5. Gordon Allport, *Becoming* (New Haven: Yale University Press, 1955), p. 30.

the adolescent."[6] The key word, according to Maslow, is "selflessly." The full development of human potential is contingent upon a person's ability to avoid egoism and narcissism.

In his excellent treatise *The Deeper Life*, Louis Dupre observes that the renunciation of desire must "be motivated by what lies beyond man, rather than by an egocentric concern with moral progress. An ascetic pursuit of virtue for its own sake has no part in Christian mysticism. Even the desire of spiritual perfection must be *God-centered* from the start. Too great a concern with one's own condition in no way profits spiritual life."[7] Experts in both psychology and ascetical theology emphasize the need for authentic motivation in spiritual development.

The issue of intentionality in spiritual development is perhaps the most difficult issue to resolve. Each person must look at himself or herself in all honesty. Only when honest evaluation occurs is it possible to escape the perils of spiritual narcissism. Religious educators must also seriously examine themselves in terms of the relentless passion for techniques that characterize some of their number; they must ask themselves if their thinking about spirituality tends to be superficial and whether their discourse about spirituality tends to be framed in church jargon.

My critique of the current interest in spirituality may not at all be applicable to the reader. Indeed, the kind of person who would read the essays in this volume probably is more critical than those who eschew serious discussions of spirituality in print. But the critique needed to be stated as a prolegomenon to my reflections on spirituality.

Spirituality: An Introduction

Spirituality, for me, refers to nothing less than a theory of human existence, a theory founded on the dynamics of ultimate concern, a theory that functions as a ground for a particular mode of being-in-the-world. The two principal elements of this description—the notions of theory and ultimate concern—require elaboration. This elaboration, in turn, serves as a preface to the explication of my understanding of spirituality.

---

6. Abraham Maslow, *The Farther Reaches of Human Nature* (New York: The Viking Press, 1971), p. 45.

7. Louis Dupre, *The Deeper Life: An Introduction to Christian Mysticism* (New York: Crossroad Publishing Company, 1981), pp. 70-71.

The Notion of Theory

The word theory is pregnant with multiple meanings.[8] Theory can connote: 1) a perspective from which a person experiences reality; 2) a paradigm or complexus of values that affects what is experienced from a particular perspective; 3) a nondiscursive vision of reality that obtains from experiencing reality from a particular perspective and with a specific set of values; 4) a series of propositions that describe the vision; and 5) the actual behaviors or practices that constitute an instantiation of the vision.

1. *Theory as Perspective.* Each of us has a particular vantage point on reality in time and place. The reference point of a medieval peasant is not the same as the reference point of someone who lives in the latter part of the twentieth century. Those who dwell in America, the Middle East, Europe, and Asia have different points of reference for seeing reality (note that the metaphor "to see" is employed to express "to experience"). The reference point of a fifty-year-old person is different from the perspective of an eighteen-year-old. Human beings may live physically in the same world but they experience different worlds perceptually and conceptually. What is experienced from one vantage point is not available to those who are situated at a different reference point. Does this imply that truth is relative? No. Truth as ontological truth is one; the individual's grasp of truth (logical truth), however, is partial, limited, and conditioned by his or her perspective. Truth is one. The apprehension of truth is manifold. We know truth relatively. Only God knows absolute truth absolutely because God's knowledge is constitutive of reality.

2. *Theory as Paradigm.* A paradigm is a "set of beliefs, axioms, assumptions, givens, or fundamentals that order and provide coherence to what is and how it works."[9] Simply stated, a paradigm is a complexus of values we bring with us to the act of experiencing reality. Two persons from the same culture, the same temporal location, and with generally the same backgrounds may experience the same reality differently because of the values and beliefs that affect their apprehension of reality.

When we view or experience anything from a particular perspective we introduce into the experience all of beliefs we have acquired. I can

---

8. A fuller treatment of the notion of theory can be found in my book *The Religious Education of Adults* (Birmingham, Ala.: Religious Education Press, 1982), pp. 104-114.

9. Peter Schwartz and James Ogilvey, *The Emergent Paradigm: Changing Patterns of Thought and Belief* (Menlo Park, Calif.: SRI International, 1979), p. 38.

share a perspective with another person and yet actually see something not seen by the person. Likewise, the other person can observe something I cannot possibly see. This is because in the act of experiencing or knowing each of us is actively receptive.

The act of knowing is characterized by the intromission of the knower's values and beliefs into the object that is known. To speak of knowing anything objectively is to fail to understand the place of subjectivity and valuing in the act of knowing. We address reality that is external to ourselves not as mere recipients but as creative agents who infuse reality with personal meanings. The relationship between knower and known is intussusceptive: Knowing subject and known object are drawn together in the consciousness of the knowing subject. When I attend to a fact, I do not know the fact as it is in itself but as it appears to me after I have intromitted my intentionality into the fact. "What a thing *is,* is to an unknowable extent determined by or influenced by what we *think* it is," writes Joseph Chilton Pearce.[10] He goes on to note that any worldview organizes a world-to-view. (It is more accurate, however, to state that one's worldview organizes a world-to-view, *and* the world one views is partially responsible for the development of one's worldview. The relationship between worldview and world-to-view is reciprocal.)

3. *Theory as Vision.* Attending to reality from a particular perspective and with a given set of values yields a vision of reality. This vision is "there" within a person in a nondiscursive and prelogical fashion. The vision is an internal landscape which reflects reality in a personal way. The vision is a source of ideas and judgments for the discursive or propositional expression of what has been experienced. Before words or propositions about reality, there is a vision of reality. This vision is a shaper of our reflective processes. Ordinarily the vision is translated into discursive language or propositional form before it serves as a guide for behavior or practice. Propositional theory is the mediating instrument that helps us move from vision to practice. Another way of saying this is that when practice is consistent with vision, practice is an instantiation of vision.

4. *Theory as Proposition.* As noted in the foregoing paragraph, when vision is expressed in words it becomes propositional theory. It is this kind of theory most people think about when they speak of theory. There are at least four major purposes of propositional theory: the explanatory, heuristic, predicative, and prescriptive purposes. Proposi-

---

10. Joseph Chilton Pearce, *The Crack in the Cosmic Egg* (New York: Pocket Books, 1977), p. 85.

tional theory may be employed to explain reality in a systematic and coherent manner. The heuristic purpose is served when propositional theory suggests research activities or raises questions for reflection. Propositional theory may be useful for predicting empirically what will happen given an intervention in a particular set of circumstances. Finally, propositional theory may prescribe a definite way of doing something.

5. *Theory as Practice.* When a given practice or particular behavior issues from the vision (which is mediated by propositional theory), the practice is a concrete instantiation of the vision. When my life activities correspond to my vision, these life activities are palpable manifestations of the vision. Theory and practice, therefore, are corelational: Vision is a source of activity and activity is an expression of vision.

Spirituality refers to a particular mode of being-in-the-world, a definite way of living. This mode of being-in-the-world is an instantiation of a spiritual vision that is mediated by language descriptive of that vision. A person's spiritual vision, in turn, is shaped to a large extent by the individual's unique perspective and by the values the person brings to the perspective. But spirituality is not just any kind of being-in-the-world. As a basic minimum, spirituality implies ultimate concern.

The Notion of Ultimate Concern

Paul Tillich averred that the faithful person is one whose life is situated in ultimate concern.[11] Tillich equated the dynamics of faith with ultimate concern. I prefer to state it thusly: The person of faith is oriented in thought and deed toward the Meaning that authenticates all of life's meanings. Without this meaning—God—my individual life and the entire cosmic process is nothing more than an exercise in futility.

Not all persons are able or willing to orient their lives consciously and consistently toward God. An individual submersed in poverty cannot often be ultimately concerned because more immediate concerns such as food and shelter are foremost in consciousness. Others expend vast amounts of psychic energy, as Ernest Becker noted, in avoiding ultimate concern.[12] The flight to the commonplace preserves

---

11. Paul Tillich, *The Dynamics of Faith* (New York: Harper & Row, 1958), p. 1.

12. Ernest Becker, *The Denial of Death* (New York: Macmillan Free Press, 1973). Becker's work is replete with brilliant insights on how human beings fabricate an imaginary world that is free from thoughts of death and ultimate concern. See especially pages 47-66.

them from wrestling with ultimate issues. To be ultimately concerned, for many people, is too arduous a task. Still others, particularly some of those involved in science and technology, develop a particular mode of reflection which inhibits the kind of thinking that reaches for ultimacy. This latter group has become fixated at a level of reflection which relates only to proximate causality. Reality is reduced to quantitative physical properties and no attempt is made to think metaphysically.

Faith as ultimate concern describes faith in a general sense that is applicable to all persons regardless of religious affiliation. Indeed, it is possible to be ultimately concerned while living outside any specific religious institution or convention. Martin Gardiner has shown this in his recent work. *The Whys of a Philosophical Scrivener*, a book that is as stimulating as it is remarkably simplistic in some of its parts.[13] Gardiner belongs to no religious tradition, but he nonetheless accounts himself a believer in God and accepts the efficacy of prayer. Of course, to say that faith is ultimate concern does not exhaust the connotative richness of the concept of faith. Faith means more than ultimate concern in a general sense, but it at least means ultimate concern in a general sense.

Spiritual development is a possibility only for those who attempt to attune themselves to the transcendent Meaning of reality, to God who is beyond all our images of God, to God who in his transcendence is nonetheless closer to us than we are to ourselves: the God who is present at times in his utter absence; the God who acts in human history through us.

Spirituality refers to a theory of human existence based on ultimate concern. Spirituality is fundamentally a vision of reality infused with ultimate concern. This vision incorporates the particular values of a person and leads to a specific mode of being-in-the-world. The values of the individual person of faith specify this way of life as Christian. Christian spirituality, then, is a particular mode of being-in-the-world defined by the Christian's commitment to the values expressed by Jesus.

An Understanding of Spirituality

Before I explicate my understanding of spirituality, it may serve the purposes of clarity to outline briefly my perspective and the paradigm

---

13. Martin Gardiner, *The Whys of a Philosophical Scrivener* (New York: William Morrow Quill Book, 1983).

I bring to that perspective. My perspective is secular or mundane in the sense that I am not a professional religionist. I am involved daily in educational administration, and in research and teaching in a graduate program of adult education. I function academically in the setting of a secular university. The vision that is permitted from this perspective, for good or ill, may be quite different from the visions of those who are actively involved in the bureaucratic life of religious institutions. While I am obviously disadvantaged by this perspective in some respects, in other respects my perspective yields experiences that are perhaps not available to professional religionists.

As for my general paradigm, I am a Christian in the Roman Catholic tradition. My faith could not be described as conventional. While I am able to profess the Apostles' Creed as a symbol of faith without reservation, my interpretations of this symbol are not identical with interpretations pronounced by Roman Catholic officialdom. I pay respectful attention to official delineations of doctrine but remain ultimately a self-defining Christian. This self-definition occurs within the context of church understood as a community of believers rather than as a hierarchical organization. To express this in a very commonplace manner, after all is said and done I operate out of my personal conscience. This is in keeping, I believe, with the best insights of Thomas Aquinas.

Two central values of my paradigm revolve around the notions of creation and resurrection. I see the world not as a place but as a process. The world is in a situation of ongoing creation and this creation, in the broad sense of the term, is the coresponsibility of God and humankind. The world can be turned toward a resurrection or new life that cannot at this point in time be fully comprehended. The criterion event against which all historical events must be measured is the resurrection (anastasis-standing again) of Jesus, a unique event that transcends the categories of historical experience and as such cannot be described adequately. I believe that the risen Jesus is the prolepsis of the absolute future, a future that awaits us beyond the denouement of the world process. I see Jesus' "standing again" as the Father's affirmation of Jesus and his teachings, an affirmation beyond which none other is possible. The teachings of Jesus, therefore, are the postulates for human activity vis-à-vis the ongoing exodus of the world process.

My Christian faith, again for good or ill, is Abrahamic in that it is a searching faith. I try to go forth trusting in God and not knowing what awaits me over the next hill. My faith may be described as critical, skeptical, and suspicious of the capacity of human language to express ultimate meanings. I accept the proposition that the institutional church is in need of continual reformation. I see the bureaucratic apparatus of the church as a means to an end and not as an end in itself. What is truly important for Christianity, and by implication for the world process, is not what happens in the councils of hierarchs and theologians, but what occurs in the lived experience of ordinary Christians and in the lived experience of those who do not profess Christian belief.

This outline of my paradigm is all too brief, but to explain the paradigm more completely would take us far afield from present purposes.

There is a marvelously insightful passage in Nikos Kazantzakis' *Report to Greco* that captures succinctly my understanding of spirituality.[14] Kazantzakis states that a great Cry is blowing through heaven and earth, and in our hearts, and that this Cry is called God. Plant life long ago wished to sleep peacefully next to stagnant waters, but the Cry shook its roots. "Away, let go of the earth, walk!" The plant, had it been able to speak, would have responded, "I don't want to. You are demanding the impossible."

After thousands of eons life escaped the motionless plant and worms appeared. They made for themselves a secure home in the mud. And the Cry relentlessly came to them: "Leave the mud, stand up, give birth to your betters." The worms answered, "We don't want to. We can't." But eventually they left their muddy home.

Again, thousands of eons passed. "Man emerged, trembling on his still unsolid legs." And the Cry mercilessly urges man to transcend himself.

Man calls in despair, "Where can I go? I have reached the pinnacle, beyond is the abyss." And the Cry answers, "I am beyond. Stand up!"

Ultimate meaning is implicit in every life situation we encounter. The Word of God is inherent in every situation. This Word calls to us and invites a self-transcending response, a response that brings in its wake authentic spiritual growth. The challenge implicit in every situation elicits our collaboration in the work of bringing to fulfillment the process of individual and cosmic evolution. We participate in this process by *attending* to the Word, by *interpreting* the Word, and by

---

14. Nikos Kazantzakis, *Report to Greco*, trans. P. A. Bien (New York: Bantam Books, 1971), pp. 278-79.

responding affirmatively to the Word. The spiritual life encompasses these three actings of attending, interpreting, and responding to the Meaning that is clothed in the events we experience.

Attending

Attending to the Word in life situations is impossible for some persons and difficult for all of us. A theoretical atheist, for example, cannot attend to the Word because of a rejection of God in the speculative realm. The atheistic theory of life forecloses the very possibility of events as revelatory. A practical atheist may profess a belief in God as a social convention, but issues of ultimate concern are seldom, if ever, regarded. Contemporary agnosticism, which is fundamentally an epistemological position, is reducible to practical atheism. Persons who have accepted the assumption that knowledge, by its very nature, does not transcend empirical data, are not able to view events except in their immediate concreteness. They are unable to see life events as symbols or mediating instrumentalities of the Word of God.

The act of attending to the Word is also impossible for those who are overwhelmed by the circumstances of poverty. A starving person who is in dire need of clothing and shelter cannot attend to the Word in life situations because these situations drain from the person the ability to concentrate and to reflect on meanings. Basic human needs must be filled before an individual is capacitated to deal with his or her spiritual actualization.

The nominal Christian is, by definition, unable to attend to the Word. The nominal Christian may be attuned only to the surface of events and does not attend to the deeper significance of life events. Such an individual lacks commitment and the insight that comes with commitment. Life situations are taken merely at their face value.

Curiously, another type of person is unable to attend to the Word because of a fixation on the sacred. This is curious precisely because one would expect that those who are actively involved in religious life would also be definitely inclined to attend to the Word. There are those, professional religionists among them, who have become accustomed to thinking about reality in terms of the Platonic dichotomy of the sacred and the secular. They find no difficulty in attending to the Word when they are engaged in explicitly religious activities such as worship or bible study, but pay little or no attention to the Word when it is vested in purely secular contexts. This bifurcation of reality into the sacred and secular domains has led to a kind of schizophrenia. For religious persons the concept of spirituality associates exclusively with liturgical celebrations, formulas of prayer, bible study, devotional discussions, and other activities that may be identified as "churchy." What is not "churchy," in their minds, is worldly, commonplace, a sort of ersatz reality. They would never expect to find the Word of God in the domain of the secular. This observation is important, I believe, because some religious educators are attracted to the work of religious education because of their predilection toward "churchy" activities and religious romanticism.

Even when we are not weighed down by limiting assumptions about how God communicates with us, we must nonetheless struggle to attend to the Word of God. We get carried away by the immediacy of our experiences. The joy we experience at a social gathering, the pain we feel in an illness, the fear we experience prior to a surgical operation, the rage that possesses us at the sight of gross injustice, the anger that surges up at a business meeting that has gone awry, all of these normal human reactions distract us from attending to the Word in these life situations.

At the very minimum spiritual development requires that we attend to the Word in the events of daily life. In its initial stages, therefore, spiritual development implies the development of a habit of consciousness that opens a person to the Word as it is present in life events. But attending is not enough.

Interpreting

The act of hearing requires both attending to the content of what is spoken and interpreting the message. It is one thing to discern the Word in a given situation and quite another thing to interpret the meaning of the Word. What is the meaning of the Word in this particular context? What is the nature of the invitation that is being extended to me by the Word? What response is being elicited?

In some situations the Word can be interpreted with relative ease. Suppose a hungry person comes to my door and asks for food. In this situation the Word is obviously inviting me to respond in such a way that the needs of the hungry person will be satisfied. In other more complex situations the interpretation of the Word becomes extremely difficult. Suppose I enter a voting booth to cast my ballot for a candidate who supports the budgeting of public money for abortions, a policy I judge as genocidal vis-à-vis society's outcasts. At the same time the candidate espouses an effective policy of public assistance that I perceive as representing Christian values. What is the Word saying to me as I prepare to vote?

There are no easy answers when the Word addresses us in complex situations. We can only struggle with the existential hermeneutic in the light of Christian tradition (written and oral) and in the light of our previous experience of the Word. If attending requires a special focused consciousness of life situations, interpreting calls for the critical application of Christian principles to the life situations. Often we will arrive at interpretations that are not altogether clear. The Word is frequently ambiguous, simultaneously disclosing and hiding aspects of meaning. This is because God wants us to work with him, not simply as unskilled laborers who function mechanically at the bidding of a straw boss, but as creative agents who are actively involved in a partnership which aims at the building of a New Heaven and a New Earth.

Responding

After we interpret the Word and gain some sense of the direction that the Word counsels, we respond by means of intentional action. That is, we choose to move in a given direction. This act of choice is no less difficult than attending and interpreting. Occasions arise wherein we are called upon to sacrifice selfish interests in favor of a choice we discern to be proposed by the Word.

The response is not something that is merely internal. While the choice is ideally internalized as a personal value, what is important is the action that issues from the intention to collaborate with the Word.

The concept of struggle is again apposite. All of us at times have been placed in situations that call for a response entailing the costs of discipleship. Occasionally we are called upon to take risks or to experience a loss of some kind because we choose to respond to events precisely as Christians.

Attending, interpreting, and responding to the Word in life events constitutes both a dialogue and an exodus. The Word is symbolized in life situations and our deeds in response to the Word symbolize our part of the dialogue. As the dialogue continues we move toward a promised land of cosmic and personal newness. Our exodus in spiritual development centers no less than on our participation in the process of creation.

Spirituality and the Roles of the Religious Educator

We develop spiritually to the extent we attend to the Word in life situations, interpret the Word as honestly as we are able, and respond to the Word as generously as we can. The field of our spiritual development is coterminous with life itself. Spiritual development can occur in the aspects of life we label secular and in the aspects of life we call sacred. Spiritual development takes place in the personal aspects of our lives and in the professional aspects. What we do as persons affects spiritual development; what we do as professionals affects spiritual development.

When we consider the religious educator as a professional we arrive at the following suggested norm for spiritual development: Spiritual development occurs in proportion to the degree the religious educator fulfills his or her professional roles. Obviously we cannot separate the professional and personal aspects of the religious educator's life. We can, however, distinguish professional roles from personal life at a notional level in order to focus on the spirituality of the religious educator as a professional.

It is not difficult initially to devise a strategy for spiritual development relative to the situations that typically exist in the religious educator's professional life. All that is necessary is the identification of the professional roles of the religious educator and what these roles require by way of appropriate response. This is to say that religious educators develop spiritually by fulfilling their professional roles to the best of their abilities.

Years ago a story of a now-forgotten saint impressed me greatly. The saint was taking recreation and was asked what he would do if he know he would die in one minute. "I would continue taking recreation," he said, "for that is what I am supposed to be doing." The moral of this hagiographic anecdote can be summed up in the old adage, "We advance spiritually not by doing extraordinary things but by doing ordinary things extraordinarily well." Following the logic of the anecdote I submit that religious educators can advance spiritually by doing what they are supposed to be doing. This principle does not prescribe arcane and dramatic stratagems for spiritual growth. For this reason some will dismiss the principle as commonplace and renew their search for esoterica and for a norm that appears more "mystical" in the neo-gnostic sense of the word. Nevertheless I espouse the principle as a norm that provides the surest direction for religious educators.

What are the professional roles of the religious educator that give us some sense of what religious educators are supposed to be doing? While I have little trouble identifying these roles out of my own understanding of religious education, I recognize that the field of religious education is neither soundly defined nor well developed in terms of philosophical foundations. Given this state of affairs there is room for differences of opinion regarding the roles of the religious educator. I suggest, however, that the practice of religious education involves six major roles: content specialist, researcher, curriculum developer, administrator, instructor, and counselor. There is no significance to the order in which these roles are listed here.

The professional situations that arise in the local church or parish call for responsive competence in each of these six professional areas. By competence I mean both knowledge in these six areas and the ability to apply knowledge to concrete situations in a fruitful manner.

Content Specialist

The religious educator must be competent as a content specialist in his or her religious tradition and, since we live in a pluralistic society, the other major religious traditions that are lived in our society. This competence implies understandings in theology, scripture, and liturgical studies. What the religious educator does with this specialized content is extremely important. The religious educator is not a transmitter of theological propositions; the religious educator is not a theologian-in-residence who teaches theology to people. Instead, the religious educator helps learners interpret their experiences in the light of their religious tradition. The religious tradition is something that is *lived* but nonetheless needs, at appropriate times, elucidation in respect to theological understanding. There are occasions when it is necessary for the religious educator to explore the meaning of the normative religious tradition before he or she can help learners interpret their experiences in the light of the tradition.

During the entire lifespan persons need to refer their experiences to their religious traditions. This is especially important in childhood. Children need meaning structures and norms to enable them to escape ambiguity and to develop a religious identity. As learners move from childhood to adulthood, and as they develop a capacity for critical awareness, they need help in evaluating the religious tradition that preserved them from intellectual and moral ambiguity. Not only must experience be evaluated in terms of tradition; tradition also must be evaluated in terms of lived experience if the tradition, or major aspects of it, are to be internalized in the hearts of believers. The process of religious education for adults, and even for adolescents, involves enabling learners to question, to evaluate, to search, and to arrive at a personal faith. This observation is perhaps most apposite for Roman Catholic religious educators. There has been an almost pathological tendency in the Roman Catholic Church for its leaders to equate teaching with the issuance of authoritative theological propositions. (Some Protestant fundamentalist traditions practice their own versions of this with the difference that theological propositions are replaced by absolutist interpretations of biblical passages.) Teaching, however, is ordinated toward learning. And significant learning occurs only when people inquire, evaluate, and think critically.

Researcher

Basically there are two kinds of research. Conclusion-oriented research is undertaken to generate knowledge that can be extrapolated to an entire field of study and practice. Decision-oriented research yields information that can be used for decision making relative to a particular location. A study of the values of religious educators in several dioceses relative to their academic backgrounds would be a conclusion-oriented study. The results of the study would be published or shared broadly. A study of the educational needs of adults in a particular parish would be a decision-oriented study. The results of the study would be useful only for developing a parish program.

Conclusion-oriented research is necessary for any field of study and social practice before that field can lay claim to the designation "professional." A professional field of study and practice is a field in which a body of knowledge is generated by means of research and "professed." This knowledge is analyzed, critiqued, and applied. For the sake of the professionalization of the field of religious education those religious educators with advanced academic degrees should contribute to the field's body of knowledge. All religious educators should be able to read published findings of conclusion-oriented research and apply these findings to their own situations. This means that religious educators should be knowledgeable about research design and procedures and the statistical treatment of data.

Religious educators should be able to conduct systematic decision-oriented research. This includes studies preliminary to curriculum development, evaluative studies of educational interventions and programs, and other studies that yield findings in respect to the values that are operative in their particular social contexts. Again, this requires a working knowledge of research design and procedures and statistics.

I have no illusions that my observations here will produce a revolution in the field of religious education. At face value it seems silly that any concept as lofty as spirituality could be related to something as mundane as, say, statistics. Of course, any perceived silliness in this regard is associated with the meanings attached to "lofty" and "mundane."

Curriculum Developer

The religious educator should be a curriculum developer and not merely a consumer of curricula developed by publishing companies or central administrative offices of the church. Nothing is less advantageous to learning than a teacher who "teaches the book" or simply covers pages in a teacher's guide. Published resources such as curricula and textbooks are means to an end. Quite often these resources become ends in themselves. Material resources are aids that help learners achieve specific instructional objectives. It seems imcomprehensible, particularly in adult religious education, that the objectives determined by a publishing company are appropriate for adults of different ages, abilities, concerns, needs, and social contexts.

The religious educator must be a curriculum developer at least to the extent that he or she is able to adapt packaged curricula to the exigencies of particular local churches. In order to effect necessary adaptations in packaged curricula it is necessary to evaluate these curricula in terms of what is known about the learners as they exist in a specific social context. Again, the need for applied social research comes to the fore. There is also a need for personal creativity and imagination. Curricula and materials that are used without adaptation are ordinarily used in a manner that is mechanistic and spiritless.

Administrator

The tasks involved in educational administration are less than glamorous. These tasks frequently become tiring chores that offer little opportunity for personal gratification. But without the completion of administrative tasks it is virtually impossible to maintain effective programs. Administration involves a number of different operations. These operations include but are not limited to:

1. The budgeting of fiscal resources and the accountability for cost effectiveness.
2. The recruitment and training of volunteer teachers.
3. The scheduling of rooms and the allocation of material resources.
4. The promotion of the educational program.
5. The supervision of instructional processes.
6. Strategic long-range planning.
7. The development of a climate that supports beneficial interpersonal relationships among teachers, between teachers and learners, and between teachers and parents.

Generally, administration involves decision making relative to the coordination of people, fiscal resources, materials, space, and time. Administrative work may be filled with tedium, but such work is the buttress for the entire educational enterprise.

Instructor

Religious instruction is more than the transmission of theological information. Any formalized instructional process must be cogently planned and implemented adequately before learning is effectively facilitated. The religious educator, therefore, must be able to formulate instructional objectives correctly, identify the resources that are to be used, determine appropriate teaching-learning techniques, sequence instructional activities to maximize the potential for learning, and establish a psychosocial climate that supports learning. In brief, the religious educator must provide a structure for the teaching-learning process that brings together a host of elements that facilitate learning. This implies that the religious educator is well-prepared in the technical aspects of the instructional process.

The management of the instructional process is easy and uncomplex only for those who fail to recognize that teaching is ordinated primarily to learning, that different types of learning can take place, and that systematic planning and implementation of instruction is crucial to religious instruction. A false mysticism which maintains that the good intentions of the religious educator are alone important, and that the Holy Spirit will intervene to salvage poor instruction, is perhaps the primary source for ineffectual instruction. The technical aspect of instructional planning and management must be mastered.

Counselor

Anyone who has functioned as a teacher knows that individual learners often seek guidance regarding their instructional experiences and/or personal problems on a one-to-one basis with the teacher. As with the other educational roles of the religious educator, the counseling or helping process is complex. Much more is involved in the helping process than listening and giving advice. Indeed, one has to know *how* to listen and help learners discover their own paths for the resolution of problems.

As counselor the religious educator should help learners explore their situations and should know how to manifest empathy, respect, and warmth. The religious educator should help the counselee arrive at understanding by emphasizing concreteness, genuineness, and self-disclosure. The religious educator should assist the learner to determine his or her own course of action by means of the appropriate interchange of ideas.[15]

---

15. For a summary of a worthwhile approach to the counseling process see George M. Gazda's *Human Relations Development: A Manual for Educators* (Boston: Allyn & Bacon, 1973).

Once again, it takes more than good intentions to facilitate the helping process. Counseling requires an expertise that is acquired only through study and practice. One cannot simply engage in counseling in an "off the cuff" manner and hope to provide real help for those in need. Frequently an "off the cuff" approach to counseling aggravates problems and does more harm than good. There are different stages in the counseling process that must be recognized and different interventions that may be actualized after a diagnostic examination of the conditions which brought the counselee to seek help. The religious educator must be knowledgeable about counseling theory and adept at selecting appropriate helping stratagems.

We grow spiritually as persons by attending to, interpreting, and responding to the Word of God present in the concrete situations of life. We grow spiritually in the professional dimensions of our personal lives by attending to, interpreting, and responding to the Word present in special situations that require professional performance. I have delineated the above selected roles of the religious educator on the basis of my attention to, and interpretation of, some of the typical situations in which religious educators find themselves. Obviously, I view the professional roles of the religious educator largely in terms of education. I would argue strongly that the view of the religious educator as content specialist in theology or theologian in residence is inadequate. This perspective may not be attractive to many religious educators. It is, however, a point of view that should be examined seriously.

Conclusion

One cannot overstate the importance of spirituality in an age that seems adrift on the seas of immediate pragmatic concerns, an age wherein issues of ultimate concern are overshadowed by the story lines of soap operas, an age in which everything seems touched by the process of trivialization. We are required to become self-transcending animals lest we perish. And self-transcendence is possible only for those who seek an authentic spirituality. I return again to what I consider the most important theme of this essay: the quest for a spirituality that is worthy of religious educators, a spirituality devoid of pop psych distractions. Such a spirituality must be founded on critical reflection. Critical reflection, in turn, is most surely facilitated in the give and take of dialogue and in the sharing of ideas and perspectives. The particular perspective offered in this essay may be somewhat different from viewpoints offered elsewhere in this volume.

In any event, all of these points of view should be studied, analyzed, discussed, and evaluated. The fruit of such a study may be an entirely new and more critical theory of spirituality, a theory of spirituality that serves as a basis for personal and collective enrichment.

3

Process Spirituality and the Religious Educator

RANDOLPH CRUMP MILLER

I
Introduction

"Spirituality" is a "weasel word." It has such a variety of meanings and emotional associations as to be almost meaningless. At its worst, it is reflected in the prayer of the Pharisee, who "stood and prayed thus with himself, 'God, I thank thee that I am not like other men, extortioners, unjust, adulterers, or even like this tax collector. I fast twice a week, I give tithes of all that I get'" (Lk. 18:11-12, RSV). Some spiritual experts teach with this goal, and we find similar expectations in some educational programs in churches and synagogues where the emphasis is on external behavior and formal spiritual exercises.

The popularity of a surface spirituality is a cause for concern. It was illustrated by a book in the Eisenhower era, *Piety Along the Potomac,* when church attendance was a mark of respectability. There are prayer groups in some churches where this same outward appearance of spirituality is substituted for the real thing.

Lest this judgment seem too harsh, in many cases there is deep yearning backed by sincerity in many spiritual adventures. Some of them may misfire, and in other cases there is a growing dissatisfaction with the lack of reality in the experience. Also, it needs to be recognized that there are honest differences in interpretations of both the term and the experience. We need to work for a unity that encompasses honest differences of opinion and the variety of experiences that provide a depth of awareness of the presence of God.

There is a genuine spirituality which we must look at carefully. It is free from false glosses, hypocrisy, and false pride. It is genuine because it deals with the mystery of God and the full meaning of humanity in the presence of God. It avoids assumptions of fixed beliefs about the nature of God, who is essentially mystery, but finds its anchor in the firmness of ultimate commitment to a deity never fully known. It leads to fulfillment in spite of all the setbacks of life and it promises salvation.

II
The Nature of Spirituality

Rachel Hosmer and Alan Jones, in *Living in the Spirit,* make some of the points listed above. Spirituality, they remind us, is an "umbrella" word, covering anything from exploring Zen to astrology. It may include many activities that are not normally considered religious, such as sports events and the spirit of the crowd. Hosmer and Jones seek to extract spirituality from "a stained glass quality" that makes it unreal for many people.[1]

"The point is that everyone has a spirituality—from Mother Teresa of Calcutta to the late Chairman Mao. Our choice of a particular spirituality, a particular way of arranging and gluing together our scattered lives, will determine the shape of our character and personality. Everyone struggles toward wholeness."[2]

Dorothy Dixon has approached the issue by saying that "if we define spiritual development as growth in awareness of unseen reality (including the vast unconscious realms of the human psyche), and the way the individual relates to these ineffable dimensions of existence, we have a working field for exploration."[3] This leads to a consideration of what F.S.C. Northrop calls "the undifferentiated aesthetic continuum." He suggests that awareness of spiritual reality is a "radi-

---

1. Rachel Hosmer and Alan Jones, *Living in the Spirit* (New York: Seabury Press, 1979), pp. 47-49.
2. Ibid., p. 49.
3. Dorothy Dixon, in *A Dictionary of Religious Education,* ed. John M. Sutcliffe (London: SCM Press, 1984), p. 329.

cally immediate experience, with all the differentiations of sensing and sensation removed, signifying nothing beyond itself."[4]

Such an experience is so lacking in differentiation that it exists, as William James suggested, at the periphery of experience. But there are moments when one is swept into a sense of oneness, when one is overwhelmed by the vastness which engulfs one, and when one is at one with whatever reality God is conceived to be. This is a description closer to some of the Eastern religions than to Christianity or Judaism, but it is common to all mystics and perhaps in a vague way to all persons.[5]

W. A. Auden, in his foreword to Dag Hammarskjöld's *Markings,* says that "Professor Whitehead was a very wise man, but he once said a very silly thing: 'Religion is what a man does with his solitude.' "[6] Auden was objecting to the privacy of such an experience, but he had not read far enough. The actual quotation is: "Religion is what the individual does with his solitariness. It runs through three stages, if it evolves to its final satisfaction. It is the transition from God the void to God the enemy, and from God the enemy to God the companion. Thus religion is solitariness."[7] There are the passing forms of religion which may be useful or harmful. There are the expressions of dogma, as well. "Expression, and in particular expression of dogma, is the return from solitariness to society. There is no such thing as absolute solitariness." It is in community that our solitary experiences are validated, for what is "known in secret must be enjoyed in common, and must be verified in common."[8]

Religion begins with a vision of something beyond our reach. "The fact of the religious vision, and its history of persistent expansion, is our ground for optimism," writes Whitehead. "Apart from it, human life is a flash of occasional enjoyments lighting up a mass of pain and misery, a bagatelle of transient experience. The vision claims nothing but worship; and worship is a surrender to the claim for assimilation, urged with the motive force of mutual love."[9] William Temple asserts

---

4. F.S.C. Northrop, *Nature, Man and God* (New York: Pocket Books, 1962), p. 189.

5. See Randolph Crump Miller, *The Language Gap and God* (New York: Pilgrim Press, 1970), p. 43.

6. Dag Hammarskjöld, *Markings,* Foreword by W. H. Auden (New York: Knopf, 1964), p. xxi.

7. Alfred North Whitehead, *Religion in the Making,* (New York: Macmillan, 1926), pp. 16-17.

8. Ibid., pp. 137-138.

9. Alfred North Whitehead, *Science and the Modern World* (New York: Macmillan, 1925), p. 275.

the same thing: "But when God is revealed as love, this can no longer be a solitary experience; it becomes an incorporation into the fellowship of all those whom God loves and who in answer are beginning to love God."[10]

Thus we have moved from solitariness to interpersonal relations, for the expression of spirituality is acted out in our relations with others. The two commandments of Jesus are equal: "Thou shalt love the Lord thy God with all thy heart, and with all thy soul, and with all thy mind. This is the first and great commandment. And the second is like unto it: Thou shalt love thy neighbor as thy self. On these two commandments hang all the Law and the Prophets."[11]

A genuine spirituality, then, is worked out in relation to others. Recognizing the distance that is between persons, there are certain qualities that emerge in treating others as persons and not as things. Through one's relation with a deity of love, there is a development of authentic personhood. One is able to be open to the other, to listen in a genuine dialogue, and to maintain that relationship in spite of disagreements. One stands on one's own feet, and yet is capable of being flexible and adaptable. Each one becomes present to the other. This is obvious in sound marriages, but it is an expresson of the spirit in every human relationship. There is risk in such a relationship, for one may be betrayed, ridiculed, or misunderstood, and this may lead to withdrawal and refusal to take further risks. But when the person has deep faith, one is enabled to face criticism, be open to the challenge of another's opinions, and to reveal oneself to others. Thus there is developed a mutuality between persons. This requires a degree of discipline, holding ourselves from seeking to overcome the other so that we may accept the other's contribution, and assuming responsibility when our action is called for.[12]

The focal point of spirituality is common worship, but it does not always become real to the participants. Isaiah made this clear many years ago:

> What to me is the multitude of your sacrifices?
>   says the Lord;
> I have had enough of burnt offerings of rams,

---

10. *William Temple's Teaching*, ed. A. E. Baker (London: William Clarke & Co., n.d.), p. 95.

11. *Book of Common Prayer* (New York: Church Hymnal Corporation, 1977), p. 324.

12. See Reuel L. Howe, *The Miracle of Dialogue* (New York: Seabury Press, 1963), pp. 67-83.

and the fat of fed beasts;
I do not delight in the blood of bulls,
  or of lambs, or of he-goats.
When you come to appear before me,
  who requires of you
  this trampling of my courts?
Bring no more vain offerings;
  incense is an abomination to me.
New moon and sabbath and the calling of assemblies—
  I cannot endure iniquity and solemn assembly.
Your new moons and your appointed feasts
  my soul hates;
they have become a burden to me,
  I am weary of bearing them.
When you spread forth your hands,
  I will hide my eyes from you;
even though you make many prayers,
  I will not listen;
  your hands are full of blood.
Wash yourselves; make yourselves clean;
  remove the evil of your doings
  from before my eyes;
cease to do evil,
  learn to do good;
seek justice,
  correct oppression;
defend the fatherless,
  plead for the widow.
                    (Isaiah 1:11-17, RSV)

Many people stay away from the worship of the church because there is an empty formality about what seems to be going through the motions. It is a false spirituality on a corporate basis.

Contrast this with the 145th Psalm:

I will extol thee, my God and King,
  and bless thy name for ever and ever.
Every day will I bless thee,
  and praise thy name for ever and ever.
Great is the LORD, and greatly to be praised,
  and his greatness is unsearchable.
One generation shall laud thy works to another,
  and shall declare thy mighty acts.
On the glorious splendor of thy majesty,
  and on thy wondrous works, I will meditate.

Man shall proclaim the might of thy terrible acts,
  and I will declare thy greatness.
They shall pour forth the fame of thy abundant goodness,
and shall sing aloud of thy righteousness.
                              (Psalm 145:1-7, RSV)

Whitehead saw this clearly. "The worship of God is not a rule of safety—it is an adventure of the spirit, a flight after the unattainable. The death of religion comes with the repression of the high hope of adventure."[13]

There are many things that keep us from worship. We have dry periods when we have little sense of God's presence. We have moods that separate us from God and from other people. We build walls around ourselves when we are too negligent to care about ourselves or others. We are sometimes bored with everything, and we say with Malachi, "What a weariness this is!" (Mal. 1:13, RSV), or we are rebellious and angry at God and the world, or we are suspicious and become paranoid in our mistrust of others. We become dead to the world and to people, and we have no desire to worship.

Yet all life is a constant process of becoming and perishing, and there is emerging novelty challenging us to make new decisions. The imagery of the dying and rising Christ is a rich part of the Christian heritage. A husband and wife become "dead" to each other, and so the marriage dies; but they may become alive to each other again, and so the marriage rises again. The same motif appears when the lost son is found, is dead, and is alive again. The lonely are restored to fellowship, sinners are reborn, transgressors are forgiven, enemies are reconciled.

When we worship, we are drawn into a fellowship that is aware not only of God's presence but of the relationship of the worshipers to each other as a supportive community. We experience ourselves as unacceptable to others and to God, and thus we are separated from them. What we hope for is reconciliation, and this is something we cannot command. Dying and rising are not under our control. But in worship we have the gift of being accepted even while we are unacceptable. "While we were yet sinners Christ died for us" (Rom. 5:8, RSV). The Easter faith comes alive for us in the recognition that death and resurrection provide the central motif for living in this world. The relationship of God's persuasive love is constantly offered to us through worship and is channeled through other people as well as through the direct relationship we may have with God. Thus we are

---

13. Whitehead, *Science and the Modern World*, p. 276.

restored to wholeness and are enabled to align our aims with God's in our moral, social, and political behavior.[14]

This points to what Whitehead calls our sense of worth. Running throughout the biblical story is the emphasis on human beings as valuable in the sight of God. Humanity is created in God's image. The psalmist wrote that we are "little lower than God" (Ps. 8:5, G). In my *This We Can Believe*, I wrote:

> Each of us is a society, made up of many processes which are becoming and perishing, and we are parts of a larger society that ultimately includes the cosmos. We are the products not only of our inner societies but also of the society we perceive. Yet we endure with a self-conscious identity, so that we know who we are, as we affect and have an effect on whatever is around us. The social system operating within us is not different from that operating in an animal, except that there is a tension between the bodily and mental poles which is different at our level of existence.
>
> In this process of becoming and perishing, we move toward novelty. Life offers us the bid of freedom whereby we may build on what has perished as we become new creations. These novelties may be introduced for any reason or none, but when they are guided by purpose, ideals, and value they point to the major difference between human beings and other animals. We grow as individuals in relationship, and we are constituted by the relationships we experience and affect. We do not control our environment, we are not creators, and ultimately we do not determine the world's destiny, but we do learn to align our aims with God's so that we respond to a love that is beyond us and experience the transforming power of God's grace.
>
> At the center of our consciousness is the sense of worth. To be human, to exist at all, is to feel worthy. This confidence in our worth gives us a basis for moral action and for belief in God. We are enabled by recognition of the worth of others to trust, and ultimately to trust God as well as ourselves and others. When we lose this sense of worth and come to despise ourselves, we find that our ability to relate to others and to God vanishes.[15]

Our spirituality expressed primarily in worship but also through supportive mutual relations keeps alive the sense of worth. It becomes a basic factor for the religious educator, who deals with the students in

---

14. *The Upper Room Disciplines, 1978* (Nashville, The Upper Room, 1977), p. 101.

15. Randolph Crump Miller, *This We Can Believe* (New York: Hawthorne and Seabury, 1976), pp. 120-121.

such a way that they know they are persons of worth! This is crucial for the sake of the interpersonal relations which provide the environment for religious teaching, but it also exposes them to the convictions that underlie the specific communication from teacher to pupil and vice versa in genuine dialogue.

III
Prayer

One of the significant books of the last generation was Harry Emerson Fosdick's *The Meaning of Prayer*. The starting point for Fosdick was that everyone has been "touched" by God, and prayer is the response. It is "latent," he wrote, in all people, but it is not readily recognized. It is in our impulses even when it is not expressed. In a whimsical simile, Henry Ward Beecher said: "I pray on the principle that the wine knocks the cork out of the bottle. There is an inward fermentation and there must be a vent."[16]

There is a dim awareness of God, of the Holy, which causes a response of awe, an uncanny emotion that is hard to describe. It is something like Northrop's "undifferentiated aesthetic continuum." Whitehead says that there is "no direct vision of a personal God" for it is only an inference.[17] We need to be cautious in speaking of God as personal, recognizing that it is an analogy drawn from human relations.

Yet we address God as personal. God as love is always thought of as personal, and our relationship with God is thought of as interpersonal. Concerning Theodore Parker, a Boston preacher, his biographer writes: "In his *theology* God was neither personal nor impersonal, but a reality transcending these distinctions. In his *devotions* God was as personal as his own father or mother, and he prayed to him as such, daringly indifferent to the anthropomorphisms of his unfettered speech."[18]

Prayer is always the spoken or unspoken expression of the deepest feelings of devotion. The concerns of our prayer are to be expressed in the presence of the holy one. This lifting up of our needs and those of others in the presence of God purifies them. As George MacDonald has written: "Anything large enough for a wish to light upon, is large enough to hang a prayer upon; the thought of him to whom that

---

16. Harry Emerson Fosdick, *The Meaning of Being a Christian* (New York: Association Press, 1964), p. 229.

17. Whitehead, *Religion in the Making*, pp. 62-63.

18. Fosdick, *The Meaning of Being a Christian*, p. 62.

prayer goes will purify and correct the desire."[19] Of course, the words of some prayers are insincere or strictly for show, but this is not our concern here.

The words of genuine prayer are what J. L. Austin calls "performatives."[20] They do things. They ask, praise, tell, confess, commit, promise; they express an attitude; they open up the worshiper to the leading of God. This may be in terms of spoken words, or in silent meditation. It may be in an atmosphere of solitariness, in a crowd, or corporately in a group, family, or congregation.

Praying is more difficult than it seems. There are many barriers. One is described as follows: "So if you are offering your gift at the altar, and there remember that your brother has something against you, leave your gift there before the altar and go; first be reconciled to your brother, and then come and offer your gift" (Mt. 5:23, 24, RSV). Vindictiveness can interfere with prayer. Alienation can keep one from attempting to pray. Sheer fatigue or apathy may get in the way.

We may use prayer as a last resort, and because we do not know from practice how to pray, we have difficulties. Psalm 107 describes a storm at sea, so that the crew "reeled and staggered like drunken men, and were at their wit's end. Then they cried to the Lord in their trouble, and he delivered them from their distress" (Ps. 107:27-28, RSV). It has been said that there are no atheists in foxholes. But such prayer is spasmodic, and thus does not provide the constant sense of God's presence.

There are those who think of prayer "as a form of spiritual gymnastics—what Horace Bushnell called 'mere dumbbell exercise!' They lift the dumbbell of intercessory prayer, not because they think it helps their friends, but because it strenghtens the fiber of their own sympathy. . . . But this kind of prayer is not likely to persist long. A thoughtful [person] balks at continuing to cry 'O God,' simply to improve the quality of [one's] own voice. . . . It is not prayer."[21]

We need to develop the habit of prayer. A slogan on my father's church bulletin used to read: "Put habit on the side of religion." If human beings are "praying animals" and this is one important function that marks them off from other animals, we need to nurture this activity. As William James said, "The reason why we do pray is simply that we cannot help praying."

---

19. *George MacDonald: An Anthology*, ed. C. S. Lewis (New York: Macmillan, 1947), 1974, 1978), No. 94, p. 42.

20. J. L. Austin, *How To Do Things with Words* (Oxford: Oxford University Press, 1962), pp. 1-24.

21. Fosdick, *The Meaning of Being a Christian*, p. 238.

I remember driving over a little used dirt road to Chaco Canyon in New Mexico. There were only two ruts, the going was slow, and we got stuck in the sand that had blown over the road. Prayer is like a road, but when it is little used we may get stuck. But unlike the road that needs to be fixed by the highway department, we can keep the road to prayer open by frequent use.

> But maybe prayer is a road to rise,
> A mountain path leading toward the skies
> To assist the spirit who truly tries.
> But it isn't a shibboleth, creed, nor code,
> It isn't a pack-horse, it's only a road.
> And perhaps the reward of the spirit who tries
> Is not the goal, but the exercise![22]

Prayer is a means whereby we place ourselves consciously in the presence of God. In this dialogue with deity, the great gift to us is God. In God's presence we can express any and all of our concerns. This can be a continuing sense of being in communion with God. "Be happy in your faith at all times. Never stop praying. Be thankful whatever the circumstances may be," wrote Paul (1 Thess. 5:17, P).

One prayer for those we love is the following: "Almighty God, we entrust all who are dear to us to your never-failing care and love, for this life and the life to come, knowing that you are doing for them better things than we can desire or pray for; through Jesus Christ our Lord."[23] For ourselves, no prayer is more inclusive than the one popularized by Reinhold Niebuhr:

> O God, give me the serenity to accept what cannot be
>   changed;
> Give me the courage to change what can be changed;
> And the wisdom to distinguish the one from the other.

The one big question that faces us is why our prayers sometimes lead to failure to overcome suffering. The most dramatic one is the prayer of Jesus in the Garden of Gethsemane.

"My heart is nearly breaking. . . . Stay here and keep watch for me."
Then he walked forward a little way and flung himself on the ground, praying that, if it were possible, he might not have to face the ordeal.

---

22. Edmund Vance Cooke, "Prayer," *The Uncommon Commoner* (New York: Dodge Publishing Co.), 1913.
23. *The Book of Common Prayer* (New York: Church Hymnal Corporation, 1977), No. 54, p. 831.

"Dear Father," he said, "all things are possible to you. Please—let me not have to drink this cup! Yet it is not what I want but what you want."

(Mk. 14:34-36, P)

The prayer of Habakkuk is also one of unfulfilled desire.

> How long, O Lord, have I cried to thee, unanswered?
> I cry, "Violence!" but thou dost not save.
>   Why dost thou let me see such misery,
>   why countenance wrongdoing?
>
> Devastation and violence confront me;
> strife breaks out, discord raises its head,
>   and so law grows effete;
>   justice does not come forth victorious;
>   for the wicked outwit the righteous,
>   and so justice comes out perverted. . . .
>
> O Lord, it is thou who hast destined them to execute
>   judgment;
> O mighty God, thou who hast destined them to chastise,
>   thou whose eyes are too pure to look upon evil.
>   and who canst not countenance wrongdoing,
>   why dost thou countenance the treachery of the wicked?
> Why keep silent when they devour men more righteous than
>   they?
>   Why dost thou make men like the fish of the sea,
> like gliding creatures that obey no ruler?

(Hab. 1:1-4, 12b-14, NEB)

Henry Ward Beecher gives us a wry comment on prayer: "A woman prays for patience and God sends her a green cook."

Fosdick recounts the story of Adoniram Judson, who wrote: "I never prayed sincerely and earnestly for anything, but it came; at some time—no matter how distant a day—somehow, in some shape—probably the last I should have devised—it came." And Fosdick relates what happened to Judson. "But Judson had prayed for entrance into India and had been compelled to go to Burma. He had prayed for his wife's life, and had buried both her and his two children. He had prayed for release from the King of Ava's prison and had lain there months, chained and miserable. Scores of Judson's petitions had gone without affirmative answer. But *Judson* had always been answered. He had been upheld, guided, re-informed. Unforeseen doors had been opened through the very trials he sought to avoid. The deep desires of his life were being accomplished not in his way but beyond his way."[24]

Out of such misery and difficulties come emerging novelties that enrich our lives or the lives of others. Samuel Rutherford put it beautifully: "When I am in the cellar of affliction, I reach out my hand for the king's wine."[25] In this context also we can assimilate the meaning of the phrase ascribed to Jesus: "I have come to let them have life, and to let them have it in abundance" (Jn. 10:10, G).

Prayer is a way of coming to decisions. William Temple once described a process he had gone through:

> I had once to make a choice which I found very difficult. I was very much interested in the work I was doing, believing it to be of some value. I was asked to take up another post which was certainly more conspicuous in the eyes of the world. I tried to avoid it. I asked all the friends of whom I could think, and they all said I had better stay where I was. I had to make a decision in time to write a letter by a certain post, and having weighed up the question as carefully as I could—and we must always do that—and having come to no conclusion at all, I began at eight o'clock in the evening to say my prayers, and for three hours, without pause, I tried to concentrate all my desires on knowing clearly what was God's will for me. I do not know how those three hours went; they did not seem very long; but when eleven o'clock struck I knew perfectly well what I had got to do and that was to accept; and I have never had a shadow of doubt since that I was right. One might go on. Other people, of course, have experiences far more striking and intimate. But there it is; there is no general rule that settles things for everyone. Each [one] has to find [one's] own vocation.[26]

Henry Nelson Wieman used to speak of problem-solving mysticism, of approaching our decisions through coming into God's presence. This is the "experience of discerning how things which were made for one another fit together." It is a sensing of the organic connection between the believers and those who make up one's world. Where this organic relationship is not yet discerned, where there is a disintegrating situation or conflict, the normal channels of reasoning cannot eliminate the problem, as it could not for Archbishop Temple. Wieman proposes that we face the problem "without any formulated thought but in a state of receptivity and responsiveness, waiting for some clue that will lead on to a new line. It is a state of waiting but

---

24. Fosdick, *The Meaning of Being a Christian*, p. 270.
25. Ibid., p. 140.
26. *William Temple's Teaching*, p. 127.

without preconception of what one is waiting for." So one becomes open to new thoughts, new ways of doing things, and new relationships. The result may prove to be useless, and one may try again. Or there may come a clue that resolves the problem.[27]

Prayer is an important element in the vocation of the religious educator, who is in some kind of relationship with the students, both children and adults. One has to make some difficult decisions, where the direction of action is not clear or susceptible to rational choice. The kind of prayer suggested by Temple and Wieman is important, for out of it new insights may emerge. It is also a process that can be utilized by the members of the class, including the teacher, as they face problems together.

We need to remember also that in the few references to prayers that Jesus prayed for the children. "Then some children were brought up to him so that he might lay his hands on them and pray" (Mt. 19:14, G). Jesus told Simon, "I have prayed that your own faith may not fail" (Lk. 22:32, G). Because there were few to reap, he said, "Pray to the owner of the harvest to send reapers to gather it" (Lk. 10:2, G). At the end, there were three prayers: "My God, my God, why have you forsaken me?" (Mk. 15:34, G); "Father, forgive them; for they know not what they do" (Lk. 23:34, RSV); and "Father, into thy hands I commit my spirit" (Lk. 23:46, RSV). Also concerned with his own death, Jesus was willing to ask God to forgive his enemies.

Religious educators also have enemies for whom they should pray. Nothing can assist a teacher more than to think of the persons in class by name in prayer. Prayers for others are an expression of our love for them, a way of entering into their lives without interfering with them.

Much of what we have said about prayer is summarized in Jan Struther's wonderful hymn:

> Lord of all hopefulness, Lord of all joy,
> Whose trust, ever childlike, no cares could destroy,
> Be there at our waking, and give us, we pray,
> Your bliss in our hearts, Lord, at the break of the day.

> Lord of all eagerness, Lord of all faith,
> Whose strong hands were skilled at the plane and the lathe,
> Be there at our labors, and give us, we pray,
> Your strength in our hearts, Lord, at the noon of the day.

---

27. Henry Nelson Wieman, *Methods of Private Religious Living* (New York: Macmillan, 1929), pp. 185-190.

Lord of all kindliness, Lord of all grace,
Your hands swift to welcome, your arms to embrace,
Be there at our homing, and give us, we pray,
Your love in our hearts, Lord, at the eve of the day

Lord of all gentleness, Lord of all calm,
Whose voice is contentment, whose presence is balm,
Be there at our sleeping, and give us, we pray,
Your peace in our hearts, Lord, at the end of the day.[28]

In 1976 at the 70th anniversary of the publication of the first volume of *Religious Education,* at a luncheon in Los Angeles, Bert S. Gerard gave the following invocation:

God and God of our fathers: God of Abraham, Isaac, and Jacob; God and God of our mothers: God of Rachel, Leah, Sarah, Rebecca, and Mary; God of our brothers and sisters: God of Noah, Job, and John the 23rd; God of Hanna Senessh, Teresa of Avila, and Harriet Tubman; God of Abraham Heschl, Gene Debs, Jane Addams, Bobby Kennedy, and Martin Luther King, Jr., grant us the sanction to discover you while looking for ourselves.[29]

[For a Protestant approach to spirituality and prayer, certain books have proved valuable over the years. The nearest to a Protestant classic is Harry Emerson Fosdick's trilogy, *The Meaning of Faith, The Meaning of Prayer,* and *The Meaning of Service.* Excerpts from all three were reprinted in *The Meaning of Being a Christian* (New York: Association Press, 1964). The best collection of prayers in the Anglican Communion is *The Book of English Collects,* ed. John W. Suter, Jr. (New York: Harper & Row, 1940). *Prayers of the Spirit,* by John W. Suter (New York: Harper & Row, 1943) contains more recent prayers, mostly by Dr. Suter. *Challenge and Power,* compiled and edited by Wade Crawford Barclay (New York: Abingdon, 1936), is a book I have made use of in the past forty-five years. *Lift Up Your Hearts,* by Walter Russell Bowie (New York: Macmillan, 1939), contains a variety of prayers and litanies which have significance still. *Come Sweet Death,* by B. Davie Napier (Philadelphia: Pilgrim Press, 1967), is a delightful commentary on Genesis, full of humor and insight. His *Time of Burning* (Philadelphia: Pilgrim Press, 1970), deals with other characters in the

28. From "Lord of all hopefulness" by Jan Struther, in *Songs of Praise* (London: Oxford University Press, 1931), No. 565. Used with permission.
29. Bert S. Gerard, "Prayer at the 70th Anniversary Luncheon," *Religious Education* 71, No. 4 (July-August 1976), p. 362. Adapted.

Jewish scriptures. *Prayers of the New Testament,* by Donald Coggan (New York: Harper & Row, 1967), covers everything that can be called a prayer. Also, *Prayers for a New World,* compiled and edited by John W. Suter (New York: Scribners, 1964), should be considered for its concern with contemporary problems and for its consistent literary style. It is ecumenical in its inclusiveness.

For other treatments of prayer among my books, see *The Clue to Christian Education* (New York: Scribners, 1950), pp. 120-137, 150-151; *Living with Anxiety* (Philadelphia: Pilgrim, 1971), pp. 118-128; *This We Can Believe* (New York: Hawthorne-Seabury, 1976), pp. 138-153.]

IV
Finding God

Seek the Lord while he may be found,
    call upon him while he is near;
let the wicked forsake his way,
    and the unrighteous man his thoughts;
let him return to the LORD, that he may have mercy on him,
    and to our God, for he will abundantly pardon.

(Isaiah 55:6-7, RSV)

But what kind of God are we seeking? Is God something beyond us? Where do we look for the divine? Whitehead writes, "If the modern world is to find God, it must find him through love and not through fear."[30] The simplest definition is that "God is love," a theme that runs through both the Jewish and Christian traditions, although frequently obscured by a variety of misunderstandings. We have tried to find God through reason, beauty, law and order, or even a vague pantheism. Some people have a religious experience and simply do not recognize it as such, or they recognize it but are unable to make use of a suitable concept and therefore do not recognize that they have been with God or God has been with and in them all the time. Fosdick reminds us that "the presence of God can be experienced only within our own hearts. *All the best in us is God in us.* . . . No [one] should ever grope outside of [one's] best self to find God."[31]

Why should you say, O Jacob,
And speak, O Israel:

---

30. Whitehead, *Religion in the Making,* p. 76.
31. Fosdick, *The Meaning of Being a Christian,* p. 258.

"My way is hidden from the LORD,
And my rights are passed over my God?"
Have you not known? Have you not heard?
The LORD is a God everlasting,
The Creator of the ends of the earth.
He does not faint, nor grow weary,
His insight is unfathomable.
He gives power to the fainting,
And to him that has no might he increases strength.
Though the youths faint and grow weary,
Though the young men fall prostrate,
They that wait upon the LORD shall renew their strength,
They shall mount on wings like eagles,
They shall run and not be weary,
They shall walk and not faint.

(Isaiah 40:27-31, G)

God is loving, compassionate, sympathetic, supportive, persuasive, earnest, and righteous. But God's judgment requires that righteousness also be at work. "What does the LORD require of you but to do justice, and to love kindness, and to walk humbly with your God?" asks Micah (6:8). "Let justice roll down like waters, and righteousness like an over-flowing stream," says Amos (5:24). At the same time we are reminded that "God so loved the world that he gave his only Son" (Jn. 3:16). God is like a shepherd who seeks his lost sheep, who forgives an erring son, who is concerned about the little ones. God is one who cares deeply about human beings and indeed about the whole creation.

So we are faced with what Whitehead calls "the brief Galilean vision" of a deity of persuasive love. Where there is sin, or evil, or suffering, a loving God shares and is affected by it, just as God is affected by our joys and our achievements of value. God as love does not coerce us, for we remain free and susceptible to all kinds of forces including the persuasive love of God. God works through us to influence us, to transform us, and to share his love with us, And when things go wrong he does not become a dictator by taking over. The cross stands at the center of Christian faith and makes it clear that God suffers for and with us, with the resurrection as a symbol of ultimate victory.

But things do go wrong, and this is where judgment comes in. Ideal parents love their children and do everything to assist them to fulfill their hopes and dreams; they provide guidelines along the way. When children ignore these guidelines, they may suffer, and the judgment is mostly impersonal and legal. If the child ends up in jail or in the accident ward, the parents do not cease to offer their love. They may be hurt, they may share the child's suffering, they may pay the child's bail, but they stand by and offer their transforming and supportive love. This analogy needs to be taken seriously as we reflect on God's judgment on us.

Spirituality emerges from the awareness of a deity in whom "we live and move and have our being" (Acts 17:28, RSV). The reality of God is, I think, an acceptable conclusion for most of us, but the varieties of religious experience and the cultural contexts in which we interpret the data lead us to concepts that sometimes seem to point to different Gods. The traditions of Protestantism, derived mainly from our Jewish biblical heritage and reinterpreted by the apostolic writings and the giants of the Reformation, come to us in the twentieth century in new trappings. For me, a Protestant in the Episcopal tradition and with a grounding in empirical and process theology, the roots of spirituality are as described above.

But the certainties of faith lie in one's commitment rather than in one's beliefs. Ian T. Ramsey wrote: "Being sure in religion does not entail being certain in theology."[32] Loyalty and commitment operate in areas where we only have a high degree of probability, and often our action results in further proof of our beliefs. This leads to a warning to all religious educators: "Let us always be cautious of talking about God in straightforward language. Let us never talk as if we had privileged access to the diaries of God's private life, or expert insight into his descriptive psychology so that we may say quite cheerfully why God did what, when, and where."[33] Horace Bushnell thought that all language about God was metaphor, poetry, and richly imaginative. The creeds, he thought, were primarily metaphorical, and he believed that we should accept as many as possible, letting them qualify each other so that we may reach some tentative conclusions.

Horace Bushnell worked on the use of religious language long before the arrival of linguistic philosophy, He wrote: "Words are legitimately used as signs of thoughts to be expressed. They do not literally pass over a thought out of one mind to another."[34] Words may distort

---

32. Ian T. Ramsey, *On Being Sure in Religion* (London: Athlone Press, 1963), p. 47; see Ramsey, *Christian Discourse* (London: Oxford University Press, 1965), p. 89.

33. Ian T. Ramsey, *Religious Language* (London: SCM Press, 1957), p. 91.

34. H. Shelton Smith, ed., *Horace Bushnell* (New York: Oxford University Press, 1965), p. 91.

meaning because they give form to what has no form. They carry with them the risk of error or partial truth. They can be used to point or show, but they do not say anything. Therefore, we as teachers must beware of using literal language when only metaphor and poetry will do.

V
Teaching

The theory and practice of religious education runs in cycles. From an emphasis on content and evangelism at the turn of the century, the scene changed to a focus on social action and the "democracy of God." Then it moved back again to an emphasis on a neo-orthodox theology and content, ignoring the social demands of faith. This is a simplification of the great variety in the field, but the churches felt the impact of such constant shifts in emphasis.

George Albert Coe was for some years the guru of the religious education movement and of the interfaith Religious Education Association, Douglas Clyde Macintosh wrote that for Coe "personal religion in the sense of an individual approach in private prayer to a God numerically distinguishable from humanity, an essentially personal God who is transcendent as well as immanent, is definitely discouraged."[35] This position of Coe was dominant especially at Union Theological Seminary in New York and at the University of Chicago. But there were dissenting voices. Luther Allan Weigle of Yale struck a mediating position. "Education becomes religious," he wrote, "when it is conscious of the presence, power, and love of God as the ultimate condition and supreme motive of human life, which includes and integrates all lesser values and motives whose proximate end is some form of human welfare."[36] Macintosh knew that the old evangelism in education and the emphasis on social education would not mix, and it did not. Macintosh looked forward to a new mixture of evangelism and religious education that would be both theocentric and related to the world situation. We need to "work for the conversion of individuals to the Christian life, and work for the establishing of a just and essentially Christian social order."[37]

Our starting point comes from the Jewish scriptures, in the book of Proverbs:

---

35. Douglas Clyde Macintosh, *Personal Religion* (New York: Scribners, 1942), p. 294.

36. Luther Allan Weigle, *Religious Education* (April 1923), p. 91.

37. Macintosh, *Personal Religion*, p. 331.

> Listen, my sons, to a father's instruction,
> consider attentively how to gain understanding;
> for it is sound learning I give you;
> so do not forsake my teaching. . . .
> The first thing is to acquire wisdom:
> Gain understanding though it cost you all you have.
> Do not forsake her, for she will keep you safe;
> love her, and she will guard you;
> cherish her, and she will lift you high;
> if only you embrace her, she will bring you to honour.
> She will set a garland of grace on your head
> and bestow on you a crown of glory. . . .
>
> My son, attend to my speech,
> pay heed to my words;
> do not let them slip out of your mind,
> keep them close in your heart;
> for they are life to him who finds them,
> and health to his whole body.
>
> (Prov. 4:1-2, 7-9, 20-22, NEB)

Wisdom is understood here as coming from God. It is a practical moral and religious intelligence (what religious educators call *"praxis"*). "In wisdom the LORD founded the earth" (Prov. 3:19, NEB). Wisdom is personified as feminine.

> For wisdom is a kindly spirit,
> And will not acquit a blasphemer of what he says,
> For God is a witness of his heart,
> And a truthful observer of his mind,
> And a hearer of his tongue.
> For the spirit of the LORD fills the world,
> And that which embraces all things knows all that is said.
>
> (Wis. Sol. 1:6-7, G)

> For God loves nothing but the man who lives with wisdom.
> For she is fairer than the sun,
> Or any group of stars;
> Compared with light, she is found superior;
> For night succeeds to it,
> But evil cannot overpower wisdom   (Wis. Sol. 7:28-30, G)

Wisdom, so described, is a major goal of the teacher. Both to acquire it and to teach it is an essential part of the spirituality of the religious educator. What happens is that the teacher's faith becomes contagious. It becomes so essential to the life of the teacher that the students sense it. It shows itself in a variety of ways through the interpersonal relations of the classroom, of meetings, of social contacts, and on the playing field. Because the teacher treats each person as an end rather than a means, the student comes to the conclusion that the teacher is someone to be trusted.

Even when the interest of the students has been aroused, such enthusiasm does not last without a contagious enthusiasm in the teacher. "But there he was; a strong man talking with a knowledge and a sort of dark enthusiasm: and, sentence by sentence, he enforced the high contagion."[38] William Alexander Percy described one such teacher, whose curriculum was life itself. "We don't absorb the multiplication table (at least not the seventh and the eleventh), but those things that are vitamins and calories of the spirit, the spirit seizes and transmutes into its own strength, wholly and forgetfully. Tolerance and justice, fearlessness and pride, reverence and pity, are learned in a course on long division if the teacher has those qualities, as Judge Griffin had."[39]

When the religious educator is grounded in a sound spirituality, the teacher becomes one who seeks dialogue with the students. A remarkable section in Reuel L. Howe's *The Miracle of Dialogue* describes what he calls the dialogical teacher. First, no matter what method is used, the principle of dialogue is served. The competence in the subject is kept in relation to other disciplines and to the response of the students. Second, such a teacher is alert to the meanings brought to the situation by the students, listening to them and trying to imagine what is going on in them. Third, the teacher helps the students formulate their questions and meanings so that the information offered will fit their capacities and hopes. Fourth, the teacher provides the resources, wisdom, and skills to assist the students in coming to their own conclusions. Fifth, such a teacher seeks for opportunities for the students to engage in dialogue with one another in order to test their grasp of the subject matter and their conclusions. "The dialogical teacher also understands that implicit in dialogue between [persons] is a meeting between God and [persons]." To love God, one must also love one's neighbor. Sixth, the teacher is not defensive about the content that is offered, for it is formulated out of life and is related to life. Seventh, the teacher is suspicious of conformity and offers the students the gift of relationship so that their personal qualities and capacities may be

---

38. Quoted by Houston Peterson, *Great Teachers* (New Brunswick: Rutgers University Press, 1946), p. 342.

39. Ibid., p. 344.

realized and confirmed. Eighth, "the dialogical teacher speaks and acts in [the] the capacity as educator and departs from [the] plan without anxiety because he [or she] trusts both the working of the Spirit and the inner workings of [the] students."

This approach, says Howe, is achieved through the language of relationship, which is the language of "mutual address and response, of trust and love," which can be correlated with words. If one's spirituality includes the I-thou relationship of which Martin Buber speaks, it can lead to a relationship also with God.[40]

What emerges from this is a creative transformation of some of the students and sometimes of the teacher. It gives them a new perspective whereby there may be an increased awareness of the meaning of life and an expanded range of knowing and valuing. Second, various perspectives are integrated as mutually sustaining activities modify and add to one's values. Third, there is an expansion of the appreciable world and one comes to understand that God is truly cosmic in relationship to all that is. Fourth, there is a growth of the sense of community as interrelationships are transformed and deepened.[41] Paul summarized it: "Do not be conformed to this world but be transformed by the renewal of your mind, that you may prove what is the will of God, what is good and acceptable and perfect" (Rom. 12:2, RSV).

To achieve something like this, we need to get away from professionalism. Henry Nelson Wieman wrote that

> religion, in one sense, is like baseball or any other form of play or art. The professionals who play in the big leagues render a great service to baseball. Baseball would certainly not pervade our national life as it does, if it were not for these big leagues. But if you want to find out the true spirit of baseball in all the glory of a passion, you must not go to the big leagues. You must go to the back yard, the sand-lot, the side street, and the school ground. There it is not a profession, it is a passion. When a passion becomes a profession, it often ceases to be a passion. That is as true of religion as it is of baseball. Among the professionals you find a superb mastery and a great technique, but not too frequently the pure devotion. Perhaps in baseball the passion is not too important, but in religion it is all important. A religion that is not passionate simply is not worth

---

40. See Reuel L. Howe, *The Miracle of Dialogue* (New York: Seabury Press, 1963), pp. 136-141.

41. Henry Nelson Wieman, *The Source of Human Good* (Chicago: University of Chicago Press, 1946), pp. 58-69; also, Randolph C. Miller, *The American Spirit in Theology* (Philadelphia: Pilgrim Press, 1974), p. 87.

considering. Therefore, I say, we need more sand-lot religion. The professional, whether White Sox or Methodist, controls inordinately our baseball and our religion.[42]

To keep passion alive and to avoid the professionalism of the religious educator, we need to be grounded in the spirituality of the amateur so that our passion may be kept alive to share with others who are also amateurs. When our roots are deep enough so that we have a faith to share because it is contagious, we are capable of fulfilling our vocation as religious educators.

My father had a profound influence on my religious development. I came to my acquaintance with religious education in the parish of which he was the rector for thirty years. I do not remember any false piety or holier-than-thou attitudes in his life, my mother's, or in the parish. There were no revivals or appeals for conversion. But there was an atmosphere at home and in his parish that was comfortable and reassuring. There was an unspoken spirituality (although we would not call it that) that was contagious. It was a liberal faith, and he was an unabashed liberal. I listened to his sermons for many years, and they were consistent with his life. When he was in his forties he wrote his one book, and it ended as I am ending this essay, with a description of

A LIBERAL FAITH

A liberal faith is a great faith. It constantly, like the chick, breaks the old faith, and walks into new life. But, mind you, it takes the essence of the old life with it, leaving only the shell. A truly liberal faith leaves nothing of any value behind. It is not some mere tangent, a starting point, a divergence that means another sect. "These things you ought to have done," said Jesus, "and not to have left the other undone." A man who calls himself a liberal and slinks back out of sight in the face of some crisis, is not a liberal; he is only a coward. A man who calls himself a liberal and lives an openly bad life, is not a liberal; he is only a libertine. A liberal is one whose blood is growing warmer, whose charity is growing broader, whose vision is growing clearer; who, in the last analysis, is deeply in love with life.[43]

---

42. Henry Nelson Wieman, "How I Got My Religion," *Religious Education* (December 1931), p. 844; reprinted, *Religious Education* (January-February 1974), p. 33. See Miller, *The American Spirit in Theology,* pp. 91-92.

43. Ray Oakley Miller, *Modernist Studies in the Life of Jesus* (Boston: Sherman, French & Co., 1917), p. 52.

4

Ecumenical Spirituality and the Religious Educator

JOANMARIE SMITH

Introduction

Each fall I teach a course entitled "Spirituality and Education." The course begins much as one begins working a jigsaw puzzle: simultaneously turning right side up all the parts of the puzzle and gathering together those which constitute the framework within which the subject will be pieced together. This essay will begin the same way. I will lay out the parts with which I will be working and construct a framework in which a model of spirituality will be pieced together.

The jigsaw analogy does not hold up very long, however. While it illuminates the initial method of the course and of this chapter, the analogy is at odds with their aim and objectives. Jigsaw puzzlers do not aim at a change of life—just the satisfaction of seeing a picture emerge from their efforts. But teaching or writing on spirituality aims to renew, deepen, or extend the spiritual life of those it engages. Conversion is the objective. May the mutual efforts of the reader and writer help to realize those aims.

Part I
Education and Religion

Modeling

Before you say anything about anything it seems to me you must be prepared to answer the question, "How do you know?" and, the even more fundamental question, "What do you mean by 'know'?" So, I will.

Traditionally, knowledge has been described as "justified true belief."[1] The operative words are "justified" and "true." In insignificant matters we generally apply what is called a correspondence theory of justification, validation, or truth. To illustrate this correspondence theory: If I believe it is raining out, I check outdoors, and if it *is* raining I am justified in saying, "I *know* that it is raining." This theory is obviously adequate enough when one is talking about rain. But what if we are talking about spirituality? Can we *know* what spirituality is? Under what circumstances are we justified in saying, "This is what spirituality truly is."? Another, broader way of framing this question is, "How do we have access to the real?" The answer to this question has changed down the ages.

From the beginning of history until the sixteenth century, in the West at least one had access to the *really real*, or one knew a belief to be true if God or the gods had revealed it as true—either through a sacred scripture or through persons like kings and popes who, by their anointed status, represented God and re-presented God's truth on earth. In the sixteenth century, however, there was an explosion of knowledge—a scientific revolution (scientia=knowledge). It was accomplished by justifying beliefs through experiment and experience.

Empirical verification was our access to the real or the true. The confrontation of these two methods of justifying beliefs, namely, authority (preferably divinely appointed and anointed) and experience (preferably visible and tangible) is dramatically underscored in Galileo's trial. Galileo "knows" that the earth moves around the sun because his instruments and experiments have revealed it to him. The churchmen, on the contrary, "know" the sun moves around the earth because God revealed it to them in the scriptures. The churchmen won that clash, but they lost the war. Most of us today are convinced that we *know* the earth travels around the sun regardless of what the bible says. From the sixteenth century up to the beginning of the twentieth century the experience/experiment method of justifying beliefs as true, as giving us access to reality, prevailed. In fact, at least

---

1. *The Encyclopedia of Philosophy,* s.v. "knowledge and belief."

one influential school of philosophy, the logical positivists, concluded that unless a belief could be verified experientially, it was simply not true, it was meaningless.[2]

In the beginning of the early years of the twentieth century there was another revolution in science. It took place in physics, the "hardest" science—the science most removed, apparently, from spiritual things. As a result of this revolution it was concluded that knowledge did not reflect the findings of our senses (experience) and certainly not the dictates of authority (revelation), but rather the probings of our imagination. In other words, the data with which science validates or invalidates its hypotheses, which was previously considered completely objective, is now recognized to reflect not only the instruments, but also the imagining framework of the inquirer. In yet other words, "All data is theory laden."[3] In other, other words, *all* experience is interpreted experience,[4] which is to say that the cognitive or awareness element of our experience (without which there is no experience) reflects the imaginative schemas we impose on our interaction with the environment.

Let me illustrate this. Look at the figure below. What do you see?

If you answer a triangle, or three lines, or even black on white you must soon discover that you do not *see* these. Triangles and lines are very sophisticated mathematical concepts. Even "black" and "white" are abstractions or ideas. You will realize that you cannot say what you *see* because you do not experience "raw" reality. Reality is mediated by the ideas you bring to it. The data is experienced as laden with whatever theories one has been educated or socialized to. The theories and ideas that mediate reality to us seem to reflect the power of imagination more than that of any other faculty.

We may be more familiar with the fact that our experience of ourselves and other persons is filtered through our self-image and the

---

2. A classic discussion of the pros and cons of this position is found in *New Essays in Philosophical Theology*, ed. Antony Flew and Alasdair MacIntyre (New York: Macmillan, 1955).

3. Norwood Hanson, *Patterns of Discovery* (Cambridge: Cambridge University Press, 1958), p. 18.

4. Ian G. Barbour, *Myths, Models and Paradigms* (New York: Harper & Row, 1974), pp. 51-56.

images we have of others. Historians and philosophers of science have convinced many of us that a similar phenomenon is operating in *all* our engagements with reality.[5]

My colleague, Gloria Durka, and I have called these imaginative constructs through which we experience reality "models."[6] We have then gone on to describe education as *commitment to better and better models of reality.*[7] Let me unpack some of the terms.

"Better and Better"

To describe education as commitment to *better* models implies that one model is not as good as another, that some models are better than others. It also implies that it is possible to discern the better—if not with certitude, at least with certifiable conviction. Finally, the expression "better and better" places an ongoing evaluative process at the very heart of education. The expression also highlights the significance of elaborating the criteria according to which one is evaluating any model.

A model of spirituality is a major imaginative construct. It minimally involves theories of God, of human nature and their relation to each other. I am convinced that a model of spirituality is best judged by the kind of criteria with which we judge those imaginative constructs that go by the name "works of art." The critical questions we bring to these works are appropriately if analogously applied to a theory of spirituality. Does it explore all the possibilities of the medium? (A great work of art, whether a play by Shakespeare or a painting by Picasso, taxes and strains the potential of its medium until former limitations are transcended.) Do the elements of the art piece contribute to the whole, and are they, in turn, enhanced by participation in the whole? Is the artwork seminal? That is, does it generate novel, enriching experience? And, finally, does it illumine existence? Do we understand more about more because of it? A "better" model of spirituality should compel affirmative answers to such evaluative criteria.

Commitment

The term commitment has connotations which recommend it as hardly less central than evaluation in the educational enterprise. First,

---

5. No one has done more to publish this thesis than Thomas S. Kuhn in *The Structure of Scientific Revolutions* (Chicago: University of Chicago Press, 1962).

6. Gloria Durka and Joanmarie Smith, *Modeling God* (New York Paulist Press, 1976), pp. 3-4.

7. Gloria Durka and Joanmarie Smith, "Modeling in Religious Education," *Religious Education* 71 (March-April 1976), p. 132.

commitment connotes some cognitive content. We speak of the loyalty of pets but not of their commitment. There is in the notion of commitment the suggestion of intellectual insight into the objects of one's loyalty.

But there is also an emotional dimension to the term. Precisely the loyalty, the doggedness, if you will, the energy and grasp of desire-in-choice which is associated with the committed person. There is the sense of passionate engagement to what one sees.

Finally, there is the behavioral aspect. To commit means above all to do something. Commitment is "acting" on one's insight with conviction. A fidelity to the processes of inquiry and evaluation characterizes the educated person because the realization is central that *no model of reality is coextensive with the reality being modeled*. Religion, on the other hand, can be described as *commitment to the more of reality*.

Religious Education

The expression the "more of reality" reflects a panentheistic model of God's relation to Creation. "In God we live, and move and have our being" (Acts 17:28). Not that reality exhausts deity (pantheism), but that all reality is in and of God. Religion is the binding and bonding to the divine in reality. Religious education is commitment to better and better models of this pervading/pervasive deity.

Having laid out this framework, I will begin to put together a picture or model of spirituality that is consistent with the color and shape of the education, religion, and religious education pieces as they have been described.

Part II
Ecumenical Spirituality

Faith

Faith is central to any theory of spirituality, especially if one believes, as I do, that faith is the fundamental category of existence.[8] Lately there seems to be some consensus among those examining the phenomenon of faith that it is essentially a dynamism; it is relational, and it is specifically human. I have been toying with the image of faith as a tropism. It seems to be a particularly fruitful image.

Tropism, like faith, is a noun, but it names movement, an involuntary movement of an organism or its parts toward an external stimulus. It is most familiarly found in the phototropism of plant life. Plants

---

8. Durka and Smith, *Modeling God*, p. 1.

turn toward the light. Could faith be a tropism toward the good; the God, of ourselves and our environment which is symbolized, ritualized, and conceptualized (modeled) more or less appropriately? If so, spirituality can properly be described as cultivating engagement to that which faith discerns.

Considering spirituality in this light offers a number of advantages. First, it sidesteps all the dichotomies too often perpetuated in notions of spirituality; the dualisms of body/spirit, mind/matter, world/other-world, even the dichotomy of good/God.

"Whatever is true, whatever is honorable, whatever is just, whatever is pure, whatever is lovely, whatever is gracious, if there is anything worthy of praise . . ." (Phil. 4:8) provides an experience of the divine. The tropism toward physical nourishment, for example, is simply a dimension of faith—a reality recognized by Christians and most radically by Roman Catholics when they say that bread and wine is not simply good, but is God. Faith is the condition of being, and communion with object of faith is being's purpose.

It makes sense then that according to Erik Erikson's stages of development[9] unless infants experience goodness/Godness in their environment, their trusting drive (I would say, faith) is thwarted and, in extreme cases of deprivation, withdrawal and death occur. Despair, the opposite of faith, has always been considered the last, worst sin, possibly the only verifiably *mortal* sin.

Imaging faith as a tropism also provides a fertile context for the pluralism of our times. There is not an Islamic faith, a Christian faith, or the no faith of the secular atheist. No more than there is a Russian or Canadian instinct to nourish oneself with food; there is a human instinct which is realized in different dishes. So there is a human dynamism which reaches out and is nourished by the good/God of reality. The objective is construed differently, and responded to differently in beliefs and rituals. But, what we realize today is that the object of faith is *not* our beliefs but the good/God they approximate. Since this good/God suffuses us and our surroundings, a spirituality which promotes communion with the world is appropriate. Hence, an ecumenical spirituality, or perhaps, more accurately, a worldly spirituality.

Ecumenical derives from the Greek *oikemene* meaning world, but with the sense of world as home (*oikas* means house in Greek). Ecumenical today describes attempts by proponents of different belief

9. Erik Erikson, *Childhood and Society,* 2nd ed. (New York: Norton, 1963), pp. 247-274.

systems to foster communion among themselves. In that sense the term seems particularly apt to describe a spirituality for religious educators embracing many different belief systems. But it is the "worldly" connotation on which I wish to concentrate. The spirituality I will describe is worldly because it focuses on the now and the here and it is inclusive.

Now

Our worldview sponsors our spiritual theory and vice versa. In a three-tiered universe in which God's will unfolds like construction from an architect's blueprint, one awaits release from the geotropism of original sin. One longs to leave this earth and go *up* to heaven in order to be with God. First and second century apocalyptic thought in the West gave an urgency to this longing. Rosemary Ruether describes the effects of the Persian and Greek dualism which engendered what has been called an angelic spirituality.

> Heaven was no longer seen as breaking in and disrupting the order of a disobedient society, overthrowing its evil structures and creating the new possibility of a redeemed life on earth. Rather, heaven now was seen as located statically "above," as the spiritual realm that corresponds to the "soul," just as the earthly realm corresponds to the body. The ethic of the Kingdom of Heaven now comes to be seen as the Platonic ethic of "mortification" (Phaedrus 66, 67). Salvation is seen as the adoption of a death ethic of lifelong struggle to withdraw from social and physical processes and to live the "angelic life," "as though not in the body." The seeker after perfection withdrew not only from economic, political, and cultural processes, but even from the physical processes of life, such as eating, sleeping, bathing, all physical enjoyment, and especially from sex, as the expression of those life processes that "keep the world going."[10]

We realize with Ruether that this worldview, with its psychological, anthropological, and theological underpinnings, has evaporated. Current psychological, anthropological, and theological insights urge us to attend to the here and now. There is the sense that it is in the here and now that we engage the good/God or we never do. This insight also underscores the relative arbitrariness of separating out the now and here and inclusiveness as dominating elements of an ecumenical spirituality. The here and now obviously includes our space/place, earth

---

10. Rosemary Radford Ruether, *Liberation Theology* (New York: Paulist Press, 1972), pp. 58-59.

and its environs. It also obviously and redundantly includes inclusiveness. Every point made under any one of the headings, therefore, could as easily and authentically be made under either of the other sections.

Here

That God is everywhere is not a particularly novel thesis. Interpreting the nature of that presence is the fundamental theological enterprise. I have already indicated that an ecumenical spirituality subscribes to panentheism. That is not a particularly novel interpretation either. Certainly Thomas Aquinas is working from that perspective when he compares the presence of God to the light of lighted air.

> . . . as light is caused in the air by the sun so long as the air remains illuminated. Therefore as long as a thing has being, so long must God be present to it according to its mode of being. But being (esse) is innermost in each thing and most fundamentally present within all things. . . . Hence it must be that God is in all things, and innermostly.[11]

What Thomas seems to be saying is that the "is-ing" (esse) of anything that is, is the "God-ing" of that thing. This is a profound and compelling insight and one that gives a metaphysical basis to Augustine's claim that "God is more me than I am myself" and Eckhart's "My truest I is God." Yet it can sponsor a personal and privatized mysticism that is antithetical to the ecumenical spirituality I am describing. Thomas' image also has a nonmaterial spin on it, while for ecumenical spirituality God is not simply *on* the earth, but *in* and *of* it, even as we are.

Twentieth century science has changed our worldview by convincing us that nothing exists separately; that in fact, there are no "things" that *have* relationships; "things," including persons, *are* relationships. The quality of existence is characterized by the nature of these relationships.

This description of reality is remarkably similar to the way the Fathers of the Church described the inner life of the Trinity. The Greek Fathers used the expression *perichoresis*, a term which indicates "reciprocity of life" or "community in relationship." The Fathers of the West used the Latin word *circumincession*. This is interpreted to mean: "The Father is in and of the Son but is not the Son; the Son is in

---

11. *Summa Theologica* I, q.8 a.1.

and of the Father but is not the Father; the Holy Spirit is in and of the Father and Son but is not the Father or the Son." It seems stunningly appropriate that a centuries-old model of God should serve scientists now as a model of all of existence.

To exist on the simplest biological level, one must be immersed in the earth. The same one hundred or so elements that make up our universe are also what we are made of. The truth in the truism, "You are what you eat," often escapes us. We eat the universe! Literally. If, through sickness we are unable to take the universe *in* and have it become *of* us, we quickly cease to exist. Our remains revert back to their original form until, perhaps, they are again, in the great recycling of energy that we call the "conservation of matter," *in-corp*orated, embodied, in another living being—nourishing a carrot seed or an astronaut.

To exist as a person one must be in and of the person-universe, that aspect of the universe marked by culture, by love, and by thought. In order to think, we probably must have a language. But language comes from our immersion in the person-universe. If some problem like that of Helen Keller prevents interpenetration with others' minds, we may exist biologically but we are hardly persons. At that marvelous moment when Helen Keller and her teacher's minds are *in* and *of* one another through the recognition of water being represented by Anne Macy Sullivan's hand signal, she emerges into the person-universe.

Personal existence seems to be a more intense form of existence. The "in-ing" and "of-ing" is more total. If we are images of God, does not the image of God as sheer *in* and *of* reality appear less inadequate than others? This does not imply that everything is God or that God is everything. But, just as carrots are *in* and *of* us but we are not carrots, and just as our being *in* and *of* other people's personhood is constitutive of our personhood but we are not other persons nor they us, so is God *in* and *of* the world but is not the world and the world is *in* and *of* God but is not God.

The most dramatic consequence of this interpretation of God's presence to us is that the good can be adored and served in its own identity, not as some veil of the deity. The good things of this earth can be loved, not because they are manifestations of God, or even because they are God, but because they are good things of this earth. Though our profoundest relationships most profoundly constitute our identity, paradoxically, the depth reflects the degree to which we can appreciate the other *as other*. A mother who treats a child as the extension of herself or a lover who sees a beloved in this way has a most superficial relationship. Communion requires difference. Identity is sterile. Confusing identities is deadly. It has in fact given charity a bad name. A term that once simply meant love has come to describe that demeaning (to its recipients at least) activity we engage in with those less fortunate than we are for God's sake. Who wants to be invited to a party "out of charity" or "for Christ's sake"? We can assume, I think, that people do not relish receiving food or clothes for that reason either. I suppose it is better to do something for someone because you see God in them than not to do it at all. But just. That the other is God can only be experienced as a surprise or it cannot be experienced.

Inclusive

The problem with many of the traditional dualisms in spirituality was not their twoness. It was that the relationship between them was seen as one of opposition: heaven versus earth, spirit versus matter, mind versus body. For the most part this opposition has dissolved, in some cases by dissolving the dualism into a distinction.

There are still dichotomies which an ecumenical spirituality must address. Not to dissolve the poles one into the other, but to resolve the opposition between them. They are: manifestation theology versus the proclamation theology found among Christian thinkers; the West versus East—a geopolitical anachronism—as well as a religious one; and, finally the male versus female split that pervades the human community.

Manifestation versus Proclamation

David Tracy has popularized the examination of theologies from the perspective of whether they emphasize the "always-already" or the "not yet" of God in the universe. In fact, he claims most religions can be classified by the contrast between two ideal types: "religions with a mystical-priestly-metaphysical-aesthetic emphasis and those religions with a prophetic-ethical-historical emphasis."[12]

So far, spirituality as I have described it in this essay is certainly in the manifestation camp. I have emphasized that the universe is sacramental; it is the always-already locus of the divine; it is theophanic. To leave it at that, to ignore the ill-fed, ill-clothed, ill-housed, the oppressed, the undereducated, and the underemployed in the here and now is obscene. To disregard the polluting of the earth and its imminent disappearance in a nuclear holocaust is lethally ignorant. It is not enough to see in these aberrations the good/God suffering *in* the

---

12. David Tracy, *The Analogical Imagination* (New York: Crossroad Publishing Co., 1981), p. 203.

world or God suffering *as* the world. It is not enough not to contribute to nor collude in this suffering. As those who emphasize proclamation realize, we must relieve it.

If one were to ask where ecumenical spirituality is most likely to be found, it is significant that the answer is: among those dissidents pressuring the rest of us for the rights of all humans and peace with justice over the whole earth. Their demonstrations have reappropriated many traditional disciplines. Pilgrimages and fasting as well as chanting and prayer vigils are common "tactics" of such groups. It is significant, too, that more often than not, persons within these groups represent different religions; invariably, they represent different denominations. Their spirituality also reflects ecumenism in the more common use of the term today.

It is in the spirituality of many human rights demonstrators and members of the peace movement that we find a happy wedding of the manifestation and proclamation insights. There is simultaneously a celebration of the "always-already" coupled with the prophetic perspective which recognizes the "not-yet."

West versus East

Most of the major religions of the Western Hemisphere are rooted in the East-West border which we now call the Middle East. But the development of Christianity especially has been part and parcel of the development of the West. The categories of Christianity and the West have so interpenetrated that they are, and have been, frequently indistinguishable to the periodic exaltation and embarrassment of either and both. The identification of cultural values with religious values made colonialists of Christian missionaries from the West. That identification has also made us too slow in adopting and adapting (at least intentionally) from the East "whatever is true, whatever is honorable, whatever is just, whatever is pure, whatever is lovely, whatever is gracious" (Phil. 4:8).

Wilfred Cantwell Smith cites examples which illustrate the interpenetration of religions that continues constantly though unattended by most of us. He traces the use of prayer beads from the Hindus to the Buddhists through the Moslems into Christendom of the Middle Ages and winding up as the Rosary of today's Roman Catholics. Smith also records the fact that the Buddha has been venerated as a Christian saint (Saint Baclaam) for centuries.[13] In a "global village," howev-

---

13. Wilfred Cantwell Smith, *Towards a World Theology* (Philadelphia: Westminster, 1981), pp. 7-13.

er, we cannot afford *not* to attend to the insights into the good/God which are the special province of any section of the globe.

Intentionally turning to the East is becoming acceptable. The writing of Thich Nhat Han[14] the Vietnamese Buddhist Zen master, has been popularized in the United States and Canada by James Forest and Daniel Berrigan, the peace activists. Han's involvement in the international peace movement, coupled with his profoundly contemplative stance toward reality, is also a marvelous paradigm of the manifestation-proclamation fusion.

While we have, as early as the Transcendental movement, begun to see the value of incorporating Hindu and Buddhist faith responses, we have yet similarly to study Islam and we have hardly taken even first steps with regard to the faith responses of the Native American or African tribal religions. Such explorations can only enhance and revitalize our own faith and move us more deeply into an ecumenical spirituality.

Male versus Female

The most pervasive and unhealthy dualism with which we must deal is male/female dualism. That people come in two basic models is not the problem; the sexism this dualism has led to is. Sexism is the consideration and treatment of females as alien, less than human, or invisible. All subsequent oppressions can be traced to it.

> Sexism is the elementary human sin. If the essential human molecule is dyadic, male/female, the perversion of one part of the dyad perverts the other. And, to distort femininity *and* masculinity, the constitutive ingredients of humanity, is to distort humanity itself; nothing will be spared the fallout from so radical a corruption. Here is *original* sin. Here is the fundamental lie that will have to mark all human ideas, customs, and institutions.[15]

When knowledge was construed as that which is revealed, those who had direct access to this revelation were almost invariably male. When knowledge was construed as that which is experienced, it was men's experience which was taken as the norm. Now that knowledge is construed as that which is imagined, it is all the more obvious that women's images must be included.

Yet, a glance at bibliographies and footnotes will indicate where the

---

14. For an example of his contribution to spirituality and the peace movement, see Thich Nhat Han, *The Miracle of Mindfulness* (Boston: Beacon, 1976).

15. Daniel C. Maguire, "The Feminization of God and Ethics," *Christianity and Crisis* 42 (March 15, 1982).

bias of male as authority still lies. Maria Harris, addressing this issue, explores the ramifications:

> [It] reveals, at a deeper level, the power to frame questions, to decide issues, to choose those areas which are important. For authority refers not only to those cited; it refers to the power to determine what considerations or studies will be pursued, and perhaps most important, the right to define the meaning of our most profound human experiences: love, faith, sin, hope, justice.[16]

In the realm of spirituality, the spiritual directors, the gurus, the "masters" have overwhelmingly been males. Current research, however, alerts us to the fact that women speak in a different voice. Carol Gilligan's work in moral development[17] illustrates the different pattern according to which women seem to develop. Earlier research[18] had failed to factor in women's experience. When moral stages were distilled from this research and applied to women, they were found (not too surprisingly) to be essentially undeveloped.

Jean Baker Miller makes a similar point. She demonstrates that the psychology we have been studying for over a century is the psychology of *mankind*—literally.[19] Valerie Saiving's contribution to this research would convince us that women's sins have been different from men's. Women have not been tempted to pride but to self-hate and trivialization.[20]

The findings of these feminist researchers and scholars have yet to wash through our psyches. Moreover, I am convinced that as significant as their contributions are to the study of humankind, no significant shift toward a truly inclusive worldview will occur until we confront the effects of our male imagery of the Deity. "Where God is male, male is God."

It is almost impossible not to collude with this all-encompassing sexism. I myself have, by using the term "God" in this article. Check

---

16. Maria Harris, "The Imagery of Religious Education," *Religious Education* 78 (Summer 1983), p. 369.

17. Carol Gilligan, *In a Different Voice* (Cambridge: Harvard University Press, 1982).

18. Lawrence Kohlberg and Robert Kramer, "Continuities and Discontinuities in Child and Adult Moral Development," *Human Development* 12 (1969), pp. 93-120.

19. Jean Baker Miller, *Toward a New Psychology of Women* (Boston: Beacon Press, 1976), p. 1.

20. Valerie Saiving, "The Human Situation: A Feminine View," *Womanspirit Rising*, ed. Carol P. Christ and Judith Plaskow (San Francisco: Harper & Row, 1979), pp. 25-42.

the dictionary. "God" is a male deity. Theoretically, we know that the Unnameable is neither male nor female. Yet, it is our images more than our theory that shape our spirituality. To see how rooted in maleness our images of the Deity are, I have suggested replacing the term God with Goddess for a month.[21] Most people find it a difficult to impossible task. They do not find it repellent to use apparently neutral terms, like the Unnameable, or Life of the Universe. It is my conviction that these latter addresses are palatable precisely because they do not reveal and painfully shatter the identification of Male and the Divine that is cemented in our psyches.

Granted, there are a number of feminine roles ascribed to the Deity in the Hebrew and Christian scriptures: God as seamstress (Gen. 3:21), God as mother and nurse (Num. 11:12), God in birth pangs (Is. 42:14), God as midwife (Ps. 22:9), God as homemaker (Lk. 15:8-10), Jesus as hen (Mt. 23:37). A more radical assertion of the female dimension of the Deity is called for. These allusions to the feminine activities of God smack too much of the old song, "Daddy, You've Been a Mother to Me."

I am afraid that, in order to see a world that really gives equal weight to the experience of women and men, we must petition with Meister Eckhardt. "I pray God to free me of God."[22]

Part III
Spirituality and Religious Educators

Is there *a* spirituality specific to religious educators? I do not think so—any more than there is a health specific to religious educators. We think of health as a rather universally and similarly acknowledged state of well-being. There are not Eastern and Western healths. Nor are there male and female healths. There are, however, health needs that differ due to genetics, environment, or profession. So, while every culture needs nutritious food, one part of the world may seek its protein in rice, while another finds it in chicken. Similarly, we all need to exercise. Some persons may obtain it through membership in a health club while others inadvertently get their exercise by walking the streets looking for work.

Spirituality, I maintain, is as universally identical as health. But, as with health, specific needs reflect a person's genetic make-up, one's

21. Joanmarie Smith, "Hen, Homemaker and Goddess," *PACE* 14 (December 1983).
22. Cited in Dorothee Sölle, "Mysticism, Liberation and the Names of God," *Christianity and Crisis* 41 (June 22, 1981), p. 184.

environment, and finally, the area with which we are most interested in this article, one's profession. As with any profession there are both hazards and opportunities to be considered.

Professional Hazards

Irregular Hours

A movement to promote equal pay for comparable work assigns points to various elements of a job; e.g., responsibility, education and skills required, and so forth. Jobs that have the same number of points are considered comparable even though they are not identical. Extra points are given to jobs where the hours are irregular. The computation recognizes that not being able to plan one's time with confidence is psychically draining. Yet this is the situation of many religious educators. One's day and week are fragmented by meetings "after work," counseling sessions on the way to class, as well as emergency visitations. Prayer can appear to be a personal luxury. It is the easiest appointment to squeeze out of a packed and irregular schedule.

The Dailyness of the Sacred

Work in the innards of organized religion can be disenchanting. That is, like Dorothy seeing how the Wizard constructed his production numbers in Oz, one may feel the magic is gone. Or, the glut of religious imagery within which religious educators live and move and have their being can become so overwhelming that one loses interest. Even as being abandoned on an island teeming with fruit one can lose the taste for fruit. How to retain the awe and fascination that must be a dimension of true religion? How can one manage to maintain a relish for the religious images through which the good/God is mediated to us? Ironically, the very hazards of the profession provide opportunities.

Professional Opportunities

Irregular Hours

The hours of those religious educators who work outside of school situations are the most irregular. Yet they may have an opportunity to shape the irregularity more than most. Participating in the preparation of calendars and daily schedules, they are in a position to build in time for prayer and meditation on an annual, monthly, and day-by-day basis. These religious educators can, more than most people, place a prayer schedule inside their work schedule. In so doing, they emphasize the realization that religious education is not a job but a work, an *ouvre*. Artists spend the bulk of their work time creating artfully if they are lucky enough to earn their living through their art. Religious educators are lucky enough to earn their living cultivating what we may presume is a central passion in their lives; that is, the religious dimension of existence. Prayer for them as for all of us must be as necessary as food.

Publishing one's prayer schedule has the effect of helping others to see the religious educator's availability includes availability to the divine in one's self. The published prayer schedule is an educational tool. It alerts people to that need in their own faith life.

The Dailyness of the Sacred

While the risks of dealing every day with religious imagery are obvious, the opportunity it offers should be just as obvious. In a spirituality that emphasizes the now and the here as well as everyone and every culture, the sacred must be a daily experience. But that need not profane it. A regimen of prayer that empties the imagination, study that stretches it, and fasting that keeps it off balance, can heighten our appreciation of and relish for the sacred in which we work and also have our jobs.

Since we are so immersed in religious imagery, there seems to be a greater need to cleanse our palate, so to speak, on a regular basis in order to heighten our taste for these images. The prayer called "centering" can provide this service. In centering we take time to relax our being in the presence of God. Then we focus on one word: "God," "Mother," "One," "Forgive." We pray these words over and over. We "pray until we are prayed," to paraphrase a Zen proverb. As we conclude this time of quiet presence to the Nameless, a familiar prayer such as the Our Father/Mother can bring us back to our myriad concerns.[23]

Study—preferably in community—is the research and development dimension of the religious educator's work. Books are not the only object of study as Richard Foster reminds us so beautifully in *The Celebration of Discipline*. But, whether we are studying books or persons, four steps are involved: repetition, concentration, comprehension, and reflection.[24]

---

23. Basil Pennington, *Centering Prayer* (Garden City, New York: Doubleday, 1980).

24. Richard Foster, *The Celebration of Discipline* (San Francisco: Harper & Row, 1978), pp. 56-57.

Repetition, perhaps, is the least appreciated. Foster says, "The mind is renewed by (repeatedly) applying it to those things that will transform it."[25] We see an effect similar to what occurs in the centering prayer. *"Our thought processes take on an order conforming to the order in the tree or book."*[26] Concentration requires our focusing on the object of our study, and comprehension on our understanding it. Finally, in reflection we look for the meaning in our study—the difference this thesis, this person, or this flower makes. Study can take us out of ourselves and then replace us so that we see nothing in the same way. By broadening our perspective and giving us new perspectives, study almost guarantees that we will not become inured to an ecstatic environment.

The fasting, I propose, is not the fanatical fasting of the second century desert dwellers. Neither is it the fasting that combined with prayer recommends some petition to God. And, of course, it is not the fasting one does to lose weight. Rather, it is the periodic abstention from one to two meals simply to break the routine, or better, to heighten one's sensitivity to the routine. It is to dehabituate us to the dailyness.[27]

There is a certain sameness to our diet, but missing even one meal usually can reestablish our hunger, can enable us to relish the most prosaic of foods that break our fast. The exercise can also have the effect of providing a space in our life that puts us, for however short a time, into a different rhythm.

Even among those of us with the most irregular hours, a rhythm of living is discernible. Fasting can so drastically alter the beat in a melody that it springs a new tune. When our rhythm changes we put different emphases on the situations in which we live and work; new patterns emerge and we begin to live another song.

Conclusion

Completed jigsaw puzzles usually have one of two fates. They are either laminated and displayed or broken again into their separate parts to provide the piecing-pleasure another day. Theories—even of spirituality—can have equally uninteresting fates. But only if we forget the derivation of theory: *Theo* and *eros*.

---

25. Ibid., p. 54.
26. Ibid., p. 55. Italics are Foster's.
27. See Margaret R. Miles, "The Recovery of Asceticism," *Commonweal* 60 (January 28, 1983), pp. 40-43.

Theoria implies a journey, a passion to "see" the divine that moves one. "The departure and separation of the journey are to render available in a new way, the self, the world, the divine."[28] So be it.

---

28. John Navone, Towards a Theology of Story (Slough, England: St. Paul Publications, 1977), p. 97. Navone uses the scholarship of Bernd Jager in "Theorizing, Journeying, Dwelling," *Duquesne Studies in Phenomenological Psychology*, II, ed. A. Giorgi, C. Fisher, E. Murray (Pittsburgh: Duquesne University Press, 1975).

Part II

Paths of Spirituality Fonts

5

Western Contemplative Spirituality and the Religious Educator

M. BASIL PENNINGTON

Introduction

The word "education" comes from the Latin word *educare*, which means to lead forth. In order to lead someone forth it is necessary to go where they are and lead them, as it were, by the hand. It is also necessary to know where the person wants to go. Sometimes the person has a very clear vision as to where he or she wants to go. It is probably more often true that the one to be educated does not. It is for the religious educator to be in touch with the deep aspirations of the human spirit and thus to know the true needs of the one who is to be led forth.

If the religious educator is fully in touch with humanity he or she knows that the human mind and heart has infinite capacity, that they are made for the Lord God and in him alone can they find fulfillment and rest. This knowledge is attainable to unaided human reason. The Apostle Paul assures us of this.[1] So does one of the greatest of Christian thinkers, Thomas Aquinas, but he also reminds us that few—very few—are ever able to attain to this in surety because of a lack of time, perseverance, and mental perspicacity.[2]

---

1. Rom. 1:19-20.
2. *Summa Theologiae*, I, q. 1.

As Christian religious educators, we do have revelation. Through it we know that by baptism the human person, already participating in the divine being, goodness, and beauty through creation, is made an even more complete participant in divine life. The human spirit is now able to know God as he knows himself, though not in every way the same, and to love God as he loves himself. In a word, to enter into the inner life of the Trinity, enjoying a union with the very Son of God that is beyond anything we can ever fully grasp, a oneness that has its archetype in the unity of the Father and the Son within the most Blessed Trinity: "That they may be one, Father, as I in you and you in me, that they may be one in us."[3] It is toward the fulfillment of these divine aspirations that the Christian educator is to lead forth his disciples, whether the disciples are yet aware of them or not. They are written into their very nature by baptism.

Some Outstanding Religious Educators

If we are to ask who has been the most significant Catholic religious educator in our times in America, we would probably get a number of different answers. I am sure that many older Catholics would answer Fulton J. Sheen. As a boy I waited hours to have a seat below his pulpit. I listened to him weekly on the popular radio program called The Catholic Hour. Later millions viewed him weekly on television. His books sold in the millions. He lives on in them and in audio and video cassettes. Sheen, as an educator, was primarily a philosopher. He held the chair of philosophy at the Catholic University of America for many years. But he was a Christian philosopher. His was Christian philosophy, a philosophy of life, in the fullest sense of the words, in the sense in which it was used by the early Fathers of the Church. It was in truth a theology. One of the early great teachers of the Christian tradition, Evagrius Ponticus said: "The theologian is the man who prays; the man who prays is a theologian."[4] In this sense, too, the late Archbishop was a great theologian.

Christians of other traditions undoubtedly would point to other great religion teachers of our times. I think of Douglas Steere, the spiritual father (if I may use that term without offending his tradition) of the Society of Friends (Quakers). A professor of philosophy by profession, he has lectured throughout America and the world, always leading his hearers into the deeper realms of the spirit, seeking to create peace and communion. He has published many books, pam-

---

3. Jn. 17:21.
4. Evagrius Ponticus, *Chapters on Prayer*, no. 60, in *Praktikos*, Cistercian Studies Series, 4 (Spencer, Mass.: Cistercian Publications, 1972), p. 65.

phlets, and articles and has organized ecumenical meetings and organizations as well as colloquia between Zen masters and Christian spiritual leaders and between Hindus and Christians.

But a younger generation might not so readily name these great men. Their very rational, concise, and clear philosophy lost much of its hold around the time of the Second Vatican Council, when Christian thought, especially within Catholic circles, returned to a more patristic mode. It is probably sadly true that most younger Christians would not be able to point to anyone as a really significant Christian educator in our times, simply because they have had little or no contact with Christian education as such. But for those younger people who have sought such an education the one name that I believe would be most frequently brought forward by young Catholics would be that of Thomas Merton. Though this great modern contemplative monk died in 1968, his books continued to sell in the millions. He is without doubt the most widely published Catholic author in modern times, if not in all times, excluding, of course, the writers of the New Testament. Merton never received the media coverage that Sheen did, for he had chosen a life apart as a Cistercian monk. Indeed, his constant quest was for ever greater solitude and apartness. Yet he did not bury his exceptional talents. In obedience to superiors and to the immediate promptings of grace he used his mind, his heart, and his most effective pen, to enliven the spirits of a multitude of Americans, Christian and non-Christian alike. And translations have brought him to many other lands and peoples.

Merton was first and foremost a monk, a full Christian humanist, but as an educator his first medium was the written word. However, he also exercised other active and effective educational roles. For some years he was the Master of the Scholastics at the large Abbey of Gethsemani (Trappist, Kentucky) and then for ten years the Master of Novices. Each of these roles required of him regular lectures or classes. Even when he retired from these and entered into a more eremitical life, he descended each Sunday from his hermitage in the woods and gave a lecture to his brothers in the cenobium. Happily, most of his lectures and courses over the years were printed or recorded so that they are now available.

To understand the elements of Thomas Merton's most effective ministry as a religious educator we could analyze this vast and rich heritage. And that is something well worth doing. However such an immense task need not be placed on us here. Merton himself did, on a number of occasions, speak directly and immediately about Christian religious education. Looking at these contributions I think we can say that we are getting the essence of Merton's educational theory.

The concern of this present volume is the spirituality of the religious educator as that individual is a religious educator. My particular chapter approaches this concern from the vantage point of Western contemplative spirituality, as it flows from the undivided church. One of the important theological thrusts of our times is the renewed realization that we best contact reality through story, especially the story of persons' lives. The gospels are full of Jesus' stories and they are essentially the story of his life. That is why I have chosen to come to our subject and to my particular focus through a particular person, his expounded theory, and how it is reflected or incarnated in his life. I have chosen Merton because he has been one of the most effective Christian contemplative educators of our times and because I know him best among those who might be chosen, both by his copious writings and tapes and also by personal acquaintance and fraternal collaboration.[5] Seeking to live essentially the same sort of monastic contemplative life that he lived I can more easily enter into this story.

A Modern Western Contemplative View of Religious Education—Merton

When Thomas Merton decided to become a Cistercian monk he put his whole heart into it, and the whole of his genius. He entered deeply into the Cistercian heritage, and made the wisdom of the Cistercian Fathers his own. Among these Fathers one with whom he seemed to develop a special affinity was the late twelfth-century novice master, later abbot of Perseigne, Adam.[6] Drawing from Adam's writings Merton wrote an essay on formation—the monastic word used most frequently for education. The title is telling: "The Feast of Freedom. Monastic Formation according to Adam of Perseigne."[7] In it he gives his most formal statement of what he saw Christian education to be:

> To form . . . is then to draw out the inner spiritual form implanted in his soul by grace: to educate—that is to say, to "bring out"— Christ in him. It is not a matter of imposing . . . a rigid and artificial

---

5. In the last year of his life Merton and I worked together to establish Cistercian Publications. In the preceding years we shared ideas on a number of other projects.

6. Adam, the son of a serf, was born around 1145 in Normandy. He was educated at Rheims or Sens and ordained a priest. He became a Canon Regular, then a Benedictine, and finally a Cistercian. As abbot of Perseigne he was frequently employed by the Holy See for delicate missions. He died around 1221.

7. This essay can be found in *The Letters of Adam of Perseigne*, Cistercian Fathers Series, 21 (Kalamazoo, Mich.: Cistercian Publications, 1976), pp. 4-48.

form from without, but to encourage the growth of life and the radiation of light within the soul, until this life and light gain possession of his whole being, inform all his actions with grace and liberty, and bear witness to Christ living in him. It takes account of the whole man, called to find his place in the whole Christ. It is realistic, simple, supremely spiritual, that is to say, attuned to the inspirations of the Holy Spirit. It is based on the great and fundamental truths of the Christian life—our union with Christ in his mysteries, through the meditation of Our Lady.[8]

Merton comes back to this in many ways in his writings and in his talks. It was a basic theme for him. In his last talk, given only hours before his tragic death, he said that Christianity looks

primarily to a transformation of consciousness—a transformation and a liberation of the truth imprisoned in man[9] by ignorance and error. . . . The traditional religions begin with the consciousness of the individual, seeking to transform and liberate the truth in each person, with the idea that it will then communicate itself to others.[10]

He then turns his attention to the educator:

Of course the man par excellence to whom this task is deputed is the monk. The monk is a man who has attained, or is about to attain, or seeks to attain, full realization. He dwells in the center of society as one who has attained realization—he knows the score . . . he has come to experience the ground of his own being in such a way that he knows the secret of liberation and can somehow or other communicate this to others.[11]

Merton is here speaking in the context of an international monastic meeting. But it should not be difficult to translate his teaching into a broader Christian context, for we must remember that for Merton, and in fact, the monastic life is just the Christian life lived with a certain intensity. In his essay on the "Renewal of Monastic Education" Merton insisted that "the monastic life is not only *contemplative* but

---

8. Ibid., p. 9.

9. In reading Merton we have to remember that he wrote some fifteen or twenty years ago, before our sensibility to exclusive language became what it should be; therefore we should not be surprised to find him using words like "man" the way he does.

10. Thomas Merton, *The Asian Journal of Thomas Merton* (London: Sheldon Press, 1974), p. 333.

11. Ibid.

prophetic."[12] It is to seek to live the Christian mystery with a certain fullness and obviousness that is to be a sign and an encouragement to all other Christians.

Merton then is pointing to what is fundamental in an education if it is to be worthy of the name Christian—and if the product of one's life is not Christian, how can one be truly called Christian. "A tree is to be judged by its fruit."[13] Christian religious educators must be directed, no matter what be their subject or the environment in which they are teaching it, toward truly educating, calling forth the Christ nature that lies deep within every human person. And they can hope to do this only if they themselves have in some way seriously moved toward full realization of themselves. Merton is very gentle here, knowing full well the human condition. He says "who has attained, or is about to attain, or seeks to attain." One has to "know the score" enough to know that this is the direction in which the true answers are to be found. The religious educator has "come to experience the ground of his own being in such a way that he knows the secret of liberation and can somehow or other communicate this to others."

This is the key to the role of the educator's own "spirituality" in his life precisely as an educator. Before I go on to speak more concretely about how the educator can come to this "experience of the ground of his own being" let me interject two notes.

First, from Merton. This emphasis on the radical elements of Christian education with its rootedness in the perduring tradition, must not be interpreted to imply a rejection of the contribution and content of modern thought. Rather this will often be the context within which the religious educator will be imparting true Christian education. Indeed it is one of the great contributions the religious educator can make: the critical and balanced acceptance of modern thought. Merton speaks of this in a talk which he gave to fellow novice masters and to a group of abbots, the primary monastic educators:

> In opening our minds to modern thought (and after all this means recognizing that we too are "moderns") we must also realize its limitations and its own peculiar hazards. Above all we must be aware of its complexities, its variations, its confusions, since "modern thought" is not a harmonious unity. Modern man is not in agreement with himself. He has no one voice to listen to, but a thousand voices, a thousand ideologies, all competing for his attention in a Babel of tongues. Our responsibility to modern man goes

---

12. Thomas Merton, "Renewal in Monastic Education" in *Cistercian Studies,* vol. 3 (1968), p. 248.
13. Lk. 6:44.

far beyond playing games with him, learning some of his lingo in order to tell him what we imagine he wants to hear. Our responsibility to him begins within ourselves. We must recognize that his problems are also ours, and stop imagining that we live in a totally different world. We must recognize that our common problems are not solved merely by logical answers, still less by official pronouncements. Yet in taking the modern temper seriously we must not accept all its myths and illusions without questions, or we will end up by echoing slogans without meaning, substituting sociology, psychoanalysis, existentialism and Marxism for the message of the Gospel. We must use the insights of modern thought, but without deceiving ourselves.[14]

Second, I would like to express my reservations with the word "spirituality" which I have placed in quotation marks above and here. I am a little bit afraid of the word. If spirituality means, as Merton said in one of the quotes above, attuned to the Holy Spirit, acting in the Spirit and under his guidance, then that is fine. We ourselves are not spirits; we are very incarnate humans. We do have a spirit, but that spirit must always live and act within the context of our human existence, except for those rare moments of true transcendence when like Paul, we do not know if we are in the body or out of the body.[15] But we certainly do not want to restrict our spiritual life or our spirituality to such transcendent moments. Indeed they are not properly even the goal of such a life. The goal is love. Such moments certainly do nuture true love of God and all our fellow humans, who in such moments are truly experienced in their participation in him. Our "spiritual life" must be seen to be our real life, the fullness of human life, open to all that we are and are called to be. "Spirituality" is a way of coming to integration, of gaining the freedom to be who we are and to act out of that reality.

With that understanding I will use the word, still fearful that the reader might want to make his or her spirituality a part of life, a dimension, instead of the very fabric, the whole substance, of life.

Some Practical Orientations Toward the Religious Educator's Spirituality

How then do we practically cultivate an integral spirituality, one that will make us true religious educators, according to the Western contemplative tradition?

---

14. Thomas Merton, "Monastic Vocation and Modern Thought," in *Monastic Studies* 4 (1966), pp. 17-18.

15. 2 Cor. 12:2.

As Christians, we share with our Jewish brothers and sisters the great privilege of being sons and daughters of the Book. We have received the revelation and been called forth by it to be "a chosen people, a royal priesthood, a nation set apart"[16] to be specially taught by God. The essence of all Christian spirituality has to lie in hearing the Word of God and keeping it, i.e., responding to it, to the reality it opens out to us.

First we must hear the Word of God—truly hear it.

Merton, in the essay on Adam quoted above, says:

His knowledge of Scripture, far from being mere piety or dry pedantry, entered deeply into the very substance of his everyday life so that, like St. Bernard, Adam viewed and experienced everything in a scriptural atmosphere. He heard God's word in everything that happened. He was one who saw all things . . . centered in the mystery of Christ. Because of this unity of outlook, Adam's theology of the spiritual life is not merely a collection of devout abstractions or a synthesis of ideas: it is a *sapientia,* a wisdom which is rooted in life.[17]

Christian spirituality begins by letting ourselves be formed by Sacred Scripture, by letting that "mind" be in us which was in Christ Jesus.[18] For this to become a reality, a daily encounter with the Lord in the scriptures becomes essential. I would like then, at this point, to share with you a very simple, practical, and traditional way of doing this. This method is based on monastic practice that goes back at least to the fourth century and probably earlier.

Existential Encounter with the Bible

First we take our bibles. We should always treat our bibles with great reverence. They should not be simply put on the shelf with other books, or tossed on the desk. They should be enthroned in our homes, in our rooms, in our offices. We see in many churches today the Sacred Text given a special place, sometimes with a lamp burning before it, proclaiming a real Presence—for God is truly present in his Word, waiting to speak to us.

We begin this method of sacred reading, of encounter with the Lord, by taking our bible and reverencing it. We might kiss the Sacred Text, or kneel before it, or just hold it reverently in our hands, realizing the Presence—but let us bring our bodies into our act of

---

16. 1 Pet. 2:9.
17. "The Feast of Freedom," p. 8.
18. Phil. 2:5.

homage and presence, making it a fully human act. Then, aware of the Presence, we call upon the Holy Spirit, who dwells in us and who inspired the Sacred Text, to help us to hear the Lord as he now speaks to us through this text.

Now, ready, we begin to listen to the Lord speaking through the text. It is not a question of reading, so much as listening. Letting him speak to us through the words. No rush. We set aside a bit of time for this—ten or fifteen minutes, or more—whatever we can afford. We don't press on to finish a page or a chapter or even a paragraph, but rather listen and respond as we are moved. If he speaks to us power-fully in the first word or sentence we stay there and let the conver-sation unfold. We are not seeking knowledge, we are seeking commu-nion.

At the end of the time we have allotted ourselves for this meeting with the Lord we thank him. It is really wonderful that we can get the Lord of heaven and earth to sit down with us whenever we want and to speak to us. The scriptures are a great gift of Presence for which we can never thank the Lord enough. And we take a word with us from the listening. Not necessarily a single word, but a word, a phrase, a sentence, a thought that he has given us. Some days he will speak a word with power and we will not have to take it, it will have been given to us. Such a word might well abide with us as long as we live. Other days we will have to choose a word. If each day one of his words of life goes with us and becomes a part of our lives, or our response to life, we will come to have the "mind" of Christ, his outlook toward life and all that is.

To sum up then this very simple method for daily encounter with the Lord in scripture:

1. We take our bible, come into Presence, do reverence, and ask for the help of the Holy Spirit, who is dwelling in us.
2. We listen to the Lord speak to us through the words of scrip-ture for ten minutes (or whatever time we decide to give him).
3. And then we thank him for being with us, and take a word along with us.

Beyond Concepts to Experience

Certainly it is not enough to know God conceptually. Even as we begin to know him in this way we cannot but be attracted to him. Affections will come forth and they will lead us to seek an ever fuller union of knowledge in and through love. An insatiable desire will begin to grow in us. If we wish to respond to it, the way leads to experiential or contemplative prayer, to going beyond our thoughts and feelings to the deeper levels of our being. Merton speaks much of this, and obviously out of lived experience. Let us listen to this master:

> Unless we discover this deep self, which is hidden with Christ in God, we will never really know ourselves as persons. Nor will we know God. For it is by the door of this deep self that we enter into the spiritual knowledge of God.[19]
>
> The fact is, however, that if you descend into the depths of your own spirit . . . and arrive somewhere near the center of what you are, you are confronted with the inescapable truth that, at the very root of your existence, you are in constant and immediate and inescapable contact with the infinite power of God.[20]
>
> . . . an immediate existential union with Him in our souls as the source of our physical life.[21]
>
> . . . an immediate existential union with the Triune God as the source of the grace and virtue in our spirit.[22]
>
> This perfect union is not a fusion of natures but a unity of love and of experience. The distinction between the soul and God is no longer experienced as a separation into subject and object when the soul is united to God.[23]
>
> It starts, not from the thinking and self-aware subject . . . Underlying the subjective experience of the individual self there is the immediate experience of self-consciousness. It is completely nonobjective. It has in it none of the split and alienation that occurs when the subject becomes aware of itself as a quasi-object. The consciousness of Being . . . is an immediate experience that goes beyond reflexive awareness. It is not "consciousness of" but *pure consciousness,* in which the subject as such "disappears."[24]
>
> The dynamics of emptying and of transcendence accurately define the transformation of the Christian consciousness in Christ.[25]
>
> The charity that is poured forth in our hearts by the Holy Spirit brings us into an intimate experiential communion with Christ.[26]

---

19. Thomas Merton, *The New Man* (New York: Farrar, Straus & Cudahy, 1962), p. 32.

20. Thomas Merton, *The Contemplative Life* (Springfield, Ill.: Templegate, 1976), p. 28.

21. Merton, *The New Man,* p. 84.

22. Ibid., p. 85.

23. *A Thomas Merton Reader,* ed. Thomas P. McDonnell (New York: Harcourt, Brace & World, 1962), p. 515.

24. Thomas Merton, *Zen and the Birds of Appetite* (New York: New Directions, 1968), pp. 23f.

25. Ibid., p. 75.

26. Thomas Merton, *No Man Is an Island* (New York: Harcourt, Brace, 1955), p. 137.

A man cannot enter into the deepest center of himself and pass through the center into God unless he is able to pass entirely out of himself and empty himself and give himself to other people in the purity of a selfless love.[27]

This going beyond thought and concepts may seem like a very mysterious thing and a very difficult thing. Actually it is not. It is quite simple—simple but not easy, in the sense that it calls for stepping out in faith.

The Practice of Centering Prayer

Through all recorded history among the classical religious traditions we find men and women turning to the masters of their tradition seeking guidance in the quest of the true self, of the true meaning of life, of the transcendence that will alone satisfy the infinite longings of the human heart. For us Christians it has been a quest to be who we are, as men and women baptized into Christ and brought into the inner life of the Trinity, it is a quest to experience our true being in God, our true oneness with him.

Merton, in his thought and in his practice, draws upon the earliest of Christian traditions, the Fathers of the Desert. In the fourth century, as in ours, men and women set forth toward the East to find spiritual teaching. These early Christians turned to the spiritual fathers and mothers in the deserts of Egypt, Syria, and Asia Minor. From thence they brought back to the West, to be disseminated by the monastics through the ensuing centuries, the teachings on prayer that these fathers and mothers had learned from their fathers and mothers. This living tradition goes on. Merton learned it from his spiritual fathers at Gethsemani and shared it in his writings.

We have sought to share it more widely through a simple method which has received the popular name of "Centering Prayer"—inspired by Merton's insistence about going to the center. Like the method for sacred reading it can be summoned up in three points:

1. At the beginning of the prayer we take a minute or two to quiet down and then move in faith and love to God dwelling in our depths; at the end of the prayer we take a couple minutes to come out, mentally praying the Our Father or some other prayer.

2. After resting for a bit in the center in faith-full love, we take

---

27. Thomas Merton, *New Seeds of Contemplation* (New York: New Directions, 1962), p. 64.

up a single, simple word that expresses this response and begin to let it repeat itself within.

3. Whenever in the course of the prayer we become aware of anything else, we simply gently return to the Presence by the use of our prayer word.

Let me add just a few words of explanation here. The whole essence of the prayer is, in the first movement, a turning to God in love. The rest of the method is to enable us to remain with him peacefully. By faith we know the Lord dwells in us: "If anyone loves me, he will keep my commandments. And my Father will love him and we will come and dwell in him."[28] For a moment we recall this indwelling and respond to the Lord dwelling in us with love. We rest with him. We give ourselves to him. We want to stay with him for these few minutes, and let everything else go by, and give him a chance to reveal himself to us. As lovers, again and again we breathe his name or whatever little word says for us: I am all yours. I love you. You are mine. It is a most intimate expression of love, this prayer word. We don't necessarily repeat it constantly, as one might a mantra, but we use it only as we need it, only as it spontaneously reaffirms and intensifies our being to our Beloved in love.

But, alas, that interior TV will simply not turn off. Very soon perhaps, and perhaps again and again, we are drawn away from the Presence by some mundane affair, by our wandering desires or fears or concerns. No harm done. As soon as we become aware of this, we simply, and most gently, return to the Presence with the use of our prayer word. Each time we do this, it is a pure act of love, a real option for the Lord, and a growing detachment from things that have tended to pull us away from him.

It is important not to judge the quality of our prayer by the presence or absence of thoughts or the use of the word, or indeed anything else. There is no place for judgment here. We are simply spending some time with our Beloved. What happens, happens. The important thing is that we are making time for him, giving ourselves to him. We are not there to get anything for ourselves, especially not some sort of self-satisfaction or feelings of peace or the like. This is a very pure prayer. It is a very Christian prayer. It is a real dying to self to give self in love to God.

When one is first learning this prayer we suggest that they try to set aside twenty minutes for it, and try to find a place where they are not likely to be disturbed during that time. Most find twenty minutes a

---

28. Jn. 14:24.

good period. The stresses and strains of the day fall away, and we are refreshed in the Lord. Two periods, though, are certainly far better than one. Our aim, of course, is not just to have some periods of good prayer, as important and blessed as this might be. What we are seeking is that transformation of consciousness, leading to a wholly centered life, to constant prayer, that is, to a state where we are always coming out of the center and always resting in God's love. Are twenty minutes twice a day and ten minutes more for the meeting with the Lord in scripture—less than an hour—too much to give ourselves for cultivating the most important relationship of our lives, for cultivating the most important dimension of our lives?

I could say a great deal more to develop these three points. I have written extensively about this form of Centering Prayer elsewhere, and for the moment I would rather simply refer you to those writings.[29] What is important is the fact that we do not know how to pray as we ought, especially when we begin to open ourselves to this deeper form of prayer. But the Holy Spirit will teach us all things.[30] This prayer form opens us to make space and be attentive to the movement and leading of the Spirit. It would be a great mistake to try to do the prayer "right." It is rather making space in our lives, both in regard to time and in regard to mental attitude and desire, to allow God to reveal to us our true selves in the eyes of his love and to bring us to the freedom of the sons and daughters of God. Some things can only be known by experience. This is true of this kind of experiential prayer. "Be still and know that I am God."[31] "Taste and see how sweet is the Lord."[32]

Through the regular practice of this sort of prayer we can come to that experience of ourselves in Christ and our true freedom in Christ, of which Merton spoke, which will enable us as educators to communicate these realities to others and lead them into an experiential knowledge of them—the goal of all true Christians' educating.

Conclusion—The Context of Joy

One of the things that made Thomas Merton such an effective educator was his great empathy. This flowed, of course, from his

---

29. M. Basil Pennington, *Daily We Touch Him* (New York: Doubleday Image Book, 1979); *Centering Prayer* (New York: Doubleday Image Book, 1982); *A Centered Life. A Practical Course on Centering Prayer* (Kansas City, Mo.: NCR Cassettes, 1979).

30. Rom. 8:26.

31. Ps. 46:10.

32. Ps. 33:9.

contemplative experience. He was deeply in touch with his own feelings, and he was deeply in touch with those of others because of the love he had for them in Christ through his experience of oneness with them in the contemplative experience. He was not afraid to express his feelings, his love, his anger, his pain, his confusion, his bewilderment and searching, his hope, and ultimately his intense joy. He knew all the human emotions and he knew how to express and share them, but in the end, as one who "knows the score," he held all in the context of joy. So people listened to him, as one who knew where they were and who knew the answer. His abiding joy, which so constantly bubbled forth and which expressed itself in so much good humor and in appreciation of the creation, was not basically an emotional thing, nor was it idealistic or unrealistic. It was based on a true perception of reality held firmly in faith and experienced more and more in contemplation.

Some years ago we had in our monastery a Zen retreat, what they call a sesshein. I do not think such an event could have taken place if Thomas Merton had not courageously shown us the way to open to the East according to the mind of the Second Vatican Council. Our "retreat master" was Josha Sasaki Roshi, an eminent Zen master from Japan. He did not have much English so I gave him a Japanese-English New Testament, for he wanted to conduct this sesshein as a Christian-Zen retreat. He studied these scriptures with care and challenged us with many striking insights and many key texts for our "koan" meditation.

On the fifth night of the retreat I had a most moving experience. I went in to see the Roshi. He sat there before me, very much a Buddha. As he smiled from ear to ear and rocked gleefully back and forth, he said: "I like Christianity. But I would not like Christianity without the resurrection." Then he added: "Show me your resurrection. I want to see your resurrection." In his simplicity and clarity the master had gone straight to the heart of things. With his directness he was saying what everyone else implicitly says to us Christians: You are a Christian. You are risen with Christ. Show me and I will believe.

Reality is that we are risen with Christ. Staying too much on the surface, we are all too often only conscious of the passing experiences of the disintegration of sin in our lives. It is when we stop and go to our deeper selves, we find ourselves one with Christ, the object of the infinitely caring and tender love of the Father. This is the true Christian perception. This is where Merton was. And this is why he was so effective as a Christian educator. He came out of reality. And he touched what was truest in his disciples. When they heard him, when they saw him, they sensed their deepest longing and they sensed a hope that here was someone who could lead them to find their true selves and the fulfillment of their deep, undecipherable longings. Even though he shared very fully the anxieties of our times—he wrote on one occasion: "I am up to my eyes in angst"—Merton was able to constantly hold life in the context of joy—its true context—because each day he heard in the gospels the proclamation of the good news and in his prayer he experienced the all-affirming, creative love of God at the ground of his being, in each one of his brothers and sisters, and at the heart of the whole creation.

Rather fittingly, I am writing the closing lines of this essay on December 10, 1983, the fifteenth anniversary of the death of Thomas Merton. Certainly Merton stands as a wonderful example and a powerful witness of the potential of the Western contemplative tradition to bring a religious educator to a personal fulfillment that will mightily empower him as a religious educator, as one who calls forth the learners to the full realization of who they are in Christ.

6

Jesuit Spirituality and the Religious Educator

WILLIAM E. REISER

The spirituality which has come to be characteristic of the Society
of Jesus can be traced to the religious experience of Ignatius Loyola, a
sixteenth-century Spanish saint whose spiritual awakening and development unfolded within the European context of the Renaissance and
Protestant Reformation, and against the wider Catholic background
of the Christian ascetical tradition. Ignatius and a closely knit band of
companions who had grown to share his apostolic vision and enthusiasm joined themselves to serve Christ and his church as members of
"*la Compañía de Jesús*," the Company of Jesus.[1] The distillation of
Ignatius' religious conversion and spiritual journey is reflected in a
short book of retreat notes, directions, and meditations entitled *Spiritual Exercises*.[2] The dynamics lying behind these Exercises spring to

1. The word "company" should not be taken in a military sense, nor in the
sense of a business firm. Its sense is collegial and means companions in the
Lord. See Thomas H. Clancy, *An Introduction to Jesuit Life* (St. Louis: The
Institute of Jesuit Sources, 1976), pp. 269f.
2. The text of the Exercises from which I shall quote here is the literal
translation of Elder Mullan which appears in David L. Fleming, *The Spiritual
Exercises of St. Ignatius Loyola: A Literal Translation and a Contemporary Reading*
(St. Louis: The Institute of Jesuit Sources, 1978). Also, see Joseph de Guibert,
The Jesuits: Their Spiritual Doctrine and Practice, trans. William J. Young (St.
Louis: The Institute of Jesuit Sources, 1972), pp. 109-139.

life during an intense period of prayer and reflection which lasts about thirty days; it is generally referred to as the long retreat. The retreat is divided into four weeks, and corresponding to the meditations of each week there is a particular grace or fruit which the one making the retreat begs from the Lord.

The Ignatian Exercises engage a person both affectively and spiritually, exposing one's deepest desires and hopes, sinfulness and fears. During the course of the retreat, the strands of one's thinking and feeling are rewoven with the fibers of the gospel. The central Christian truths are appropriated experientially, not theoretically, and so the retreat can be likened to a profound catechumenate experience in which believers are schooled by the Spirit as to the meaning of the gospel and are liberated to become disciples and companions of Jesus.

Ignatius realized that not everyone was suited to making the Exercises in their entirety, but to those who were the Exercises provided a context for discovering what they should be doing with their lives, that is, what God wanted of them, provided they could learn how to hear God speaking, to trust their responses to the words and example of Jesus, and to ask earnestly for the grace of knowing, loving, and following Christ, wherever his path might lead. As they guided people—clergy and laity alike—through the meditations of the Exercises, Ignatius and his companions were carrying on a ministry to the word of God. The spirituality represented by the Exercises worked itself out in the principal writings of Ignatius and in the subsequent history of the Society, but the fruit of the Exercises and the spirituality of the Society were not intended for Jesuits alone.

From one point of view, there is basically only one spirituality known to Christians, and that is the gospel itself. As believers identify with the disciples who are gradually drawn deeply and thoroughly into the life, death, and resurrection of Jesus, their living becomes evangelical. They live as spiritual men and women, people whom the Spirit which raised Jesus from the dead leads and brings to life, people in whom the Spirit lives and intercedes (see Romans 8:5-27).[3] From another point of view, it must be admitted that there have been numerous ways of incarnating the gospel within particular cultures and historical periods. Many Christians throughout the centuries responded charismatically to the religious needs and opportunities of their age. They gave dramatic expression to the gospel in their own living

---

3. See Louis Bouyer, *A History of Christian Spirituality,* Volume 1: *The Spirituality of the New Testament and the Fathers,* trans. Mary P. Ryan (New York: Seabury Press, 1983), pp. 35-164.

by highlighting, for example, Jesus' ministry of preaching, his service to the sick and socially marginalized people of his day, his work as teacher, his poverty and simplicity of life, his prayer and contemplative union with the Father, his mission of forgiving sins. The various works which were undertaken by the Jesuits—their establishment of schools, their writing and research, their missionary and pastoral activity, and their leading people through the Exercises of Ignatius—reveal a religious group especially dedicated to ministering to the word of God.

Seven Characteristics of Jesuit Spirituality

Jesuit spirituality, it seems to me, bears at least seven important features. These features derive from the Society's sense of its mission and place in the church and the world, and from the religious insight of Ignatius and his first companions. Jesuit spirituality includes: (1) a respect for human intelligence and an appreciation of the place of critical thinking in the spiritual life; (2) the importance of discerning the movement of the Spirit within one's thoughts, feelings, fantasies, desires, and so on, and the conviction that one's inner experience, properly discerned, can be trusted; (3) a deep, personal attachment to Jesus; (4) loyalty and dedication to the church; (5) an experience of the life of faith as a companionate grace; (6) a realization that the practice of one's faith involves the pursuit of justice; (7) the ability to find God readily in whatever circumstances one finds oneself.

For several reasons this list does not mention anything related to the religious vows of poverty, chastity, and obedience. The religious vows, examined independently of the sacrament of Christian baptism, have often been regarded as marks of separation which designate certain Christians as those who have embraced a manner of following Christ which is higher and nobler than the path taken by ordinary followers. The gospel, however, does not distinguish the followers of Jesus in terms of two classes. All of Jesus' disciples are called to follow him perfectly. The religious vows of poverty, chastity, and obedience are dramatic expressions of the evangelical lifestyle to which all believers pledge themselves at their baptism. Each Christian must come to terms with Jesus' words about possessions and wealth, his insistence upon seeking to do God's will in all things and trusting in God's providential care for the world. Every Christian needs to listen closely to Jesus' insistence that we love one another purely and chastely, and to his reminder that at the resurrection people will neither marry nor be given in marriage.

Religious vows proclaim here and now the church's belief that the reign of God in this world has already begun. In a similar way, the marriage vows between Christians assume their saving significance from the fidelity and irreversible love which God has shown toward the world in Christ. These vows celebrate the church's belief that the reign of God has begun to prevail here and now in the friendship between husbands and wives. This belief is renewed whenever disciples recall Jesus' instruction to share the eucharistic bread and cup in memory of his undying friendship and loving acceptance of them. In short, vows alone are not the real basis of the spirituality of a religious community like the Jesuits. The basic spirituality informing every Christian life is determined by the gospel and celebrated in baptism.

Furthermore, even the somewhat legendary notion of "Jesuit obedience," however aptly it may have described the readiness of Jesuits to obey their superiors and the pope, is not a constitutive feature of Jesuit spirituality. There is a difference between that religious obedience which springs from a radical openness to the word of God and a thoroughgoing willingness to listen and respond to whatever God wants, and that pragmatic obedience which makes it easier to implement a plan or strategy because people have learned to conform their will to the decisions of another, in God's name. Without practical obedience a religious community would be unable to fulfill its corporate goals. However, the claim of truth upon the human mind and the claim of freedom upon the human will cannot be suspended by or surrendered to any human person, for no Christian can appropriate to himself or herself what God alone has the right and possibility to ask. No one directly represents God. "Jesuit obedience," which has sometimes been called "blind" obedience and which Ignatius himself wished to be a distinctive trait of the Society, has been a conspicuous feature of a religious community with many institutional and theological commitments. But it does not appear to be particularly evangelical. Let us return then to the list which I have proposed.[4]

---

4. This is not the place to discuss a general notion of religious obedience. Suffice it to say that the political and ecclesiastical conditions of the modern world require a rethinking of religious obedience. Some of Ignatius' emphases sound depersonalizing to men and women living in a more democratic age. Furthermore, Ignatius' concept of obedience represented a union of minds and wills, and it presupposed a high degree of self-renunciation. The purpose underlying Ignatian obedience was the carrying out of the divine will, signified by one's superior. Many today would be much less sanguine than Ignatius about the possibility of determining and representing the divine will for another. See Karl Rahner, "Freedom in the Church," *Theological Investigations,* Volume 5, trans. Karl-H. Kruger (New York: Seabury Press, 1975), pp. 89-107; "A Basic Ignatian Concept: Some Reflections on Obedience," in Raymond A. Schroth, ed., *Jesuit Spirit in a Time of Change* (New York: Newman Press, 1968), pp. 123-141; and *Ignatius of Loyola* (with a historical introduction by Paul Imhof), trans. Rosaleen Ockenden (New York: Collins, 1979), pp. 29-31.

First, the Society of Jesus has been fortunate in having attracted many intelligent, articulate, and devout Christians to its ranks. Jesuits have engaged in scholarly pursuits—theological, scientific, literary, and artistic—practically since the Society's founding. Part of the reason for this facet of the Jesuit tradition arose from the Society's early establishment of schools and its participation in the theological renewal associated with the Council of Trent and the Catholic Counter-Reformation. The habit of study and the apostolic need for intellectually competent ministers of the gospel enforced upon Jesuits the connection between the life of faith and the life of the mind. Ignatius recognized that the mind, like all creatures, was one of God's gifts, and that the mind bears a trace of the divine image.

Yet perhaps the importance of human understanding was underscored even further for Ignatius in the critical matter of the "discernment of spirits." From his experience of the conflicting movements in his own soul, Ignatius came to know the difference between those promptings, feelings, fantasies, and so on, which arose from the evil spirit and those which came from the good spirit. He learned one of the classical spiritual lessons, namely, how to distinguish the way of life from the way of death (see Deuteronomy 30:11-20). Discernment was no easy matter because the evil spirit often paraded as an angel of light. The imagery and language with which Ignatius couched his instructions about discernment—the soul's experience of "consolation" and "desolation" during its time of prayer, "good spirits" and "evil spirits"—harbor an essential spiritual insight, namely, that people come to know the truth by experiencing the truth. For truth is what is lifegiving and whatever satisfies our thirst for life comes from God, the author of life. During the course of the Exercises, the discernment of spirits becomes the key for recognizing and embracing God's will, for Ignatius believed on the basis of his own experience that men and women could really know what God was asking or inviting them to be and to do. One's inner experience can be trusted precisely because the basic movement of the soul, quickened by God's Spirit, is oriented toward life and toward God. Concretely, the image of life appears before the Christian in the person of Jesus. One learns to sort out and identify one's feelings, to understand the origins of various moods and desires. Such inner events help to pinpoint one's deepest longings. Laying bare this inner experience to prayerful examination opens the individual to the healing and transforming power of Jesus' example and love.[5]

---

5. On the discernment of spirits, see Jules J. Toner, *A Commentary on Saint Ignatius' Rules for the Discernment of Spirits* (St. Louis: The Institute of Jesuit

It is not necessary, and in fact it would ultimately prove spiritually defeating, simply to tell a person what to do with his or her life. Even with all the goodwill in the world, such outside direction would always leave people vulnerable to doubts as to whether their decisions rested finally on suggestions made by merely human voices. Ignatius believed—and this is the great fruit of the Exercises—that God himself would teach us what he wishes us to know. The soul can savor divine truth for itself and will be able from then on to recognize the taste of God. This is the surest base for genuine religious understanding.[6]

Third, Jesuit spirituality is marked by a deep, personal attachment to Jesus. In itself, this point might not appear so striking because every Christian is invited into a close personal relationship with Jesus. But Ignatius not only experienced Jesus as a living person in whose company he imagined himself walking, like one of the first disciples whom Jesus had invited to follow him; he also managed to help others share in the same experience, to discover for themselves a fresh and exciting meaning of Jesus' real presence among his followers. The request for the grace to know Jesus intimately in order to love him more ardently and follow him more closely occurs constantly in the meditations of the second week of the Exercises. Ignatius would have the retreatant plunge his imagination into the gospel scenes, to hear, to smell, to watch, to be fully present at the lanes and villages where Jesus walked and stayed, at his encounters with the diseased and with sinners, at the exchanges between Jesus and his disciples.

Behind this meditative effort of the imagination there lies an intense desire to be in the company of Jesus wherever Jesus is, to learn from him, to embrace him, to suffer with him. This desire spilled over into Ignatius' resolve to make a pilgrimage to Jerusalem in order to set foot on the land where Jesus lived and to touch the places where Jesus walked and slept, prayed and broke bread, healed and taught, died

---

Sources, 1982). Also, Karl Rahner, "The Logic of Concrete Individual Knowledge in Ignatius Loyola," in his book *The Dynamic Element in the Church*, trans. W. J. O'Hara (New York: Herder and Herder, 1964), pp. 84–170; and Hugo Rahner, *Ignatius the Theologian*, trans. Michael Barry (New York: Herder and Herder, 1968), pp. 136-180.

6. Ignatius' second annotation at the beginning of the Exercises reads: "For, if the person who is making the Contemplation, takes the true groundwork of the narrative, and, discussing and considering for himself, finds something which makes the events a little clearer or brings them a little more home to him—whether this comes through his own reasoning, or because his intellect is enlightened by the Divine Power—he will get more relish and fruit, than if he who is giving the Exercises had much explained and amplified the meaning of the events. For it is not knowing much, but realising and relishing things interiorly, that contents and satisfies the soul." (*Spiritual Exercises*, pp. 5-6.)

and was raised from the dead. In this Ignatius shared that instinct to touch the holy places which has marked many devout Christians throughout the centuries and which has brought them to journey to the Holy Land. Put in the context of the Exercises, this instinct and the imaginative leap into the gospel texts manifest Ignatius' way of ministering to God's word by guiding people to a knowledge of scripture which was experiential, personal, and spiritually satisfying because it was finally an intimate knowledge of Jesus. Ignatius wanted Jesus to notice him, to love him, and to choose him to serve the Father, as Jesus had done, under the sign of the cross.[7]

Fourth, Ignatius was both a man of the church and a man of his time. He identified the church as the "hierarchical church," and both he and his companions determined that the appropriate way to serve Christ was to put themselves at the disposal of the vicar of Christ for service to the church. The pope, Paul III, accepted their offer. The chief apostolic aims of the Society were sketched in the short formula which they presented to the pope for his approval: "to strive especially for the defense and propagation of the faith and for the progress of souls in Christian life and doctrine, by means of public preaching, lectures, and any other ministration whatsoever of the word of God, and further by means of the Spiritual Exercises, the education of children and unlettered persons in Christianity, and the spiritual consolation of Christ's faithful through hearing confessions and administering the other sacraments . . . in reconciling the estranged, in holily assisting and serving those who are found in prisons or hospitals, and indeed in performing any other works of charity, according to what will seem expedient for the glory of God and the common good."[8] All these works would be done in the church, and Ignatius appended to the Exercises a number of guidelines to help retreatants to have the right sentiment toward Catholic doctrines, practices, devotions, ecclesiastical superiors, scholastic theology, and so forth.

Within Ignatius' theology of the church we have to disengage those

---

7. This becomes evident as one reads Ignatius' autobiography. See *St. Ignatius' Own Story*, trans. William J. Young (Chicago: Loyola University Press, n.d.). For example: "One day, a few miles before they reached Rome, while he was praying in a church, he felt such a change in his soul, and saw so clearly that God the Father placed him with Christ His Son, that he would not dare to doubt that the Father had placed him with His Son" (pg. 67). Ignatius dictated his autobiography to one of the early Jesuits, Luis Gonzalez de Camara; this accounts for his speaking in the third person.

8. St. Ignatius of Loyola, *The Constitutions of the Society of Jesus*, trans. George E. Ganss (St. Louis: The Institute of Jesuit Sources, 1970), pp. 66-67.

elements which were peculiar to the state of the church in the sixteenth century from those elements which disclose what belonging to the church might have meant for the early Jesuits. The model of church to which they subscribed was primarily an institutional model, with its stress on authority, hierarchy, orthodoxy, and the administering of sacraments. But the concerns of the early Jesuits were clearly pastoral. The primary religious purpose which joined them was the service of Christ and the glory of God. Although today, in light of the background and developments surrounding the Second Vatican Council, the first Jesuits would have had a different theology of the church, they would nevertheless have considered themselves particularly blessed if Christ had accepted them to serve the people of God, which is his church. They loved the church because they loved Christ. Were he alive today, Ignatius would have proposed guidelines for thinking with the church in the modern world.

The fifth feature of Jesuit spirituality might be called the companionate grace. I have avoided the term "Ignatian spirituality" for the simple reason that the religious journey embarked upon by the first Jesuits was a corporate, fraternal journey which gave rise to a corporate spiritual history. The Society took on a spiritual tradition of its own. The Society of Jesus was not the brainchild of Ignatius; it was the graced outcome of the blending of individual histories and personalities by a group of men who soon discovered, after their individual experiences of the Exercises, that Jesus was their common friend and together they had become his companions. Together they risked the perils of traveling from Paris to Rome at a time when national armies were at war, in the severity of winter, and when they had no money. Together they resolved to sail to the Holy Land and labor there among the infidels, and when that intention failed to materialize, to place themselves at the service of the pope. Together they begged for food, they cared for one another when one of them became ill, they prayed together and enjoyed discussing among themselves the life of the gospel into which they had been newly born, and together they vowed to remain poor men. Together they came to a decision to band as companions of Jesus and to promise obedience to one of their number. Their deliberations and communal discernment gave the Society its shape and spirit.[9] While the genius of Ignatius undoubtedly inspired the first companions, and while it was Ignatius who assembled and polished the text of the Exercises and later wrote the Soci-

---

9. See Javier Osuna, *Friends in the Lord*, trans. Nicholas King (*The Way* Series 3 [1974]).

ety's *Constitutions,* one would underestimate the richness of the Jesuit spirit if one overlooked the essentially ecclesial grace that brought the Society into being. The companions had an experience of being church, people called together by the Spirit under the Lordship of Christ. Because the grace they shared was ecclesial, the companions felt the urgency of Jesus' mission and set about helping other men and women to find the kingdom of God in their lives.

Sixth, the link between faith and justice has given Jesuit spirituality today a fresh and in some ways revolutionary focus. The Thirty-Second General Congregation of the Society and its twenty-eighth superior general, Pedro Arrupe, left no doubt that companionship with Jesus in our time draws the disciples of Jesus into working on behalf of justice and for the reform of unjust social structures.[10] Indeed, this conviction is a prominent feature of contemporary Catholic thought. The Second Vatican Council's Pastoral Constitution on the Church in the Modern World (1965), the social teachings of recent popes, especially Paul VI's encyclical letter *Populorum Progressio* (On the Development of Peoples [1967]), the Medellin Documents of the Latin American bishops (1968), and the statement *Justice in the World* issued by the 1971 international synod of bishops—all these documents demonstrate that the church is growing sharply aware of the gospel's call upon Christians to pray and work on behalf of justice.[11] In their decree "Our Mission Today," the Jesuits of the Thirty-Second General Congregation wrote:

> We can no longer pretend that the inequalities and injustices of our world must be borne as part of the inevitable order of things. It is now quite apparent that they are the result of what man himself, man in his selfishness, has done. Hence there can be no promotion of justice in the full and Christian sense unless we also preach Jesus Christ and the mystery of reconciliation he brings. It is Christ who, in the last analysis, opens the way to the complete and definitive liberation of mankind for which we long from the bottom of our hearts. Conversely, it will not be possible to bring Christ to people or to proclaim his gospel effectively unless a firm decision is taken to devote ourselves to the promotion of justice.[12]

---

10. See Pedro Arrupe, *Justice With Faith Today,* ed. Jerome Aixala (St. Louis: The Institute of Jesuit Sources, 1980).

11. These documents can be found in Joseph Gremillion, ed., *The Gospel of Peace and Justice* (Maryknoll, N.Y.: Orbis Books, 1976).

12. *Documents of the 31st and 32nd General Congregations of the Society of Jesus,* ed. John W. Padberg (St. Louis: The Institute of Jesuit Sources, 1977), p. 421.

This feature of contemporary Jesuit spirituality is in some respects new. People of the sixteenth century were unaware of the dimensions injustice could assume, especially injustice which had rooted itself in social structures. Today men and women have a better grasp of the nature and effects of economic, political, and social structures. They are aware that political, military, and social policies are being shaped by national and international economic interests. The first companions were as familiar with poverty as any of Jesus' disciples down through history. They ministered to the poor by housing them, by begging food and alms for them, by nursing them back to health, by speaking to them of God. The fascinating story of the seventeenth-century Jesuit project to create among the Indians of Latin America new communities based on a Christian social and economic order remains a proud page of Jesuit history and a reminder that the connection Jesuits perceive between faith and justice is not an exclusively modern theological insight.[13] To be a companion of Jesus in the modern world requires one to be where Jesus is, and the gospel typically finds Jesus among the poor.

Finally, a seventh feature of Jesuit spirituality is its way of relating active apostolic life with religious contemplation. For Ignatius and his companions, the Society which they were experiencing did not readily fit the conventional definitions or forms of organized religious life. Apostolate and mission, they agreed, should not be subordinated to a fixed order of the day, appointed periods of community prayer, a specific style of religious dress, or one predominant religious enterprise. Jesuits had to be available for any work where there was promise of the good of souls and God's glory; they were ready to travel anywhere on earth where they might assist in building the kingdom of God. In order not to slacken in their zeal and religious effectiveness, and in order to survive spiritually outside the customary structures of community life, Ignatius knew that members of the Society would have to achieve and maintain a continual, profound union with God. Such was the grace of the fourth week of the Exercises, and what Ignatius had learned about finding God in all things wound its way into the Society's *Constitutions*. Ignatius could find God whenever he wanted—such had been God's goodness to him—and he seems to have thought that this was a special favor God was granting to the

---

13. On the so-called "Paraguay Reductions," see William Bangert, *A History of the Society of Jesus* (St. Louis: The Institute of Jesuit Sources, 1972), pp. 257-260, 350-354. Also Philip Caraman, *The Lost Paradise: The Jesuit Republic in South America* (New York: Seabury Press, 1976).

Society in order for it to achieve its apostolic aims.[14]

As amazing and singular as this feature of Jesuit spirituality may sound, it seems to me that the grace of finding God in all things is also an ecclesial grace: many Christians receive it and thereby enter more deeply the mystery of being church. The seed of such union of the believer with God is the indwelling Spirit, a grace that Jesus wanted his disciples to share: "May they be brought to complete unity" (Jn. 17:23), "May they also be in us" (Jn. 17:21), "The Father himself loves you because you have loved me" (Jn. 16:27), "We will come to him and make our home with him" (Jn. 14:23). What proved strategic about this grace for the Society was that through it the early companions were free to chart a fresh course in the history of religious life, to fashion a new kind of religious community. The companions did not imagine themselves in the presence of a Jesus who lived within a monastic enclosure or who would have been comfortable with the prevailing image of the exemplary religious man or woman. The grace of being contemplatives in the midst of action was a liberating grace for the early Jesuits, and it set the stage for later generations of Jesuits to risk mistakes, criticism, and ridicule from people inside and outside the church, for the sake of Jesus, the one whose union with God drove him to the heart of the world.

Application to the Religious Educator

Coming now to consider what contribution Jesuit spirituality might make to the religious educator, I would emphasize immediately that Ignatius and the early Jesuits were religious educators. The main objective of their work as disciples and companions of Jesus was ministering to the word of God. They taught people how to pray, instructed them about the gospel and the commandments, engaged them in conversation about the things of God, and helped them to understand

---

14. One of Ignatius' associates, Jeronimo Nadal, wrote that some of the grace Ignatius had of finding God in all things overflowed upon his companions: "That is why we believe this privilege was not only granted to Ignatius but to the whole Society and that the favor of that kind of prayer [to pray easily to the Holy Trinity] and contemplation is offered to all the Society and we hold that it is bound up with the grace of our vocation." As quoted in Clancy, *Introduction*, p. 278. Regarding Ignatius' mystical life, see de Guibert, *The Jesuits*, pp. 44ff.; Karl Rahner, "The Ignatian Mysticism of Joy in the World," *Theological Investigations*, Volume 3, trans. Karl-H. and Boniface Kruger (New York: Seabury Press, 1974), pp. 277-293; and Harvey D. Egan, *The Spiritual Exercises and the Ignatian Mystical Horizon* (St. Louis: The Institute of Jesuit Sources, 1976).

the mysteries of their faith. The presence of Christ in scripture is a particular mode of Christ's real presence to the church; the religious educator, as minister to God's word, exercises a service to the faith by enabling people to meet the Lord in his word.[15]

Furthermore, since heartfelt penetration of scripture calls for more than intellectual mastery of biblical texts, the religious educator ministers most fruitfully to God's word in the situation of faith. People must have faith, that is, they must leave their minds and hearts sufficiently open to God, if they are to understand and appreciate what the religious educator is trying to share. This means that a major task facing the church consists of teaching people how to pray: not simply what words to use in addressing God, but how one goes about placing oneself in God's presence, how to notice the way God responds to one's thoughts, feelings, fears, sins, and desires, how to deal with distractions and dryness which often undercut one's attempts to pray regularly, and so on. Admittedly there are many tasks, many gifts and ministries in the church, and no one person is expected to meet all those tasks and possess every gift. However, one of the serious difficulties religious education faces is the anomaly of teaching people about God apart from the process of spiritual direction. The Ignatian Exercises testify to the importance of linking a ministry to the word with assisting people to learn the ways of God. Certainly, the story of Ignatius should make it abundantly clear that religious educators have to be men and women of faith, open to the word of God, sensitive to their need for spiritual direction, and committed to a prayer that is more than addressing the right words to God; they must know how to listen to the God who responds.

Let me return to the seven features of Jesuit spirituality which I have proposed and develop each of them in the context of the religious educator.

First, *the importance of critical thinking in one's religious life.* One phrase Ignatius often used was "discreet charity," by which he meant that love had to be informed by prudence or discretion. An over-zealous charity could find itself misguided; it could prevent the successful outcome of

---

15. This is an important idea. For a theology of the word, see Edward J. Kilmartin, "A Modern Approach to the Word of God and Sacraments of Christ: Perspectives and Principles," in Francis A. Eigo, ed., *The Sacraments: God's Love and Mercy Actualized* (Villanova: The Villanova University Press, 1979), pp. 59-109. Also, Bernard Cooke, *Ministry to Word and Sacraments* (Philadelphia: Fortress Press, 1976), pp. 219-340. On spiritual conversation as a form of Ignatius' ministry to God's word, see Thomas H. Clancy, *The Conversational Word of God* (St. Louis: The Institute of Jesuit Sources, 1978).

apostolic work and even give rise to scandal or misunderstanding. Over-zealous charity could also drain the disciple's energies and cause the disciple to lose sight of his or her dependence on God; it could hinder superiors from making hardnosed decisions. In this regard, Ignatius proved himself to be an eminently practical man, one who learned well from his own experience and from the experience of the people he guided through the Exercises. There is no question that for Ignatius the ultimate law of the spiritual life, as it is for all people of God, was the law of love, for God is love. Yet the mind has its way of loving too. The mind loves when it thinks, and it loves best when it thinks God.

The religious educator cannot afford to neglect the role of intelligence in his or her spiritual life, nor can the educator ignore the development of religious understanding among those to whom he or she ministers. The mind has to learn how to pray, to praise and adore its Creator and Lord, and this it does by thinking, questioning, studying, seeking and reverencing the truth. Reason and faith must not be so juxtaposed that one becomes the enemy of the other. When a believer asks questions about God, human life, aspects of personal experience, the meaning of doctrines or biblical texts, the mind has to pursue those questions, to discover why those questions are of concern, how other Christians have answered them, and to learn for itself both the possibilities and the limits of thinking toward God. The mind also has a spiritual journey to make; the mind generates its own kind of spirituality. To look for God with all the powers of one's mind; to discover with the young St. Augustine that one's craving for intellectual certitude about the ultimate meaning of life, God's existence, or the resurrection of Christ, is wrong-headed; to be frustrated and disappointed upon recognizing that one's thoughts have been on the wrong track; or to realize that one has been deceived by mistaken ideas; the thrill of savoring truth or understanding for the first time a puzzling gospel passage, being grasped by the harmony of all things working together for God's purpose: these are some moments of the mind's spirituality.

But if an individual is told arbitrarily to ask no further questions, to stop thinking and simply believe God—or the church, or one's spiritual director, or one's religious superior—then the mind will be deprived of making its rightful contribution to the life of faith. The person will not experience the way God purifies our minds and draws them toward himself through teasing us to learn how to think. For the religious educator, reading, study, thinking, keeping one's mind open to the truth, are ingredients of a well-founded spirituality.

Second, *the need for discernment.* I recall a moment while teaching a course on the church when I became aware of how uninterested I was in the material being discussed. As I thought about the points under consideration I grew increasingly unhappy with my own role at that moment, concerned that the students were not profiting from the lecture (even though they were studiously filling their notebooks with my comments); I was tasting the irrelevance of some particular aspect of the theology of the church. But when I thought for a few seconds about what being a Christian meant to me, what the early disciples might have experienced as they stayed with Jesus and grew to be his community, I felt an altogether different movement. The gospel images which came to mind were stimulating and the ideas those images suggested were attractive. A renewed confidence about my role as teacher sprang from a sense that these fresh ideas were prompted by the Spirit, and the insight into what being church means felt both liberating and correct.

I hesitate to develop the classroom example any further, but the episode illustrates how a religious educator might experience an event of discernment, that is, how conflicting movements in the soul can be instructive about where God might be leading us, provided that those movements are not set aside and forgotten but are attended to, prayed over, and discerned. Even while teaching, the mind of the religious educator can experience moments of desolation and consolation. Taking seriously the fact that intelligence also prays and is also susceptible to the movement of the Spirit keeps the teacher from dismissing key interior events. Such events may be the Spirit's means of helping teachers to exercise their ministry.

Similar moments have occurred to me during the preparation and delivery of sermons, the celebration of the eucharist, or during informal discussions with students. Some ideas, thoughts, information, or practices, I would realize, should not be fussed over. When a teacher proceeds to treat them anyway because a text or syllabus requires that the matter be covered, it may be that the teacher will communicate neither ideas nor facts, only the lifelessness of material which has grown wooden and irrelevant to living faith.

Or, to take another example, the religious educator may be deeply reluctant to face a group of teenagers who have not the slightest interest in religious matters. Perhaps the prescribed presentation is not suited to them, or they are not yet ready to understand the matter which the teacher is supposed to talk about, or the teenagers simply lack a developed religious sense. By proceeding in spite of the reluctance, the religious educator might only succeed in alienating students from the church, at least for a while. The conflict one feels between the instinct that says this may not be the proper time, place, or age to be talking about some aspect of religion, and the voice of one's pastor, principal, or school board insisting the matter be covered, is an instance of the educational dilemma facing anyone who ministers to God's word. That word, if it is to be fruitful, must be accepted freely and with faith; but freedom and faith cannot be imposed on people. My point in raising this familiar difficulty is to draw attention to the feelings which the religious educator can experience. Those feelings, whether of resistance, discouragement, and disappointment, or whether of satisfaction, gratitude, and hope, need to be noticed, reflected upon, and presented to the Lord in prayer. After all, neither Jesus nor Paul, nor any of the apostles, had to face a classroom of unwilling teenage students; they would probably not have consented to do so in the first place. The apostles appear to have devoted their time to teaching and preaching to adults. The church's religious education programs often overlook this fact, and religious educators frequently get caught between their sense of what is right and workable, and what church leaders expect them to do.

I cannot offer a practical solution to the various problems besetting religious educators, but I do encourage them to pay attention to their inner experience. Feelings of conflict, enthusiasm, reluctance, or gratitude can shed light on the way the Spirit is speaking to us here and now in the context of our ministry.

Discernment, however, also carries another level of reflection. Each human being experiences the tension of being a creature, of having to choose between conflicting values, desires, goals, and courses of action. Such is how God fashioned us. In fact, the Spirit of God is still working upon us, fashioning us into the likeness of Christ. In contemplating Jesus, the believer comes face to face with his or her own best self. The ultimate decision one has to make—a decision which unfolds over a lifetime—is whether to accept that self and own it.[16] The process of spiritual growth, that is, the growth of one's own spirit, is often more dialectical than straight and smooth. That dialectic shows itself in the contest, to use Ignatius' words, between good and evil spirits. No matter how one refers to it, the contest is an inescapable part of being a man or a woman who has come to realize that God has designs on us and has his own idea of what a human being should finally look like. Even after going through the process of prayerful

---

16. For an excellent elaboration of this point, see Sebastian Moore, *The Crucified Jesus Is No Stranger* (New York: Seabury Press, 1977).

discernment there remains the redemptive struggle of putting on Christ.

Ignatius believed that we could tell where the conflicting movements of our souls stemmed from. He was convinced that the Spirit is continually drawing us toward God alone, and that each person's inner experience must be respected, for it is that experience which finally has to confirm a person in the truth. In the fifteenth annotation to the Exercises, Ignatius wrote:

> He who is giving the Exercises ought not to influence him who is receiving them more to poverty or to a promise, than to their opposites, nor more to one state or way of life than to another . . . in the Spiritual Exercises, when seeking the Divine Will, it is more fitting and much better, that the Creator and Lord Himself should communicate Himself to His devout soul, inflaming it with His love and praise, and disposing it for the way in which it will be better able to serve Him in the future. So, he who is giving the Exercises should not turn or incline to one side or the other, but standing in the center like a balance, leave the Creator to act immediately with the creature, and the creature with its Creator and Lord.[17]

God is the real director of souls; God alone should be trusted absolutely. That is why in the life of faith one's security lies not in the bible, the sacraments, ecclesiastical authorities, tradition, doctrines, teachers, or parents. In the life of faith one's only security is God. However important these other things are for guidance, correction, understanding, and support, in the end people must know God, their Creator and Lord, and not merely know about him. The religious educator respects the inner experience of the people to whom he or she ministers, and respects the religious freedom which every human being enjoys as a child of God.

In light of my own contact with the Exercises, I have found it helpful to distinguish the way of doctrine from the way of discipleship. In the process of coming to adult faith, the two ways are complementary. The way of doctrine presents what Christians believe, their answers to profound questions about sinfulness, suffering, creation, the person of Jesus, and so on. It is the way of creeds and catechisms. Many Christians are introduced to their religion through this way. Parents, teachers, and ministers of the gospel announce and explain the articles of faith. But there is also the way of discipleship or the way of experience. On this way one comes to understand who Jesus is by

---

17. Fleming, *Spiritual Exercises*, p. 12.

following him, by listening to his words and observing his example. This is how the original disciples grew in faith and understanding. The way of discipleship is, I think, the way of Ignatius in the Exercises.

When Christians are given answers without an appreciation of the questions which believers need to raise, when knowledge is imparted without sufficient attention to experience, then the basis of faith will be shaky. The two ways are illustrated in the Gospel of John. Two of John the Baptist's disciples hear him announce as Jesus passes by, "Look, the Lamb of God!" And this corresponds to the way of doctrine, the proclamation of faith. But the disciples don't yet know who Jesus is, and so they ask, "Where are you staying?" Jesus invites them to come and see. They follow Jesus, and for the next few years they are walking the way of discipleship. At the close of his gospel John tells us he has written so that "you may believe that Jesus is the Christ, the Son of God, and that by believing you may have life in his name" (20:31). In other words, John has come to his own confession; he concludes with the doctrine that Jesus is the Son of God. But the doctrine is intelligible to us only after we too have become Jesus' disciples and experienced the way of faith. Ignatius respected people's experience because human experience is the Spirit's classroom.

Third, *personal attachment to Jesus.* The spirituality underlying religious education finds its reference point in service to the word of God, which is also to serve the church's faith. Seen through the eye of Jesuit spirituality, this would imply that the religious educator above all else aims at leading men and women continually to discover what true intimacy with Jesus, the Word made flesh, really is. This Jesus is not a figure who belongs mainly to theologians and clergy; he is not someone who can be co-opted by any cause, religious denomination, or political interest. Jesus challenges the piety and beliefs of the simple faithful as well as the pretensions and expectations of those who are well-educated. Jesus is Lord of the church. Openness to Jesus, a readiness to learn daily from his words, his example, his death and resurrection, needs to be cultivated prayerfully and humbly by everyone who ministers to God's word. Everything in life, everything in religion, is relative to the Jesus whose word and presence abides in the church. The religious educator communicates this central Christian fact. The fundamental goal which unifies every aspect of his or her ministry is that of enabling people to know the Lord intimately, so that they might love him ardently and follow him closely.

If the exercise of this ministry involves helping people to understand who Jesus is and to become thoroughly versed in the gospels, it also calls for helping them to examine and reform their lifestyles. Genuine spiritual openness is an openness of the whole person— mind, heart, and will. Jesus challenges our piety, our routine manner of practicing our faith, our preconceived notions about God and what the reign of God may be demanding of us here and now.

But how do we manage to develop and maintain genuine spiritual openness? Prayer alone is not enough. We need to adopt a style of living which will keep us open to God's concerns. This means that the way we live, judge, and act must be constantly exposed to the gospel's clarifying light. Our attitude toward wealth, our career goals, our circle of friends, our recreational habits, our awareness of the global conditions of human life, become the doors which will open or close us to the world of God's concerns. If our lifestyle is too comfortable, if the harsh realities of our world are kept from view because we are busy about our own private affairs, then like the rich young man of the gospel who could not part with his money we shall have turned away from the road on which Jesus walks.

The point I am registering is not a passing moral fashion. The point is christological. It presupposes that the prayer to follow Jesus will lead us, if God grants the grace, to be with Jesus where he is in our world. This amounts to developing a new dimension to our spiritual growth, an international-mindedness, a heart that resonates with people throughout the world who are hungry, unjustly imprisoned, deprived of land and decent wages, persecuted for the sake of justice. Such development is the logical outcome of Jesuit spirituality as reflected in the third week of the Exercises. For the grace appropriate to the first week is that of knowing oneself to be a loved sinner. The disciple stands before Jesus on the cross, ashamed, confused, and embarrassed by the depth of God's forgiveness and love. The grace of the second week consists of the mounting desire to imitate Jesus, to be instructed by his example, and to be called by the Father into companionship with his Son. The grace of the third week is the favor of being thoroughly associated with Jesus, of being allowed to share in his experience, especially his experience of suffering and dying. This is a serious prayer, to seek a share in what Jesus feels, endures, experiences, and suffers. For the disciple this means not only sharing in Jesus' personal experience as one contemplates the gospel's Passion narrative; it also means sharing in the experience of the Jesus who has identified with us and who today suffers in his brothers and sisters because of human sinfulness. The spirituality of the religious educator includes, therefore, an instinct for being with Jesus by feeling the concerns of his people throughout the world, concerns which Jesus has made his own. The religious educator will assist people in developing this important dimension of Christian spirituality.[18]

Fourth, *loyalty to the church.* Love for the church is not made easier by the imperfections and errors of its leaders, by the poor quality of some of its preaching, by the record of its begrudging toleration of scientific breakthroughs, or by the spiritual shallowness of many of its members. But these things do not preoccupy those who love the church. The church, after all, is the people of God; it is not a group of faceless ecclesiastics, nor a collection of devout church-goers, nor a body of wayward drifters from organized religion. When individuals claim to be disenchanted with the church, one has to inquire how they are defining the church. Like the dragnet of the gospel parable, the church collects all sorts of people. But what one loves in loving the church is Jesus, and through him one learns to love all men and women for whom he gave his life. One remembers the price Jesus paid to establish the new covenant: "my body given for you," "my blood, which is poured out for you." Since the Lord has loved the world so much that he gave his life for sinners, how can we tell him that we are disenchanted with his church because it includes sinful people?

The religious educator can never afford to lose this perspective nor let it slip away from his or her ministry. Men and women have to be helped to understand that they too are church. If a local church fails to grow into a community of disciples whose love makes them one, then perhaps all must shoulder some share of the blame. However, being church is not restricted to the time spent within the walls of a church building. The experience of church occurs in families and neighborhoods, at parties and banquets and moments of forgiveness; it also occurs in parish halls, renewal weekends, marriage encounters, charismatic prayer groups, and informal gatherings for bible study. The gospels report that Jesus dined in the homes of friends and tax gatherers, and that he also worshiped and preached in synagogues. Through their companionship with Jesus, Christians grasp what the gospel means by the kingdom of God; like Jesus, they want to proclaim its possibility here and now. It is indeed possible to build a community in which people live a reconciled existence. There can be

---

18. See William A. Barry, "On Asking God to Reveal Himself in Retreat" and "The Experience of the First and Second Weeks," in David Fleming, ed., *Notes on the Spiritual Exercises of St. Ignatius Loyola* (St. Louis: Review for Religious, 1981), pp. 72-77, 95-102. Also, see Jon Sobrino, "The Christ of the Ignatian Exercises," in his book *Christology at the Crossroads,* trans. John Drury (Maryknoll, N.Y.: Orbis Books, 1978), pp. 396-424.

a community of disciples who are alert to forms of manipulation and domination that frequently affect human interactions, who reject the materialistic and pragmatic values of their society in favor of evangelical ones. They are prepared to greet others as brothers and sisters, for they have been schooled in how to forgive one another, lovingly. Such is the reality called the church. It is a way of living that witnesses to and proclaims the reconciliation Jesus won through his dying and rising; it is people called together by the Spirit under the Lordship of Jesus.

Today many Christians welcome the variety of ministries in the church and esteem forms of service beyond those exercised by clergy and religious. Hierarchy, institution, and tradition are aspects of the church, but hardly the only aspects and not the essential ones. To think with the church in the modern world requires maturity and humility. The church is surely more collegial and democratic than in the sixteenth century, yet we have not outgrown our need for guidance, to hear someone preach God's word boldly and with faith, to listen to the wisdom of the past, and to be ministered to by our sisters and brothers. We should give thanks for the renewal taking place in the church; we should praise God for the great event of modern biblical scholarship; we should praise God for liturgical reform, for ecumenical dialogue, for the social teachings of the recent popes, for the witness to justice on the part of many Third-World Christians. We should thank God for the church's voice in the debates over nuclear disarmament, for the awakening of fresh interest in retreats and shared prayer, for the renewal of religious life and the growing involvement of laypeople in church ministries. If Ignatius were composing his rules for thinking with the church today, surely they would sound like this.[19]

Loyalty to the church does not necessarily mean defending every last decision taken by the hierarchy, but it does mean placing as positive an interpretation as possible on the words and actions of another. This is simply Christian etiquette. But above all, loyalty to the church, that is, to the people of God which all of us together are, means giving one another through our conversation, action, and lifestyle, every possible ground for trusting that the reign of God in our lives has begun.

Fifth, *the companionate experience: finding God together.* The church

---

19. Compare Ignatius' text of the Rules for Thinking with the Church and David Fleming's contemporary rendition in *Spiritual Exercises*, pp. 230-237.

becomes a living reality when one discovers oneself depending on others, confiding in them, trusting them for patience and forgiveness, and wanting their love. Not only that, one also realizes that others are looking to him or to her for encouragement, to be strengthened in faith, for friendship in the Lord. The process of discernment takes an ecclesial, communal form when a group of Christians begins praying and deliberating together in order to seek the Lord's guidance for a common decision. When the group discovers, as Ignatius and his companions did, that communal discernment actually works, that the Spirit does manifest itself when two or three gather in Jesus' name, the group experiences a corporate peace and joy. This peace is a graced confirmation of the fact that the Spirit characteristically moves us toward being companions of Jesus, toward being a communion of love and faith. Communities, like individuals, experience desolation and consolation; like individuals, communities are susceptible to the movement of good and bad spirits. The community's coming to full stature as disciples of Jesus is largely a charismatic achievement, a work of the Spirit. Christian maturity cannot be institutionalized; real communion is a grace for which we must work and pray quite hard, if we really desire it. The community needs to know through its corporate experience that Jesus' promise to remain among his followers can be trusted.

No one in the church exercises a solo ministry. All gifts and graces are complementary, for such is the Spirit's way of linking us together. Thus the religious educator too depends upon a community of faith and looks to the company of believers in order to find the Jesus who dwells in the church. And so the spirituality of religious education includes a companionate grace which needs to be translated ministerially. Men and women have to be informed about the corporate nature of Christian faith: They depend on one another's charity and faith, they have to learn how to listen to what the Spirit is saying to and through the community of believers. God's designs for the world go beyond fashioning us as individuals. God is forming a single human family. God desires that all men and women should live a communion with each other through their union with the Creator and Lord of the whole human race. The theological basis of the communal deliberation is that the Spirit draws people together by showing the way toward greater freedom, greater unity, and deeper peace. The process of communal discernment is one way leading us to realize our mutual dependence in the Lord and to appreciate God's final aim for us as a people. In all their work, religious educators thematize the theology of union and communion, which is so prominent in the

Second Vatican Council's Dogmatic Constitution on the Church. Their ministry includes helping others to find God in the experience of being companions and friends in the Lord.[20]

Sixth, *the connection between justice and faith*. We saw the christological basis of this aspect of Christian spirituality while explaining that disciples must look for Jesus where he is in the world.[21] Christian doctrine about the divinity of Christ involves not only a cognitive claim about who Jesus is; it also involves a practical claim which expresses the fact that we praise him as Lord and do what he asks. In other words, there is a relationship between knowing the Lord and living the gospel. I do not mean that the Christian first accepts Jesus as Lord and then begins following his way. Rather, in the very process of following Jesus and imitating his example, one comes to understand why Jesus is the way, the truth, and the life, why Jesus is called the Lord and Savior.

At some point, religious education becomes education for justice. The companionate grace, the awareness of one's solidarity with the peoples of the world, the following of Jesus as he moves among the poor and oppressed, all these are the elements that account for the contemporary church's insistence upon linking faith and justice. Christians have always undertaken or supported charitable works, and since the time of the early Church Fathers they have recognized that what is often considered charity is actually a requirement of justice. When the rich give to the poor they are frequently merely restoring to the poor what is rightfully theirs. The church in the modern world has become increasingly critical of capitalism and free-market economic policies, of exaggerated notions of private property, and the outrageous sums spent on defense while poverty and hunger remain unchecked in large parts of the world.[22] Again, the church's sensitivity to issues of justice

---

20. Religious educators are not necessarily spiritual directors, but it is important that they should be familiar with the nature and process of spiritual direction. On this, see William A. Barry and William J. Connolly, *The Practice of Spiritual Direction* (New York: Seabury Press, 1982); and, Katherine Marie Dyckman and L. Patrick Carroll, *Inviting the Mystic, Supporting the Prophet: An Introduction to Spiritual Direction* (New York: Paulist Press, 1981).

21. This is treated in more detail by William J. Connolly and Philip Land in "Jesuit Spiritualities and the Struggle for Social Justice," *Studies in the Spirituality of Jesuits* 9:4 (1977). Also, I refer the reader to my article "Truth and Life," *The Way* 19:4 (1979), pp. 251-260.

22. Pope John Paul II has provided a critique of capitalism in his encyclical letter *Laborem Exercens* (1981). The text of this letter, with a fine commentary, can be found in Gregory Baum, *The Priority of Labor* (New York: Paulist Press, 1982).

is not a temporary ethical trend. The church's stand on behalf of justice represents a contemporary practical consequence of its belief in the divinity of Christ.

If Jesus is Lord, he is to be obeyed; if Christians live the gospel seriously, they will understand who Jesus is. This is simply a matter of correct spirituality. The religious educator will appreciate that the best way to apprehend the meaning of Christian doctrines is by living them, and the best way for people to understand Jesus is to live his words. Major questions still have to be asked about lifestyles and economic policies of the Western countries, questions that require penetrating analysis and evangelical insight. The unsettling answers which might be proposed will call for a considerable degree of evangelical freedom. The religious educator cannot prescind from such concerns because the central Christian belief about the Lordship of Jesus requires the church to ask in what way Jesus is Lord of our political, social, and economic systems.

Seventh, *the relation between action and contemplation.* The grace Ignatius wanted the one making the Exercises to ask for during the fourth week is that of rejoicing and being intensely glad because of Christ's newly won glory, to have some experience of Jesus' joy. Ignatius concluded the meditations of the Exercises with a contemplation to gain a pervasive love of God which arises from an inner experience of God's goodness. Theologically, the resurrection stories of the gospel narrate the church's easter faith that the risen Jesus now walks through a new Galilee, as it were. Jesus is now present wherever his disciples are; he walks ahead of them throughout the world, inspiring them to follow him and to spread the good news about God's kingdom, empowering them to hope that God's promise of new life will be fulfilled. The risen Jesus asks his disciples to be his witnesses, "in Jerusalem, in all Judea and Samaria, and to the ends of the earth" (Acts 1:8).

The disciples are Jesus' witnesses in two senses. First, they witness to him by proclaiming the story of his life, death, and resurrection to others. Second, they witness to him by being his disciples, his community. They are the ones who testify through their charity, their lifestyle, and their hope, that Jesus is still present in the world. By being church, Jesus' disciples present the world with an example of the Spirit's activity in its midst and provide an occasion for others to be attracted toward the prayerful source of the disciples' life.

And so the grace of the fourth week is not only the favor of sharing Jesus' experience of joy and victory; it is also the favor of being with the risen Jesus as he moves ahead of us into our neighborhoods, our cities and states, our homes and places of work, indeed, into every corner of the earth.

There is an adage attributed to Ignatius which runs, incorrectly, something like this: We must work as if everything depended on us and we must pray as if everything depended on God. The correct form of Ignatius' intention was dialectical and more challenging: We must work as if all depends on God and pray as if all depends on us. Ignatius would implore God for a particular grace like a soldier storming a fortress. He insisted, begged, asked the intercessory help of Mary and Jesus, fasted, wept, and offered Masses when he was seeking light and wisdom about some important matter. Yet when he came to his work and to accepting God's will, Ignatius demonstrated great inner peace. Not that he failed to work hard and to use all possible human means to accomplish what he believed would advance God's glory. But Ignatius' approach to apostolic work was suffused with a lively sense of God's closeness, a sense that he was cooperating with the movement of the Spirit, and with a practical acknowledgment of the limitations, compromises, and frustrations that delay or halt the holiest of human efforts. The aphorism literally reads: "So trust in God as if every outcome of things depended on you and nothing depended on God; nevertheless, so push your work toward these things as if you would accomplish nothing, God alone would do all things."[23] The dialectical relation between prayer and action suggests that for Jesuit spirituality resurrection faith—the grace of the fourth week—empowers a Christian to be a contemplative living in the world, cherishing its goodness, demonstrating that evangelical living is a human triumph, aware that everything is grace, and hopeful that God's designs for the world will one day be realized.

This touches the spirituality of the religious educator in several ways. Generally speaking, Christian life is neither exclusively active nor exclusively contemplative because both elements feature into the word of God. The one who ministers to that word, therefore, helps to create a balance between spirituality and politics, between prayer and activity on behalf of one's neighbor, between regarding scripture solely as private devotional words spoken by God for the individual and treating scripture as unparalleled theological texts which are the exclusive domain of scholars.

In fact, religious education itself is neither an active nor a contemplative ministry. The religious educator instructs men and women on how to listen to God's word and to keep it, how to be open to the Lord and to believe that in their own lives his word will be fulfilled. "Blessed is she who has believed that what the Lord said to her will be accomplished!" (Lk. 1:45). Just as one must work at learning to listen to

---

23. See Hugo Rahner, *Ignatius the Theologian*, pp. 25ff.

others, so one must learn to listen to God. In the course of a conversation, we can be so distracted by other concerns—the business that has to be done later, the appearance and gestures of the person we are speaking with, figuring out what we want to say next—that we may not hear what the other person is saying. Genuine listening is an active exercise of being open to the words of another. This also holds true for our conversation with God, both the ordinary conversations which are Christian prayer and the extended conversation with God which a human life is. The problem is letting go of oneself in order to enter into the concerns and experience of God, and so the religious educator not only assists people to understand the meaning of God's word but also how to go about opening themselves to it. Understanding without openness would collapse God's revelation into mere human words about religious things. The spirituality of the religious educator derives from the vocation to make men and women active listeners to the word of God.

To be contemplative while living in the ordinary human world requires a considerable degree of interior freedom and faith. The desire to be complete masters of the events and circumstances of our lives clouds the vision of faith which would perceive all things in their dependence upon God. Adam wanted to be like God, but his notion of being God was to have power and control. Jesus, on the other hand, did not think being like God was something one should grasp at, and so he lived the life of radical dependence upon God in all things; Jesus lived like one of God's servants (see Philippians 2:5-11). Yet something of the old Adam still exists in us. We have all been made in God's image, but we have yet to learn that the image of God is the image of the powerless one, the one who became poor for our sake. Genuine listening, prayerful attentiveness to the word of God, is impossible without spiritual freedom. Ignatius realized that real evangelical freedom was the fruit of choosing to be with the Jesus who was poor and powerless.

We also need to become free of the tendency to be looking at and listening to ourselves. Many people live as if a hundred pairs of eyes were constantly watching them, judging them, expecting them to behave in certain ways; but the only eyes watching them are their own. We have to detach ourselves from the mind's habit of reaching around and pigeonholing every facet of life and experience if we are to realize the grace of finding God in all things. The religious educator ministers to human freedom when he or she enables others to understand that their only lasting freedom consists of hearing and keeping the word of God. What I have been describing is not some Christian rationalization of life and experience. I have been describing the result of seeing creation as a gift, which is the fruit of Ignatius' final contemplation in the Exercises. The final word of God, the only word which adequately captures the divine revelation, is love.

Conclusion

If I have been correct in understanding the spirituality of the religious educator as the spirituality of the one who ministers to God's word, then the spirituality of the Society of Jesus, particularly as represented by the Spiritual Exercises of Ignatius Loyola, is a genuine resource for religious educators. Conducting the Exercises is one of the Society's ministries to God's word; it is religious education in the fundamental sense of schooling people in the ways of God. The Exercises provide the context in which the Christian makes a basic choice in favor of evangelical living. While religious education takes place over a lifetime, not just thirty days, still the spiritual moments which are central to the Exercises will keep recurring: the realization that one is a sinner yet loved by God, the achievement of that inner freedom required for choosing to remain in Jesus' company, lessons in discernment and self-knowledge, union with God, and the grace of finding God in all things.

Jesuit spirituality is also marked by an experience of being church or "friends in the Lord." It is characterized by a reverence for the mind and an appreciation of the role of intelligence in the life of faith, by a respect for religious freedom and by a confidence that the Spirit moves within human experience, by loyalty to the people of God, and by an integration of faith with justice. Religious education too creates a context in which a basic choice in favor of the gospel can be made freely, intelligently, and lovingly. While religious education is a multifaceted ministry, its underlying vision converges on the word of God, which it serves by helping people to hear God's word in faith and keep it:

"It is not up in heaven, so that you have to ask, 'Who will ascend into heaven to get it and proclaim it to us so that we may obey it?' Nor is it beyond the sea, so that you have to ask, 'Who will cross the sea to get it and proclaim it to us so that we may obey it?' No, the word is very near you; it is in your mouth and in your heart so you may obey it." (Deuteronomy 30:12-14)

Listening to and obeying God's word places us in Jesus' company, indeed numbers us among his own family: "My mother and brothers are those who hear God's word and put it into practice" (Lk. 8:21).

7

Orthodox Spirituality and the Religious Educator

ANDREW J. SOPKO

Some Basic Themes of Orthodox Spirituality

Unity in Diversity

The goal of Orthodox spirituality lies in the termination of the divisions between God and man, soul and body, man and fellow man, man and creation, paradise and the world, heaven and earth.[1] Victory in all these areas would mean nothing less than a complete unity between God and the created order. Already this hope has become a reality through manifestation of the Trinity: In the incarnation of God in Jesus Christ, not only has man been reconciled to God the Father, but the renewal of the entire created order through the Holy Spirit has begun. Orthodox spirituality flows from the reciprocity between the christic and the pneumatic. It believes that only Christ, as the divine focal point for reality, can "save" us and that the Spirit provides the milieu for this salvific activity. "To be saved" means that a person's true humanity has been preserved through communion with God.[2] Through such preservation, each person becomes the very image and

---

1. This list is inspired in part by the remarks of Maximus the Confessor, *Ambigua, Patrologia Graeca* 91: 1109CD.

2. Concerning the verb "to save," see Hans Urs von Balthasar, *Kosmische Liturgie* (Einsiedeln: Johannes Verlag, 1961), p. 254

150

likeness of God with Christ himself providing the model for this process. And, as St. Paul reminds us in Romans 8, salvation is destined not just for humanity but for all of creation through the Holy Spirit.

If Orthodox spirituality stresses unity, it also contains the paradox of polarity. The impossibility of a mixture between the uncreated and the created safeguards the integrity of man and the universe.[3] Communion with God does not mean the encroachment of the *divinum* upon the *humanum* but rather the realization of the full potential of humanity. Just as the human and divine natures in Christ retain their characteristics, so salvation or "deification" occurs for each human being without any change to what is proper to human nature.[4] The more human an individual becomes the more divine are the characteristics manifested until true personhood is attained. Maximus the Confessor even tells us that the incarnation can occur anew in every human being. With Christ as the model, man deifies himself through a natural desire to find pleasure in God alone.[5]

Life in Christ

But it is not merely the imitation of Christ which makes this a possibility but what the Orthodox tradition refers to as "life in Christ." In other words, the Pauline statement that "no longer I live but Christ lives in me" is taken at face value. The Christian life depends, not upon a personal meditation on the historical Jesus, but upon the actual attainment of the presence of God in the person through the power of the Holy Spirit. This does not belittle the historical reality of the incarnation but extends it empirically in the absence of the corporeal Christ who has passed beyond history. There has been some confusion as to what events in Christ's life provide the foundation for Orthodox spirituality. Certainly Irenaeus' view of the entire incarnation as salvific sets the tone for the Orthodox view, but what should stand at the center, the cross or the resurrection? It is not unusual to hear it said that Western Christianity stresses the cross and Eastern Christianity the resurrection and Orthodox have been especially good at perpetrating this myth.[6]

---

3. This of course does not mean to imply that man is not dependent upon God.

4. For a good discussion of this, see Lars Thunberg, *Microcosm and Mediator: The Theological Anthropology of Maximus the Confessor* (Lund: CWK Gleerup, 1965), pp. 29-34.

5. Thunberg, *Microcosm and Mediator,* p. 458.

6. See especially a book such as Nicholas Arseniev, *Mysticism and the Eastern Church* (Crestwood, N.Y.: St. Vladimir's Seminary Press, 1979).

Orthodox spirituality emanates from each Orthodox Christian's experience of the cross. While the cross and resurrection are usually mentioned together in Orthodox hymnography and the cross generally seen in the light of the resurrection, this does not undermine the preaching of Christ crucified nor the individual Christian being crucified. Rather than see the resurrection as the *terminus ad quem* of the cross, a more balanced perspective might be had by seeing the cross in its chronological position between the transfiguration of Christ on Mt. Tabor and his resurrection. The glory of the transfiguration might be said to present the potentiality of man and, by extension, creation as it could have been without the Fall. But now the created order can reach this state only through *metanoia* and this change comes only through suffering. Even the resurrected body of Christ retains the stigmata of his suffering and those who follow him will likewise suffer. This sharing in the kenotic character of Christ's suffering has in fact been very strongly emphasized in Orthodox spirituality, particularly in Russian piety.[7] It would be incorrect to think, however, that suffering alone makes God present in each life and in the world. Just as in the incarnation, from the very moment of conception, life exists with the participation of God's creative will manifested in the Holy Spirit.[8] A willingness to suffer is in fact one of the highest demonstrations of human cooperation with this will.

When the Orthodox Christian affirms in the Nicene-Constantinopolitan Creed that God is the maker of all things "visible and invisible," this does not mean that these are two created realms which stand apart from one another but that they co-inhere. In man, the visible or sensible is manifested in the body while the invisible or intelligible is manifested in the soul, the life force which animates the body. Both are mutually dependent upon one another and personal spirituality is in fact a quest to assure that they remain "in contact" so that full communion with God is possible.[9] A long battle was fought in the Eastern monastic tradition concerning the relationship between body and soul. Neoplatonic influences evolved into Origenism and Evagrianism, both of which dismissed the body as something unimportant.[10] Obviously, such an attitude could not be endorsed by the

---

7. See particularly Nadezhda Gorodetsky, *The Humiliated Christ in Modern Russian Thought* (London, 1938).

8. Orthodox Church in America, *Women and Men in the Church* (Syosset, N.Y.: OCA Department of Religious Education, 1980).

9. See particularly the discussion in Thunberg, *Microcosm and Mediator,* pp. 100-109.

10. For a good overview of this, see John Meyendorff, *St. Gregory Palamas and Orthodox Spirituality* (Crestwood, N.Y.: St. Vladimir's Seminary Press, 1974), pp. 20-23.

church if the doctrine of the incarnation was to be upheld. What stood at the root of the controversy was the concept of prayer itself. The Evagrians identified prayer with only "the mind," which they considered divine. For them, communion with God could occur only through "intellectual prayer" which carried the mind far from the corporeal.

Prayer

The replacement of the "prayer of the mind" with the "prayer of the heart" by the church reiterated that true humanity is always a psychosomatic whole. In this context, "heart" is not meant in an emotional sense but as the seat of the inner personality. Prayer, that activity which makes true communion with God possible is always the joint effort of body and soul led by the heart. The words of the prayer aligned with the rhythms of the body are meant to overcome any subject-object distinction. Hesychasm (hesychia=quiet), the attainment of mental and bodily quietude in prayer, in fact attempts to once again "circumscribe the Incorporeal in a dwelling of flesh" just as at the incarnation.[11] While there is no set methodology in attaining this goal, the most commonly accepted fashion has been to take the Pauline admonition "pray without ceasing" seriously. The Orthodox tradition has especially stressed the constant repetition of the so-called "Jesus Prayer" ("Lord Jesus Christ, Son of God, have mercy on me a sinner.") in carrying out St. Paul's instruction. The remembrance of Jesus at all times and in all things brings his "re-incarnation."

But private prayer in and of itself is not enough—the Christian who is alone is not really a Christian. Privately, the mediation between the sensible and intelligible may occur through prayer but intrapersonally, it must occur through the observance of the commandments. The stories of the saints who made peace with their neighbors before their prayers or who even left them in order to do so are legion. But how does the observance of the commandments also bring a mediation between the sensible and the intelligible? It must be stressed that the term "intelligible" refers to more than just that which can be perceived cognitively. In fact, it would be helpful to associate it with the "non-sensory." Although the intelligible is always reasonable, reasonability is rooted not in the *ratio* but rather in the Logos, the second person of the Trinity "through whom all things were made." The "reasons" behind the created order *and their interrelationships* are root-

---

11. John Climacus, *Ladder of Paradise,* Step 27, quoted in Meyendorff, *St. Gregory Palamas and Orthodox Spirituality,* p. 36.

ed in the Logos.[12] The Logos, made flesh as Jesus of Nazareth, thus becomes the reason behind ethical behavior, with the Holy Spirit providing the power of discernment.

It is through the emulation of God's love, demonstrated in Jesus Christ, that man performs the task of mediation. If love is the motivating and unifying factor behind the universe, both sensible and intelligible, man in fact becomes a microcosm of the universe when he loves God and fellowman, overcoming creation's differentiations in doing so. But the fulfillment of the double commandment might seem an impossibility if God and fellowman are conceived of as "objects," for must not man's love of God be total? Love for one's neighbor does not imply an attachment to men which is of the same character as the attachment which love for God implies. When one loves "in God," the person shares in God's "state of mind" and possesses God's charity toward all men.[13] Maximus the Confessor in fact tells us that human preferences are the result of human imperfections and that human love should be an equal love for all men brought about through the attainment of detachment which is one of the benefits of unceasing prayer.

Love

Self-love and mutual self-interest do not truly reflect love, and this is why the Holy Trinity has always remained the paradigm for human love in the Orthodox tradition. The manifestation of the Trinity in which all Orthodox Christians strive to participate takes them beyond the merely singular and dual and presents them with the reality of unity in diversity. Father, Son, and Holy Spirit have been revealed as different divine persons acting in unity through a co-inherence of love. While three, their action (energy, will, or grace) always remains one. St. Isaac the Syrian has stated that the Holy Trinity "by nature, creates, anticipates and judges that which has been made by Him," and this means that humanity has the obligation to pattern itself after the Trinity. With the Fall, however, the fragmentation of humanity began. As St. Gregory of Nyssa has observed, as human beings have reproduced, this fragmentation has accelerated. But in God no such fragmentation occurs for there is only "one and the same person of the

---

12. Such a foundation for moral theology has been absent in the Western Christian tradition but now the Roman Catholic Joseph Fuchs has been working along these lines. See James Gustafson, *Protestant and Roman Catholic Ethics* (Chicago: University of Chicago Press, 1979), pp. 102-107.

13. Thunberg, *Microcosm and Mediator*, pp. 332-33.

Father from whom the Son is born and the Spirit proceeds."[14] Humanity can regain its unity only through adoption by the Father in Christ. This would end fragmentation when all become the children of the person of the Father who neither fragments nor multiplies. Unity is restored by the Father's adoption of humanity in his Son and humanity, when it chooses to cooperate fully, will be reunited through the Holy Spirit.

This cooperation can occur only through conformity with the will of God as manifested in Jesus Christ. Just as his human will always assented to the will of God, so each individual will must do likewise for the fragmentation of humanity to end. Only then will true human freedom be manifested. Just as Christ prayed "not my will but your will be done," humanity must make its prayer the same. Will implies energy or movement, and humanity would never reach its full potential, communion with God, unless it participated in this "process." The conformity of human wills to the divine will has more than just the unity of humanity as its goal. Both human society and creation must be reunited on earth and beyond but the decision rests with man alone. As Olivier Clement has observed, "For the universe, man is its hope to receive grace and be reunited with God; Man is also the possibility of failure and loss for the universe."[15]

Culture in a Transformational Key

The interaction between man and the earth has generally been referred to as culture. Because Christianity makes the claim that the God-man interacted with our world, it feels that all cultures must be seen in the light of the life of Christ. According to Orthodox spirituality, the continuing "life in Christ" in fact provides the possibility for the transformation of culture until it too is divinized. Not even Orthodox Byzantium succeeded in such an accomplishment and culture will be fully transformed only in the Kingdom of God. Until that time, a state of tension will always exist between the claims of the gospel of Christ and the ways of the fallen order. Still, each individual Christian can have the same opportunity to interact with the world and transform it as did Christ. Obviously this cannot be reduced to only individual efforts but must remain first and foremost the collective effort of the church as "council" or more concretely, as the body of Christ.

In the church the entire life of Christ becomes a reality in which all

---

14. Quoted in John Meyendorff, *Byzantine Theology* (New York: Fordham University Press, 1974), pp. 183-84.

15. Olivier Clement, "L'homme dans le monde," *Verbum Caro* 12, 45(1958), p. 11.

can participate in their own lives and not just those who knew him in his own historical-cultural context. And while each person who strives to live "the life in Christ" possesses the potential for a new incarnation of Christ, this could not occur in and of itself without interaction with the world. Here, the "traditional" categories of scripture, liturgy/ sacrament and the Fathers become necessary models. These all deal with the interaction of persons "living in Christ" with the world around them and pay particular attention to human language and community as well as nonhuman nature.

Scripture and Sacrament

The vernacular reading of scripture in the ecclesial community presents a verbal icon of Christ which aids in the concrete realization of the life of Christ and the life in Christ. As such, *lectio divina* cannot be limited to literal readings but always remains open to an interpretation which goes beyond the author's intention and which indeed may aid in bringing the message of Christ into a new cultural context through the Holy Spirit.[16] Honor given to scripture emphasizes the theological implications of language and the value of words in themselves for all words participate in Jesus the Word. In fact, those who listen and apply the text to their everyday lives become the living gospel.[17]

Just as with scripture, Christ is also the *auctor* of the sacrament. In other words, in the life in Christ there is no distinction between historical and actual reality, but it is always the continuous presence of Christ which is stressed in every activity. Sacrament, the carrying out of the activity, and liturgy, the gathering for it, embrace not only those persons living in Christ but also affect the world through the interaction of these persons. Not only human beings but all matter is "gathered into Christ."[18] Sacramental celebration expresses the proper relationship between both man and nature and provides models for personal, social, and ecological propriety.[19] For example, baptism becomes the prototype for not just spiritual but also physical hygiene,

---

16. John Breck, "Exegesis and Interpretation: Orthodox Reflections on the Hermeneutic Problem," *St. Vladimir's Theological Quarterly* 27, 2(1983), p. 85.

17. Anton Ugolnik, "An Orthodox Hermeneutic in the West," Ibid., pp. 117-18.

18. See the remarks of Yves Congar, *Tradition and Traditions* (New York: Macmillan, 1966), pp. 11-12, 89.

19. This is especially emphasized in Alexander Schmemann, *For the Life of the World* (Crestwood, N.Y.: St. Vladimir's Seminary Press, 1973). "Social ethics" would belong in the sacramental category although even today the Orthodox tradition has no such discipline.

and the eucharist presents at its most basic level the pattern for all proper eating and drinking. In all these actions, the Holy Spirit is called upon for it is the presence of the Spirit which gives men the ability to see reality as it actually is and not as it seems to be in its fallen state.

Sacramental actions which "restore all things in Christ" find their goal in the eucharist. No sacrament is greater than the eucharist, for in it the body and blood of Christ are made available as food and drink for all from the matter of the earth. This means that each eucharist is in fact a "Mass on the world" for Christ is consubstantial with the created order. The eucharist provides a foretaste of the Kingdom because it unites the diversities of the created order. Through both the eucharistic offering and the gathered assembly, Christ recapitulates in himself through the Holy Spirit, not only the earth, but the entire cosmos as it will ultimately be. When offered, the eucharist becomes the ultimate thanksgiving: An encapsulation of the created order as it was intended to be is returned to God.

Mediation of Man with Creation

Since the cosmos still awaits its final transfiguration when Christ will be "all in all," the spiritual task of relating Christ to the current order of things is always on the agenda. While it has been usual to think of the Fathers of the Church chiefly as expositors of scripture, they have always been and always will be (for each age produces its own Fathers) the chief theologians of culture. As such, they always stand on the boundary between culture and the Kingdom, doing the heavy work of apologetics and inspiring others on their spiritual journey. Differences of opinion and even error may exist in their instruction, but the *consensus patrum* always remains: They all reflect "the oneness of the reality to which they belong and within which they think, move, and love."[20]

Beyond the boundaries of the church, mediation between man and creation occurs when each person humbly carries out his duties. Honest labor not only ennobles everyday life but enables man to build up the earth through self-forgetfulness.[21] When man forgets himself in his honest labors, he can no longer be an exploiter of the environment. While many of the Fathers have looked upon work as an absorb-

---

20. Alexander Schmemann, "The Orthodox Tradition," in *The Convergence of Traditions*, ed. E. O'Brien, SJ (New York: Herder and Herder, 1967), p. 24.

21. Olivier Clement, *The Spirit of Solzhenitsyn* (New York: Barnes and Noble, 1976), p. 47.

er of iniquity, they have never regarded it as a curse. Through the positive *ascesis* of repetitive manual labor, man can enter into dialogue with matter in nature or through man-made objects. "The union of mind and heart in work banishes all extraneous thoughts from the mind, bringing concentration on a single idea and the making of that idea, not by imposing it on matter but by yielding to the latter in order to give expression to its dynamism and construction."[22]

More than anything else, artistic creativity unites intellectual and manual labor. Intelligence is united with the heart and so with the body. The artist becomes a creator after the Creator and shares in the work of the Logos, providing meaning for the created order. Art is not just the presentation of things as they seem to be to the public-at-large but carries personally rooted experiences in its content. It exists not merely to be beautiful but rather to make us more aware of the created order through the personal awareness of others. The sharing of these personal awarenesses is in fact meant to broaden our own horizon of vision and point to a creative reality beyond ourselves. The truly beautiful icons of culture should help us realize that earthly culture itself is called to be an icon of the Kingdom of God beautifying itself through an awareness of the Holy Spirit.[23]

Before earthly culture can become the Kingdom of God, two further mediations must be accomplished: Paradise must be restored in the world and the divisions between heaven and earth must be overcome. According to Maximus the Confessor, when Christ sanctified the inhabited world through his human behavior, he entered paradise after his death as he promised the thief for, for him, there was no longer any difference between paradise and the inhabited world. Following his resurrection, Christ manifested this restored unity of the earth.[24] Individual Christians can do likewise, but this requires crucifixion with Christ throughout their spiritual development. There must be a detachment from the temptations of the sensible world and an abandonment by the mind of the contemplation of these temptations. This makes it possible to share in the body and mind of Christ and to eventually share in his divinity. In other words, the positive *ascesis* of work and creativity which brings the mediation between man and the earth must be complemented by a negative *ascesis* of denial for the earth to become paradise again.

Self-denial of sensible temptations brings with it the impossibility of

---

22. Ibid., p. 51.

23. Paul Evdokimov, *L'amour fou de Dieu* (Paris: Editions du Seuil, 1973), p. 136.

24. Thunberg, *Microcosm and Mediator*, p. 406.

natural determinism. Not only man but also nature has been affected by the fall. Through the crucifixion of the senses, the imbalance in the natural order is transcended and even death, the primary expression of that imbalance, is sensibly overcome as it was in the bodily resurrection of Christ.[25] But to crucify the senses does not mean to be unfeeling toward or unaffected by life's current problems and dilemmas. Through the possession of the mind of Christ, the perspective of the person sees reality as Christ sees it, realizing that hope for the created order is not in vain but logical, i.e., Logos-oriented. Even now, God's intention for the universe is clear to those who possess the eyes of faith given by the Spirit. As Father Zosima's brother tells us on his deathbed in Dostoevsky's *Brothers Karamazov,* "Life is a paradise, but we won't see it; if we could, we should have heaven on earth the next day."

As Christ was with the thief "in paradise" so he is now with all who crucify themselves to him and will be resurrected in him. This explains why the *parousia* has been initiated even now. The eucharistic canon of the Orthodox tradition *remembers* "the second and glorious coming" implying that with the resurrection, the eternal presence of Christ has already been initiated. At present, outside the church, the realization of the Kingdom is not a cosmic process but an individual one. Nature cannot change itself; only persons can change themselves and nature with them. This means the process toward God's Kingdom, initiated in the waters of baptism and revealed most fully in the eucharist remains a prime responsibility of individual Christians in the world. The Kingdom of God is, in fact, the Holy Spirit for the Spirit witnesses to the presence of Christ, manifesting the goal of history far in advance of its final attainment.[26] Man is in the Kingdom when he possesses body, soul, and Spirit for the Spirit shows forth the divine will which ushers in the Kingdom. As St. Seraphim of Sarov tells us in his conversations with Motovilov, "The grace of God must dwell within us, in our heart, because the Lord said: The Kingdom of God is within you. By the Kingdom of God, the Lord meant the grace of the Holy Spirit."[27]

It might be assumed that this view reduces Orthodox spirituality to

---

25. On natural determinism and the resurrection, see John Meyendorff, *Byzantine Theology,* pp. 135-36.

26. See the exploration of this idea in P. A. Florensky, "On the Holy Spirit," in *Ultimate Questions,* ed. A. Schmemann (Crestwood, N.Y.: St. Vladimir's Seminary Press, 1977), pp. 166-68.

27. Quoted in George P. Fedotov, *A Treasury of Russian Spirituality* (New York: Sheed and Ward, 1948), p. 271.

individualism, but it emphatically does not. When the fruits of the Spirit are possessed by a person, egocentrism is an impossibility. And although the Kingdom will be fully manifested only when each person is filled with the Spirit, the lives of the saints provide myriad examples as to how all can do likewise. According to Nicholas Cabasilas, it is not miracles which constitute sainthood but rather conformity of the will to the divine will manifested by the Holy Spirit.[28] Sanctity can be apprehended in the community only through personal interaction and this is why the recognition of a saint is always a local event. The environment in which the saint has lived has been transformed by his presence. In many of the *vitae* of the Eastern saints, a return to a paradisaic state is stressed. Even the relationship between the saint and wild animals is that from before the Fall.

Just as the death and resurrection of Christ have brought a mediation between the inhabited world and paradise, his ascension has done the same for earth and heaven. Heaven is that place where God's will is obeyed and through the fulfillment of the will of God, man likewise "ascends" there. While not losing his sensible faculties, he becomes like the intelligible ranks of angels, "knowing" the reasons behind God's creation.[29] The angels represent the ideal side of creation, but in becoming like them man does not pass outside the realm of the incarnation, for the body of Christ now remains the focal point of the reasons behind both the sensible and the intelligible. Furthermore, the fact that Christ has reconciled the entire created order to himself also means that the mediation between earth and heaven is in no way circumscribed by the earth but must be carried beyond the earth to the ends of the universe. Since man is a microcosm of the whole creation, the created order could itself be thought of as a cosmic "being." Through man's efforts, this cosmic being is also destined to participate in the task of terminating all divisions. Thus, the termination of divisions ceases neither with man nor with the earth but only when the entire cosmos becomes like Christ both sensibly and intelligibly.

Applications to the Religious Educator

Teaching in the Spirit

Who then are the educators for the realization of this monumental task? A practical spirituality which has concrete goals, even though

---

28. Meyendorff, *Byzantine Theology*, p. 108.
29. Thunberg, *Microcosm and Mediator*, pp. 416-18.

these may be long-term, must be rooted in theology. *Theologia* is not something imparted by professional theologians with multiple degrees and long-winded phrases but is grounded in personal experience. Through its emphasis on an apophatic or negative theology which stresses the incomprehensibility of God, the Orthodox tradition has not been trying to reduce God to a *deus absconditus* but rather attempting to remind us that "God always has something more to teach."[30] Here, the term "teach" does not refer to just intellectual knowledge but to an illumination of the entire person. Theology, or more properly, the experience of God, is not to be limited to scripture, doctrine, or writings of individual saints but always belongs to the realm of the Spirit who will lead us into all truth. Theology is the vision of God which all persons "in the Spirit" share. The fact that it is never individualistic reveals its "mystical" quality, and from this experience of God which is simultaneously personal yet collective flows spirituality.

Spirituality is a Spirit-filled behavior which fulfills the two great commandments. The private, personal experience of God in and of itself does not guarantee the manifestation of spirituality. Just as only a divine person can fully witness to another divine person as the Holy Spirit testifies to Christ, so only a human person can "educate" another in manifesting that spirituality which proclaims true personhood. Christ always remains the quintessential person and it is particularly the "Christs" of succeeding generations, manifested through the Spirit that make spiritual education possible. For this reason, the role of the spiritual educator has never been limited in the Orthodox tradition merely to the professional theologian as teacher, the bishop as the guardian of the apostolic faith, or the presider as leader of the local eucharistic community. Such limitations would, in fact, be a confinement of the power of the Spirit.

The Orthodox tradition actually finds it difficult to speak in terms of "religious education" or "religious educators." The very use of terms which have their semantic roots in the concept *religio* (ritual scrupulousness) implies a compartmentalization of the structures of faith in such a way that they would not embrace all of life. "Religion," to the contemporary mind, unfortunately connotes certain rites or beliefs which can be analyzed or compared by scientific methodology (hence, *Religionswissenchaft*) but not *a way of life*. This helps explain why, in the Orthodox tradition, it is not the scientific and methodological presentation of doctrines which connotes "religious education" but

---

30. St. Irenaeus, quoted in Kallistos T. Ware, *The Orthodox Way* (Crestwood, N.Y.: St. Vladimir's Seminary Press, 1979), p. 185.

rather Spirit-filled behavior. Those who possess the Spirit are the true "educators" teaching through their personal relationships with others. Traditionally, the "religious educator" in Orthodoxy has been the so-called spiritual elder (Greek, *geron*, Slavonic, *starets*) or director. Recognized as such by others in the community, these directors may be men or women, they may be lay or cleric, but they do not form a special caste or class within the church. A consideration of their role will aid in formulating an Orthodox understanding of the spirituality which should be manifested by today's religious educators, i.e., those who teach and relate to others in the classroom or in other educational settings.

Religious Educator and/as Spiritual Director

Most frequently mentioned in the monastic literature, the elder or spiritual director is someone sought out by another person. Spiritual directors are not institutional fixtures but charismatic guides who can fulfill a prophetic role in a particular person's life. An elder is not necessarily old chronologically but possesses the wisdom of the Spirit. Since the milieu of the Spirit assures that a true spiritual director can never become some sort of individualistic guru, it also safeguards the personal nature of his or her work—bystanders and the curious will never comprehend the director's wisdom. Pneumatic reciprocity makes the relationship between the spiritual director and the true seeker possible. Not only does the Spirit dwell in the spiritual director but it is the Spirit who has drawn people to the elder. The Spirit always dwells in the ecclesial community but it is personal communion with the Spirit in a personal relationship with another human being that strengthens Christian community, especially as it is revealed in the eucharistic assembly. Even in the relationship between the director and the seeker there is "community" for the Spirit is always present as "other."[31] Through the Spirit, person and community are dialectically united.

The relationship between the spiritual father or mother and each spiritual child is always personal. Each person is unique, each situation is different. Therefore, there can be no set rules and regulations in guiding a person in the spiritual journey. Just as spiritual guides are never appointed, so there are not guidebooks which will aid in decision making.[32] Spirituality is not based on book-learning but on trust

---

31. For more on this idea, see Dumitru Staniloae, "The Holy Spirit and the Sobornicity of the Church," in idem., *Theology and the Church* (Crestwood, N.Y.: St. Vladimir's Seminary Press, 1980), pp. 61-64.

32. See the remarks concerning a noncasuistic approach in Kallistos T. Ware, *The Orthodox Way*, pp. 128-29.

and love of God and others. The director's personal efforts to attain perfection have come to the seeker's attention, making him realize that the director has struggled in much the same way as he has. This realization brings the seeker to the spiritual director as a co-struggler in the spiritual warfare. As co-strugglers, one is not better than the other nor is there a hierarchical distinction between them. Wishing to be Spirit-filled imitators of Christ, this common goal motivates their personal relationship. Nor do the benefits conferred by the Spirit travel a unilateral path in the relationship. Spiritual growth continues on both sides of the relationship with the gifts of the Spirit distributed bilaterally.

It has been said that the true theologian is the person who knows how to pray and the spiritual director must have this ability before all else. The relationship between the spiritual director and spiritual child goes far beyond their meetings. Behind the advice which a director gives there must be ceaseless prayer on behalf of the spiritual child. Enhanced through contemplation and silence, the cares, anxiety, and even guilt of the spiritual child become the director's own. While prayer must be constant, there can be no prescribed schedule for meetings between the spiritual director and his children. Some may come once or twice in their lives, others may come daily.[33] In the first instance, the spiritual director might aid in momentous decision making while in the second, advice may be given concerning the most seemingly inconsequential daily task. The supreme importance of each human person and his actions in the sight of God means that all are treated equally by the spiritual director. What St. Augustine said concerning God could also be said of the spiritual director: "He loves each one of us as if there were only one of us."

Those who visit the spiritual director frequently generally confess their sins. This is done not to fulfill any legal requirement but to enable the elder to better guide the conscience of the spiritual child. Both in the past and even today in some monasteries, absolution is pronounced by nonordained monastics, a practice which helps demonstrate the antinomy between the institutional and the charismatic in the Orthodox tradition. The forgiveness of sins does not belong to only the "ordained" functions in the community but to all who are truly able "to call sin by its name" and initiate the process of healing.[34] Not only the private instruction and guidance but also the emulation

---

33. Ibid., pp. 127-28.

34. Meyendorff, *Byzantine Theology*, pp. 195-96. Unfortunately, this concept has been weakened in recent centuries. Now it is not uncommon for a person to go to an "ordained" minister for absolution after visiting a nonordained spiritual director.

of the spiritual director are to be carried into everyday life by the spiritual child. Prayer and active love toward others must permeate each spiritual child's calling. Teachers, doctors, scientists, and all others are called to be spiritual directors each in their own way. Alexander Solzhenitsyn has offered some interesting insights into the spirituality which should motivate particular professions. He tells us that for a teacher, the attainment of an all-encompassing sincerity will enable pupils to live life more deeply. A doctor "should have no more patients than his memory and personal knowledge can cover." This enables him "to treat each patient as a subject on his own." The scientist's research must always become "active contemplation, producing. . . . mental exaltation" that will make others aware of the ultimate meaning behind the universe.[35]

Solzhenitsyn's remarks concerning teachers leads us back to a consideration of the religious educator in light of the spiritual director's work. Solzhenitsyn himself seems to say that some sort of spiritual direction should be a cardinal function of all teachers, obviously implying that such direction certainly belongs to religious educators. The use of the Orthodox spiritual director as a model for today's professional religious educator should not be misconstrued as an exercise in anti-intellectualism but rather a clear demonstration that the presentation of theology at the rational, cognitive level is only one aspect of the experience of God and must in fact be transcended.

Paradoxically, Orthodox spirituality faces a grave crisis in the contemporary world possessing far too few spiritual directors, and it may in fact be its professional religious educators who will fill this vacuum. Spiritual directors have never been mass-produced and certainly will not be in a culture of mass production. When we read about a traditional Orthodox culture such as that of the Greek islands as described by Alexander Papadiamandis, we immediately realize that today's cultural context is very different. The encroachment of technological society on traditionally Orthodox areas is one thing, but even more problematic is the survival of an Orthodox spirituality in areas where there have never been deep Orthodox roots. Before Orthodox spiritual directors can emerge in great numbers from non-Orthodox cultures, foundations will first have to be laid using the "earthen vessels" at the command of Orthodox religious educators. But to assure that the doctrines and rites of which these educators speak will not remain merely earthen vessels, the tasks generally assigned to spiritual direc-

---

35. Oliver Clement, *The Spirit of Solzhenitsyn*, pp. 54-55. The quotations come from *Cancer Ward* and *The First Circle*.

tors will also have to become their motivating principle but on a much broader scale. Such an approach may aid not only the Orthodox religious educator but religious educators in other traditions as well.

As has already been mentioned, Orthodox spirituality has always considered interaction with different cultures necessary. Both the work of the early Church Fathers as theologians of culture and the thrust of later vernacular missions such as that of SS. Cyril and Methodius to the Slavs demonstrate this. But to transform large populations and entire cultures requires a structured "patristic" and "apostolic" effort. There is no better means of doing this than through education, but education tempered by the example of spiritual directors. In other words, the presentation of simply "academic" material is not enough. While the Orthodox Church recognizes certain Fathers of the Church as "religious educators," it also reminds the faithful that they were simultaneously theologians of culture and spiritual directors.[36] Also, it has been shown in Orthodox Church history that academic structures can aid in the revitalization of spirituality. A particularly pertinent example would be that of the Russian theological academies which adopted the curriculum of Western Christian education and succeeded through this regimen in rediscovering the riches of Orthodox spirituality.[37]

In the contemporary context, religious educators must also be both theologians of culture and spiritual directors. This implies simultaneously macrocosmic and microcosmic dimensions in their efforts. Since Orthodox spirituality stresses interpersonal relationships so heavily, bringing both aspects together can be quite a challenge. Generally, religious educators must usually relate not just to the culture-at-large but to large groups of people in formulating attitudes. The milieu of contemporary religious educators is unfortunately not the one-to-one situation of the spiritual director but multitudes of students. But without a manifestation of the personal dimension in relating to society as a whole as well as to the needs of individual students, his or her work will bear no fruit.

Working Through the Eucharistic Assembly

The "masses" with which religious educators must interact should be apprehended in terms of the eucharistic assembly and, ultimately,

---

36. For instance, The Feast of the Three Holy Hierarchs (January 30) honoring SS. Basil the Great, Gregory the Theologian, and John Chrysostom is considered a celebration of these Fathers as "religious educators."

37. See particularly George S. Florovsky, *The Ways of Russian Theology*, vol. I (Belmont, Mass.: Nordland, 1980), passim.

the Trinity. These are the only models which guarantee a spirituality which will be both personal and social.[38] In the eucharist, the gathering of the people in a common action reflects the co-penetration of unity and diversity in the Trinity, and the same movement must occur within the classroom. Without an appreciation and respect for the diversity of the assembly in working toward a common goal, the milieu of the Spirit will have no opportunity to manifest itself. As difficult as it may be to attain, religious educators must attempt to practice that same *ascesis* which Maximus the Confessor prescribes when sharing in God's "state of mind," the unique value of each person will be recognized and all loved equally.

Deepening the Educator's Own Faith Commitment

To cultivate such an attitude presupposes a faith commitment on the part of the religious educator. Religious educators who do not believe in what they teach ultimately personify the demonic. Their work could never be considered a calling but rather a profession or even worse, a job. They themselves manifest a dichotomy which a living spirituality overcomes: the divergence between mind and heart. If the work of religious educators proceeds only from the mind without the participation of the heart, the possibility of "practicing what one preaches" becomes less plausible. This, of course, does not mean that religious educators cannot proclaim personal *theologoumena* (theological opinions). There would never be any creativity if this were the case. To remain true to their calling, however, they must reflect the continuity of the corporate experience of the tradition to which they belong. If they cannot, they must relinquish their task.

Creativity on the part of the religious educators implies "the way of the cross." If religious educators hope to relate contemporary culture to theology, they and their personal presentations must undergo a continuous *metanoia*. To attempt to change the world through the experience of God implies suffering, for the world in its fallen state denies this experience. Religious educators take the challenges of the fallen order seriously, for this is the only way culture will be transformed. The suffering, alienation, and confusion which the divisions of the created order cause must be personally recognized and embraced. Only through such a process will religious educators aid in making it possible for the world to become fully eucharistic, i.e., fulfill

---

38. For more on the eucharist as a model for social spirituality, see John Meyendorff, "The Unity of the Church and the Unity of Mankind," in idem., *Living Tradition* (Crestwood, N.Y.: St. Vladimir's Seminary Press, 1979), passim.

its God-given potential. Areas of division which particularly merit the attention of religious educators today include the suffering of those at the mercy of various political-economic systems, the alienation which the ongoing opposition between the sexes continues to bring and the confusion which the scientific-technological establishment has brought to our perception of the created order in general. Like those groups with which religious educators must personally interact, these more abstract social categories must also be perceived in christological, eucharistic, and trinitarian terms.

Service as Focal Point

In bringing about the reformation of the political-economic order so that the transformation of creation proclaimed by the church may be hastened, it is the "persecuted" or those at the mercy of the political-economic order who must receive priority. Religious educators who follow and teach the example of Christ must emphasize a *diakonia* which stresses service to all the persecuted. Solidarity with those who suffer cannot be limited to just those known personally. Because Christ wants all men to be brought into the Kingdom, each human life on earth is of value for each must be given the opportunity to fulfill the potentiality to be another Christ. The obligation not just to see a potential Christ in each person but to treat all as Christ must be stressed. Since suffering means that some exist in a condition inferior to others, the inequality that accompanies suffering must be eradicated for true love cannot tolerate distances.[39] The chief temptation that arises for religious educators when transposing the attitudes which motivate individual acts of charity to encompass large social groups lies in the possible adoption of ideologies spawned by the fallen order in their presentations. A spirituality which becomes identified with only a particular political ideology or social system will inevitably fail.

Within the context of the construction of paradigms for the reconciliation of human beings, the need for a resolution of the serious division between the sexes cannot be neglected by religious educators. Unfortunately, both the development of a sprituality to overcome male/female divisions and discerning what its end result would be do not come easily. Patristic teaching states only that in their reconciliation male and female will not undergo ontological change but that the roles and relationships of men and women will be different. Reli-

---

39. Dumitru Staniloae, "The Orthodox Doctrine of Salvation and its Implications for Christian *Diakonia* in the World Today," in idem., *Theology and the Church* (Crestwood, N.Y.: St. Vladimir's Seminary Press, 1980), pp. 207-9.

gious educators must discover and convey how sexuality enhances spirituality and help disavow the misconception that spirituality ends sexuality. Once again, the eucharistic assembly may serve as a helpful point of departure for the entire problem. Its emphasis on not just diversity and unity but also on the equality of its participants needs to be expanded.

Science and the Religious Educator

Contemporary science often challenges the work of religious educators today by offering its own worldview. Many people look to it as the chief spokesman for reality but paradoxically, its measurement and classification of objects in isolation often undermines its attempts to offer a worldview. Because spiritual educators invariably offer their own holistic vision of the created order, this puts them into conflict with scientists. Science offers a type of abstraction through empiricism which religious educators from the Orthodox tradition find impoverished. It will be recalled that one of the most important mediations of Orthodox spirituality is between the sensible and intelligible, i.e., the empirical and the nonsensory. Science, by its very nature, denies the nonsensory, or at least it has up to the present. A truly spiritual accomplishment on the part of religious educators would be the rapprochement of science with the nonsensory.[40] Entering the realm of applied science or technology, the sacramental character which technological creations can ultimately possess should also be a goal of religious education.

A Summing Up—Facilitating Spirit-filled Lives in Self and in Others

These few examples have been offered to demonstrate how wide is the scope of religious educators' concerns. In other words, their concerns should embrace far more than "religion" and their presentations should convey a living experience of God, both privately and publicly. Many might express disbelief that the seemingly miniscule personal effort that occurs through the relationship of the educator with pupils can change the world let alone the entire cosmos, but there really is no alternative as a beginning. The acquisition of Spirit-filled lives on the part of educator and student is always a personal odyssey, "the way of a

---

40. This may not be as far-fetched as it sounds. Recent discoveries in physics concerning particle-anti-particle symmetry complement the sensible-intelligible view in Orthodox spirituality. See Paulos Gregorios, *The Human Presence: An Orthodox View of Nature* (Geneva: World Council of Churches, 1978), p. 93.

pilgrim." In the process, seekers will encounter many things, persons, and events along the way and it will always be the behavior displayed in these instances which really will determine the future. Because personal spirituality is not a cut-and-dried process but one open to the fluidity of the Spirit, its results and effects cannot be timed or predicted. In order for the spirituality of the true religious educator to triumph, it will always have to struggle to overcome the conventions and misconceptions of the fallen order.

Conclusion

The claim which traditional Orthodox spirituality makes upon not just the individual person but upon humanity, its functions and the environment in which those functions occur, is obviously a total one. To acquire the ability to advance "from glory to glory" means that spiritual education must be a never-ending process not just for the individual but for society as a whole. While the cosmic dimensions of Orthodox spirituality may look attractive in an age when quantum physics and its related disciplines stand at the center of attention, its anthropocentric character may not appear so convincing in a post-Copernican universe. But Orthodox spirituality is anthropocentric precisely because of its positive view of man. There is no other spiritual educator available except man himself. In an age when the discernment of the potential of humankind has itself fallen on hard times, it is instructive to remember the very positive observation of Maximus the Confessor, the inspirer of much that has been written here. He tells us that the incarnation of Christ would have occurred even if the Fall had not.[41] Although the earth did become one of the lost sheep of the universe, Christ was destined to be our educator no matter what. It is not spiritual comfort which we should obtain from this belief but rather a call for spiritual action. As he lived and died with us, he taught us both in word and deed and now that task is ours.

---

41. Meyendorff, *Byzantine Theology*, pp. 160-161.

8

Eastern Spirituality and the Religious Educator

JUSTIN O'BRIEN

Introduction

The Vedas are the most ancient source of human spirituality. They are writings from an oral tradition, more than ten thousand years old, that explored every aspect of reality. These writings are unique in that they expound the insights of enlightened beings, men and women who have attained the transcendental knowledge which constitutes the heart of human spirituality. To speak of the Vedas as Eastern misleads the reader. These writings are not sectarian promotion. They originate and belong to that eternal library of primordial wisdom that composes the Sophia Perennis. From the Vedas have come the Upanishadic literature which discloses the transcendental experiences these authors underwent in their encounter with the absolute—the universal consciousness. From the inspiration of these writings and the quest that is described in them have come many of the Eastern traditions of spirituality. Hinduism, Buddhism, Zen, Sufism, The Tao are spiritual rays that have emanated from the transcendental transformation that occurs in man when he is on the path to ultimate wisdom.

This chapter speaks from the perennial tradition that finds its reflection throughout the various schools of Eastern spirituality. At the very core of the Sophia Perennis is the experience of meditation and

170

contemplation. According to the Vedic experience of meditation, genuine spirituality contains elements of yoga. For yoga is both the means and the state that indicates the soul's union with the divine. Yoga itself is not a religion but the most ancient description of those basic practices that enable man to find the saving knowledge that liberates him into his spiritual existence.

Everyone today faces enormous challenges in attempting to live an intelligent spirituality. Insofar as an individual is a religious educator the task of spirituality spreads wider than personal piety. The professional obligations of his activity require the religious educator to recognize the social and historical configurations of spirituality; otherwise he will be out of touch with the audience. No spirituality thrives in a vacuum, isolated from society's values. The cultural complex of trends, fads, influences, beneficial or not, must become part of the educator's purview. He is obliged, as a professional, to more than sectarian preferences or parochial convictions. Spiritual traditions other than his own favorite may possess a depth whose genuine content can enable him to bring an enrichment to education that exceeds private hopes.

To view other spiritualities a priori as alien would misunderstand the opportunity at hand. Vatican II, as well as the World Council of Churches, has recognized the enduring value of non-Christian spiritual traditions:

> Men look to the various religions for answers to those profound mysteries of the human condition which, today even as in olden times, deeply stir the human heart: What is a man? What is the meaning and the purpose of our life? What is goodness and what is sin? . . . Where lies the path to true happiness? . . . What, finally, is that ultimate and unutterable mystery which engulfs our being, and whence we take our rise, and whither our journey leads us?[1]

Until the trauma and aftermath of World War II, it was intolerable for Christians of major denominations to dialogue with each other, let alone with "pagan" religions. Today, theological seminaries have interfaith faculties. Departments of religions offer credit in world religions. Ministers and priests practice Zen. Catholic nuns start their day with yoga. Divinity students study St. Thomas Aquinas and the Bhagavad Gita, while graduate students in theology take multidenominational

---

1. *Declaration on the Relationship of the Church to Non-Christian Religions*, N. 1, in *The Documents of Vatican II*, ed. Walter M. Abbott, S.J. (New York: America Press, 1966).

courses. For many years the largest proportion of students seeking a doctorate in religious studies at the University of Chicago was Roman Catholic. There are interfaith liturgies and cooperative ventures in biblical translations.

Ecumenically, the solidarity of people as human beings is slowly reaching that level of spiritual insight where no church or sectarian group can claim the exclusive right to divine favor. The Vatican document mentions that "from ancient times down to the present . . . recognition can be found of a Supreme Divinity"[2] among all peoples. It goes without saying that the religious educator must become aware of the ecumenical and cross-cultural currents influencing the spiritual consciousness of people.

In dialogue with these times, let me assume the position of a religious educator who is professionally interested in the nature of spirituality. Let me begin first by questioning some of the cultural assumptions and spiritual notions prevailing today. To this end, I will take as a critical beacon a sapiential perspective and draw upon this boundless tradition of Sophia Perennis. Finally, in part two there is a suggestive, practical program for incorporating a wisdom-inspired, holistic spirituality for daily life.

The Modern Situation

Let us begin by proposing a thesis:

Spirituality, like genuine philosophy, is primarily a way of realization.

It is a matter of being and insight rather than of thought or action. Delineated in this way, the function of spirituality is to rediscover the source—the Sophia Perennis—the summation of sacred knowledge that reveals the ultimate meaning to existence and reinstate man into perfection. Broader than confirming one's proper church membership, the tradition of sacred knowledge has influenced every spiritual legacy bequeathed to mankind.

Confronting this thesis is the dominance of modern culture. Bedazzled by titanic inventions and worried by nuclear anxiety, people forget the sapiential perspective. There are at least three elements that have shaped the attitudes and values of our age: 1) a loss of the sense of living in a sacred cosmos; 2) the technological success of reducing intelligence to reason; 3) a lack of integrating body, mind, and spirit in pursuing a noble existence.

In addition to these opposing currents, the religious educator has to

---

2. Ibid. N. 2.

take into account an unsuspected resistance to the admission of the wisdom tradition coming from Christian quarters. Among many denominations there exists an outright refusal to consider the possibility in human nature for the intelligent assimilation of a saving wisdom. Instead, the highest achievement possible for Christians is adherence to their creedal tenets. It is not difficult to grasp why Christians would harden their stance for the leap of faith when they have cut themselves apart from nature and a global understanding of spirituality. This reluctance is even more strange given the Judaic-Christian origins that included a developing wisdom tradition for centuries up until modern times.

Since the seventeenth century, Western culture has completely secularized matter and thus made nature subservient to man. The result has been the profound imbalances in nature. Our ecological plight has many irretrievable aspects that indict the greed of commerce and marketplace. Western Christianity as a whole endorsed the gulf between man and nature. It sanctioned the exploitation of environment and natural resources by science-technology.

Instead of a sacred world, man now lives in a technologically controlled one. We forget that by deposing nature to our commercial ends prevents our discerning its spirit quality. We are less human for this oppression of the natural realm for we lose the opportunity to quicken the meaning of ourselves. In our attitude toward nature, we reveal the extent of our spiritual values. By removing the sacred from nature, the idea of divinity becomes so abstract and distant that everyday life seems bereft of ultimate significance. Thus, the sentimental forms of inner experience that substitute themselves for sacred knowledge. To abolish the sacred in nature leaves a spiritual vacuum in man's self-understanding.

Modern attempts at spirituality, evidenced by the proliferation of psychospiritual offerings, suffer collectively from the same flaw: They never pass beyond their own subjectivity. The starting point for them is a spiritual half truth, namely, that man is only existential. Existentialism means that man is entirely malleable, lacking an essential order which would give him a universal nature shared by other humans. Put in everyday terms, one hears the axiom: "I do my thing, you do yours." The problem here is a confusion of effect for cause, of manifestation for principle. The grandeur of human creativity and thus spirituality would be reduced to the momentary. My mood at its physical moment of expression becomes the height of value. My identity is the collection of discreet moments of doing my thing. On this basis, intelligence would be just a collection of thoughts, a stream of discontinuous ideas. I think one thought one moment, and another one a moment later. There are no connections between things. There are no possibilities for growth, since growth implies continuity in the same agent. The world offers no unity, only unintelligible diversity.

Without a sense of radical identity, one becomes obsessed with time. Life is pursued without purpose. The intolerable sins are boredom and loneliness. This rather severe appraisal is not an extreme, for many people feel this way today, if not constantly, then at least sufficiently to hold true. There is no ultimate meaning to life for them. This existential anxiety with survival is the easy road to two substitutions. First is the lure of religious fundamentalism. Here are those who find the struggle for meaningful living too harsh. The issues of survival produce so much stress that spirituality becomes an escape from the real world. Second is the fascination with the endless variety of inner experiences. New Age churches, charismatic groups, Eastern religions, and various occult movements vie for the human search of the ultimate meaning to life. People seek out one experience after another, rarely staying long enough to test its validity. Their restless searching seems to confirm that within life there are no absolutes anymore except unstable change. Even the more traditional mainline churches and synagogues cannot elicit the reverence formerly attributed to them.

Institutional spirituality, biblical or sacramental, seems stale and irrelevant to the cultural advances in other areas of human endeavor. The dogmatic truths of mainline spirituality fly in the face of the human condition of uncertainty in life. Scientists remind us of the probability of all knowledge. Truth is ephemeral; devotion to a spiritual ideal appears adolescent. We have entered an era that promotes spiritual nominalism. Your path is no better or worse than mine. It is a gambler's outlook where there are few certainties and these are temporary.

The Spirituality of Reason

Western society is built upon an ethic of work. The inner resource for establishing the types and kinds of work is the faculty of reason. Pervading and justifying the scientific, technological, and commercial advantages in society is the guiding presence and operation of rational thought. The Greek description of humankind as homo sapiens has been eclipsed by our century's designation of homo faber. Man becomes enamored with his rational enterprises. Transfixed by the possibilities of success, he gradually shrinks his spirit to the exclusive demands of discursive approval. Implicit here is the denial that there could be cognitive activity superior to reason. Reason in its modes of business, science, medicine, education becomes so impressed with its success, it tends to generalize. When reason forgets its inherent restrictions in any of its aforesaid specialities, it announces occasional assurances like Bertrand Russell's radio message that "what science cannot tell us, mankind cannot know."[3]

Reason depends for its lifeblood upon the senses. Without sense impressions supplying food for thought, reason is out of work, even starving. In and through the senses, reason knows the material world. Our sensible environment is for nearly everyone the most real of realities. We will tolerate the mistakes, omissions, confusions, and contradictions of reason so long as it keeps its contact with the sensuous real world. Given the pressures of our values in the culture in which we live, reason has made sensual materialists of us all.

This predicament can never be manageable for the way it confines the human spirit. The religious educator would not question the self-evident validity of reason, only its comprehension of reality. Is discursive thought adequate to the diverse task of knowing reality? Is the human spirit's highest aspirations expressed in scientific reasoning? Is society's hope for a safe future best assured by technological control?

Under the contours that rationality assumes in Western culture, people need to bifurcate their lives to make tenuous sense out of them. Spiritual ways have to separate themselves into compartments, scheduled, as it were, at off-hours away from the mainstream of daily living. The rationality of the work world seems to have little in common with the discursive activities expected of spiritual endeavors.

The Problem of Culture and History for Spirituality

People cannot be blamed for seeking individual maps for locating the spiritual meaning of life. Almost every institutional form of spirituality has embarrassed itself by arriving at the pragmatic conclusion that certain parts of its spiritual program are impotent or useless.

The shock of coming to grips with a tenet or ascetic practice that no longer moves its followers forces revision. Spiritual paths occur in history and history does not stand still. The seasons may repeat themselves, but the cultural consciousness of any epoch does not replay itself. When spirituality is removed from its cultural contours and its historical context then one will find himself in a wilderness speaking and listening only to his ego.

---

3. Quoted in *Beyond the Post-Modern Mind* by Houston Smith (New York: Crossroads, 1982), p. 163.

The Forgotten Truth

According to the ancients, spirituality never originates within history. If it did, then it could not lift man beyond his own condition. Spirituality in its essence exists, first and foremost, outside of time and space. It is a given; a revelation takes place. Something within man is stirred beyond his rational anticipations. It is ineffable because it exceeds the imagination as well as conceptualization. One is taken beyond the everyday rational ways of dealing with life. Yet the experience is profoundly intelligible. The mind meets its origin face to face. In that encounter there is no darkness left, no unanswered questions, no hesitations about the meaning of life.

> Man reaches a stage where he sees
> nothing but God; see how exalted
> is that station of manhood.[4]
>   Sa'di, Persian poet

And the later echo of this experience in the Christian mystic, Ruysbroeck reads,

> Enlightened men are . . . lifted above reason into a bare and imageless vision wherein lies the eternal indrawing summons of the Divine Unity. . . . There, their bare understanding is drenched through by the Eternal Brightness.[5]

Sages, mystics, holy men and women have described it variously, for no description fits. One is forced into metaphors and analogies that evoke a glimpse, and fade like fireworks.

The quest of spirituality purports to clarify the meaning of life in its final perspective. It is not a theoristic undertaking. It is not an analysis of ideas. The goal of spirituality is nothing less than sacred knowledge, a knowledge that resides outside concepts and symbols.

There is a natural propensity for man to seek objective reality, to build a life based on the truth of things. But knowing the truth about life does not imply a psychological accommodation but a recognition of the world and beauty of things. In their rightful place created realities are indispensable aids for man to finish his spiritual journey.

With his empirical vision of the world, man forms his career. But his

---

4. The Persian poet Sa'di, quoted in *Knowledge and the Sacred* by Seyyed Hossein Nasr (New York: Crossroad, 1981), p. 182.
5. *The Adornment of the Spiritual Marriage* by Jan van Ruysbroeck, translated by C. A. Wymschenck, Dom. (London: Dent and Sons, 1916), p. 185.

eyes, in time, become myopic. The optics of his vision compress the horizon of life within the radius of self-made boundaries. He accustoms himself to a certain range of activities, and the experiences within these rational boundaries form his orientation to life's meaning. Amidst the business of everyday duties is the lost wonder that nature as well as history is an illuminating icon. The manifested world reveals divinity. The sages do not experience our insecurity. They recognize that life develops according to universal laws, for these are the dynamic expressions of the divine universe. An impeachable order prevails. Much like the way gravity exerts its universal pressure upon all bodies, the cosmic universe insinuates its ordering presence upon the intelligence of man.

The cosmos may be compared to an intelligible prism in which man's arts and sciences are but refracted rays of the divine light. It is the light that eventually draws man rather than the surface colors of the prism.

The prism metaphor is one among many that may stimulate the spiritual man to remember his divine calling. For the spiritual man, the cosmos is replete with active, symbolic meanings. To assume a symbolic essence to water, for example, is not to disregard its chemical properties, but to penetrate into the further significance of its spiritual character. Scientific knowledge of the real can become a transparent episode to the wonder of its origin. Everything in nature reveals to the eye that sees an epiphany of the sacred.

> Upon the face of every green leaf
> is inscribed for the people of
> perspicacity, the wisdom of the
> Creator.[6]

Sufi poem

In similar words, a medieval mystic says,

> Whoever, therefore, is not enlightened
> by such splendor of created things
> is blind;
> whoever is not awakened by such
> outcries is deaf;
> whoever does not praise God because
> of all these effects is dumb;
> whoever does not discover the First

---

6. Nasr, *Knowledge and the Sacred*, p. 215.

Principle from such clear signs is
a fool.[7]

St. Bonaventure

Life within a Cosmic Context

One begins a new recognition of nature by repositioning his attitudes to matter. The slime of earth is the cosmic dust out of which God brought forth his image and likeness and everything else that can inspire man to expand his horizon.

One lives in a cosmic drama. The conviction is not the romantic autopsy on a primitive myth. Its worth is the recognition that the myth never died but only suffered from neglect. The return to sacred knowledge agrees with the Greek wisdom that the cosmos, the real of earth and stars, is alive with soul and intelligence.[8] The daily, particularized experience of the cosmos can evoke for the religious educator the intimation that the events of his life possess more than a humdrum regularity. There is a sacred significance to obvious mundane appearances. The same daily routine can reveal a hidden luminosity. Placed within the light of a cosmic context, life and career beckon to find richer meanings. There exists an overall harmony and dynamic equilibrium that is very difficult to discern at times. During catastrophes that produce extraordinary turmoil and human suffering, the recognition of the cosmic character of life provokes only angry denunciations. God, the divine providence, and the world as a holy symbol are repudiated. Under the stress of the irrationality of the times, feeling the cruel course of history, few can sense the presence of wisdom in the torn order of the world.

Yet these personal and historical moments are required for wisdom to ripen. Not from divine punishment but from the consequence of his own folly does man undergo his absurd thoughts and actions. The churnings of the cosmos are not wicked, waiting patiently to trap man in his ambitions. He, on the contrary, from childhood years to senior citizenship, forges his own destiny. Within the cosmos there are unlimited possibilities for success or failure. But there is always a continuity between thought, speech, and action. The order is there untouched by the unpredictability of historical events. The intelligible order is stronger than the calculated chaos perpetrated by those acts and omissions,

---

7. *The Soul's Journey unto God* by Saint Bonaventure, trans. E. Cousins. (Indianapolis: Bobbs-Merrill, 1946), p. 67.
8. Plato, *Timaeus* 30 B.C. in *The Collected Dialogues of Plato*, ed. Edith Hamilton and Hougton Cairns (New York: Pantheon Books, 1963), p. 1163.

the sins of the human race, that afflict the hourly ambitions of every land. The cosmos is not for admiration. Its order is a symbol for liberation, for divine wisdom frees man from the chaos of stressful existence. The cosmological order expresses the divine intent. This supreme action has been beautifully portrayed in every spiritual tradition that traces its lineage to the Sophia Perennis.

An Ancient Perspective on Spirituality

What does Eastern spirituality have to say to the modern problems of Western man? Let us place the world of travail entirely within the context of ancient wisdom:

> The foolish run after outward pleasures and
> fall into snares of vast-embracing death.
> But the wise have found immortality
> and do not seek the eternal in things
> that pass away.[9]
>
> Katha Upanishad

The pursuit of life demands actions. These actions or *karma* produce consequences that affect the doer. In this way man forges his spiritual history as well as his destiny. Likewise, society.

All spiritual life is the search for union. Man seeks to unite himself to his highest aspiration. This lifelong task is the essence of yoga, for yoga means union. Yoga admits the human condition but refuses to endorse its finality. The spiritual life leads to perfection, i.e., where all the dimensions of man's nature are harmoniously unified. Thus the life of yoga is at the very heart of ancient wisdom. It orders man to himself and to the universe. Yoga believes that in knowing the eternal order, one's spirit achieves the freedom that the world cannot give. While it recognizes the pains of life, yoga refuses to accept their bondage. Compromises with the stress and strain of modern living are tolerated for awhile, but the goal is their extinguishment. For who can be happy in distress?

Spirituality from the yoga perspective may be described as the alleviation of misery in all its forms. This removal is permanent. The use of the negative form in describing spirituality's goal is deliberately chosen in order to imply a profound positivity. When the aches and pains of life are resolved, then man in his undisturbed clarity of soul will be himself. In that equilibrium of self-knowledge he will have

---

9. The Katha Upanishad in *The Upanishads*, trans. Juan Mascaro (England: Penguin, 1965), p. 62.

completed his soul's quest; he will know himself as the *atman*. And who is the *atman*? Let the Bhagavad Gita speak:

> He who dwells in the earth, yet is other than earth,
> He who dwells in the waters, yet is other than water,
> He who dwells in the moon and stars, yet is other than moon
>   and stars,
> He who dwells in all beings, yet is other than all beings,
> He is the unseen peer, the unheard hearer,
> The unthought thinker, the unknown knower.
> There is no other seer,
> There is no other bearer,
> There is no other thinker,
> There is no other knower,
> Than he.
> He is your atman, the inner controller,
> The immortal.[10]

Lest anyone doubt the force of this ancient revelation, the sage adds:

Anything else is the cause of suffering.[11]

Suffering anywhere, anytime is, according to the Buddha, the ultimate problem for the human race. Yet suffering is not an esoteric puzzle. It has a cause—ignorance—and thus can be obliterated. Many spiritualities have genuine elements in the description of their path, but how many assert the final absence of suffering this side of death? From this perspective, yoga, or the path of sapiential spirituality, may be described as the sacred science of liberation. Crucial here is the beginning insight that we are not talking about a speculative knowledge or enforced by authority. The concern of yoga is emancipation from the fundamental ignorance regarding the ultimate purpose of life that seems to shroud mankind.

Lured by the attractions of success, ambition burns in the heart of man. The flame of accomplishment can consume the energies of mind and body, twisting the spiritual thrust for good and beauty. The Spiritual man needs *viveka*, which is discrimination to know his limits and not live from his fantasies. The phenomenal universe, nature and her

---

10. The Brhadaranyaka Upanishad 3.9.26 in *The Vedic Experience Mantramanjari*, trans. Raimundo Pannikkar (Berkeley: University of California Press, 1977), p. 709.
11. Ibid.

products, the unlimited potentialities for modifying culture are the beckoning allurements that yoga calls *maya*.

There stands spiritual man: a being in the world, surrounded and stimulated by multiple opportunities for involvement. Man chooses. His act reshapes culture and himself. Then, tired from the chase of the chosen goal, he wilts *(tamas)*. Restored, he embarks enthusiastically once again, determined to succeed *(rajas)*. Finally he succeeds, resting content with his latest prize *(sattva)*. The reflecting upon his success or failure, he starts anew, and so it continues. These three conditions of man's attitude show up variously as he goes about the tasks of life. Choices and habits bind man to his decisions and their consequences. The karmic merry-go-round of life rolls on, keeping man in bondage to the pleasures and pains of its endless turning. How does one get off?

Transfixed by the excitement of being in the world, man forgets his spiritual heart. He capitulates to distractions, diversions, procrastinations, and all the other vicissitudes of human existence. Almost lost amid compelling enterprises, there flickers at times a faint questioning of the excesses of life. Something within prompts a new series of questions about the meaning of life. The party is over. Like sobering up from a bad dream, man begins critically to examine his long engagement with *maya*. Am I only a body? Is the aquisition of money or prestige the true goal of life? If my self is only chemicals and electric reflexes, how can I even ask these questions?

Eastern spirituality—including Hinduism, Buddhism, The Tao, and Sufism—recognizes that people progress in stages through the awakening process. Each has his own story to tell. But more and more the world becomes appraised from the vantage of the spirit. When the world is properly correlated with man's spirit, then human life becomes the occasion for total fulfillment.

Slowly man becomes convinced that the indiscriminate involvement with thoughts and things misshapes his development of spirituality. He feels the need to bring his own life into balance. A growing integration of body, mind, and spirit involves a reassessment of his attitude toward the external world. Instead of being embroiled in a culture of ineluctable change and a restless craving to be fashionable, he begins to measure the dispensation of his energies by their impact on his health and well-being. He enters into himself, discovering an inner life of awareness that extends to his public role. His improving health and calmness allow a better quality of choices only wished for in the past. He becomes a man of meditation, that inner journey that reveals the plentitude of life.

When the wise knows that it is through
the great and omnipresent Spirit in us
that we are conscious in waking or in dreaming,
then he goes beyond sorrow.[12]

Meditation is the spirit's indwelling upon itself. It is the strongest fount for the spiritual life. Without meditation man will never grasp the significance of the life-force that throbs within his body. Most people are only aware of their imagination. This range of awareness still keeps man in the dark about himself. Unless he turns inward, there is no escape from the turmoils of life. Spirituality can become a burden within a stress-filled society.

The mind gives only partial insights into the meaning of life. This level of awareness cannot fulfill one's highest spiritual aspirations. Just as the mystics have said that God cannot be grasped by images or concepts, likewise, to know the most profound dimensions of human nature is not available to the efforts of reason.

When one meditates, there emerges a new sense of calmness. This sense of tranquility is not magic nor is it an external gift from the outside. Meditation is self-generated, but it exceeds the boundaries of the individual mind. Hence, the spirit expands its presence. Pain confines a man to his disorder. Meditation lifts man past his sorrow. The spirit knows its immortal nature in the experience of meditation. But this living insight does not come immediately. First, the person has to struggle with settling the body in a comfortable position. Then the emotional impulses need to be assuaged. Finally the rumblings of the mind are quietly bypassed. One enters after a while into that region of inner life that lies on the other side of the rational mind. Here in the region of pure spirit the conscious life-force discovers its inner source.

Meditation is thwarted by the constant externalizing of the mental life-force. Man needs to recognize his value not only in the external world, building family and career, but he needs to balance his efforts to live an intelligent and successful life by returning to his inner source. Spirituality requires balance and discrimination. The basis of these qualities is self-control, and self-control is impossible without knowing the workings of the mind and its higher capacities. Meditation opens the door to the dynamics of consciousness. A transformation over time occurs enlivening and stimulating the latent forces of man's nature. These forces emerge in the person as qualities of inde-

---

12. The Katha Upanishad 5, *The Upanishads*, p. 64.

pendence from worldly cravings and illusions. An unsuspected self-reliance develops which gives man intuitive power to use with his rational skills. He becomes aware of himself as a free being, able to order his energies for the benefit of society.

Part II
Practical Implications for the Religious Educator

To summarize Eastern spirituality and make more explicit the consequences of the Sophia Perennis, let us compose the following theses and include the practical implications for the spiritual growth of the religious educator.

1. All Being, in principle, is knowable and unified.

This inclusion of "all" takes into account the unmanifested regions of reality that are not sensibly nor rationally discernable. The manifested event of being can be subsumed under the symbol of cosmos. The Greek worldview recognized this basic intuition regarding the world and lived from it. Later it was lost unfairly in the cultural circumstances of the last three hundred years.

The religious educator lives in a modern world that resists looking upon itself as an ordered whole. Evolutionists insist that our present world is an unchartered circumstance of blind forces and mechanical necessity. Like it or not, man has no essence, nature has no intrinsic purposes, and the future is fickle to human ambition. In the words of a Nobel laureate, "man knows at last that he is alone in the indifferent immensity of the universe whence he has emerged by chance."[13]

The cosmos is as real today as it was for the ancients. If the religious educator probes carefully enough, he would see that the complexity of forces and processes reveal purposes that are intelligible and supportive to the human aspiration to comprehend existence. The scientific eye sees too dimly, unaware of its constrictive view. It literally overlooks the splendor of the cosmos. When Einstein spoke of the grandeur of the universe, he was speaking from a broader view than his categories of relativity theory.

From blazing ardor Cosmic Order came and Truth;

> From thence was born the obscure night;
> From thence the Ocean with its billowing waves. . . .

---

13. J. Monod, *Le Hasard et la Necessité* (Paris: Editions du Seuil, 1970), p. 195.

Then, as before, did the creator fashion
The Sun and Moon, the Heaven and the Earth,
The atmosphere and the domain of light.[14]

Exceedingly wise, exceedingly strong is the Designer.
He is Creator, Disposer, Epiphany supreme.[15]

The cosmos reveals an intelligibility that can be apprehended at varying levels. The faculty of reason in its scientific expression can be certain in its knowledge but not comprehensive. The beneficial use of reason in a scientific way cannot, however, penetrate to the ultimate intelligibility of the cosmos. This deficiency in reason does not hamper its normal occupation with the everyday business of earning a living and raising a family.

By entering into meditation, the religious educator gradually realizes that there is more to his mind than his reasoning power. The perceptive quality of his mind changes, allowing for a breadth and acuteness toward the world that exceeds the dexterity of reason alone. Meditation affects a transformation of consciousness in the religious educator that now touches his self-understanding and the way he views life and its challenges. It goes without saying that this change in consciousness will color his teaching responsibilities.

Meditation awakes the dormant faculty of intellect. This intuitive power enables the religious educator to recognize that the literal, scientific way of appraising the world actually hides symbolic aspects. Reason in its discursive operations is less susceptible than intellect in recognizing the symbolic dimension in reality. The faculty of intellect, the spiritual eye of man, makes use of rational concepts as symbols to describe with certitude the sacred knowledge about reality. All the truths of reason have an inner connection, which reason cannot discern, to the vaster unity of sapiential truth, which the intellect does discern. Spirituality, prepared for by reason, pertains primarily to the intellect. It is the business of the intellect to detect the universal laws found in the cosmos that relate to man's spiritual progress. These laws exist embedded, as it were, amid the dynamics of the cosmos. When the religious educator has experienced life sufficiently, he begins to discern them. To paraphrase a scriptural axiom: When the eye is ready, it will see what has always been there to see. It is the religious educator's responsibility to pursue the cosmos at the various levels of its intelligibility and arrive at the basic unity in the diversity of existences.

---

14. The Rig Veda, 10.190. in Pannikkar, *The Vedic Experience*, p. 60.
15. The Rig Veda, 10.82, ibid., p. 812.

This growing sense of discrimination between the levels of reality and integrating that awareness is only possible when the religious educator contrives his inner growth through meditation. For it is the act of his meditation that stimulates the mind to perceive the richer symbolic dimensions of life.

2. Human nature is a dynamic composite of body, mind, and spirit.

The human spirit equals consciousness, which is the enlivening force for the entire human entity and the living principle behind the cosmos. The cosmos exists and is intelligible only because it is a partial manifestation of the order of divine consciousness. The religious educator can know himself at any level of his nature—sense, mental, intuitional—precisely because he shares with mankind the same spirit of consciousness that brought the world into actuality. In fact, the religious educator discerns the unity of his personal nature with the human community the more he enters into himself and discovers the source of the unity. In a way, the spiritual life involves man's intelligence recognizing itself, its essence, in the cosmic unfolding of nature and history.

The human constitution is not a machine, as Descartes, Hobbes, and behavioral psychology would have it, any more than a machine is a living organism. The mind is not a by-product (à la Carl Sagan) of the brain, any more than thoughts are subject to the law of gravity.

The question for the religious educator today is to recover the whole person in meeting life. He needs to recognize that the most ordinary activities of rest, bathing, eating, playing, and exercising have decisive results upon man's spiritual journey. In all things, he must give rein to himself as a *satya-kama*, a truth seeker, in life. Divine consciousness projects itself as the cosmos and man's adventure is to grasp the projection and penetrate its truth to its infinite source.

3. Man is a psychosomatic unity.

To speak this way about homo sapiens gives us the first clue of how to proceed in the study of spiritual awakening. Nothing in man's make-up is superfluous. The religious educator can discern the mineral, vegetative, animal, mental and intuitional or intellectual features. The material of man's body is unique. It is living matter. The assimilation of matter involves a transformation that enlivens matter so that it enters the domain of spirit. These features comprise an organismic whole.

Sapiential spirituality is growth by degrees. Respectful of the ordered make-up of his nature, the religious educator needs to become acutely aware of its interrelationships in daily life. The first general law of his being that needs reckoning is the reciprocity of mind and body. His bodily feelings make inroads upon his thoughts, which in turn affect his bodily disposition. His thought extends itself through his body; his body needs enlist his mind. It is not spirit against matter. The body is essentially good in every way. It is the medium for the creative expression of the mind. It incarnates the spirit.

The psychosomatic unity of body and mind opposes all schools of materialism in biology and psychology. Consequently, to neglect either side in this unity imbalances the other. Asceticism is built upon a sound understanding of physiology and psychology and the peculiar circumstances of the individual's constitution in society. One may recommend fasting to a monk on retreat, but the same advice to a mother at home with three small children may prove a hazard to her health.

In recognizing that what occurs with his body is not incidental to his spirit, the religious educator revises his appreciation for matter. In sapiential spirituality, the body is appraised as a temple of the spirit. The way he treats it—eating, recreating, posture, personal hygiene— is a revelation of his self-appraisal. As an educator, how he regards his body is unavoidably communicated to his students.

4. *The mind as the rational-spiritual principle can assume direction over the entire body.*

The entire autonomic processes, from cell repair to the aging process is capable of being under man's volitional direction. The reason for this unorthodox statement is that the spirit pervades the body. The spirit is immune from entropy. Every tissue in every organ can be influenced by the mind. This should not seem impossible when one considers that the normal activities of most of the bodily or metabolic processes proceed in their operations with reasonable order and consistency. Digestion, like cell reproduction, occurs not in a haphazard manner.

Improvement of these "automatic" processes is possible by various exercises. Exercise of the cardiovascular system, for example, tones up many of these visceral functions, rendering the person with a true sense of more energy. The adage "what you don't use, you lose" holds demonstrably true as we grow older. Therefore, spirituality places a priceless regard upon the necessity to preserve health. Thirty minutes a day on exercising the body does not seem too severe a price to pay for diseaseless longevity.

The body thrives upon exercise and man needs three kinds as he matures: the toning of his cardiovascular system through aerobics; the slow stretching of all the major areas through hatha yoga postures; and sufficient isometric stimulation of the upper-body muscles.

The religious educator is much more responsive to the mind's plans for itself when he is in sound physical condition. His bodily coordination even improves the mind's attention span and vice versa. Neglect of the bodily exercise needs will eventually impair the mental acuity. A weakened constitution and avoidable illness are not the signs of a robust spirituality. In sapiential spirituality, man's essential nature is at peace with itself. But this tranquility of order between body, mind, and spirit is a daily self-responsibility for the religious educator.

5. *The body is entirely within the mind but the mind is not entirely within the body.*

Here is where the sapiential tradition separates itself from contemporary views on the range of consciousness. The mind has a relative dependence upon the body while the body has an essential, indispensable dependence upon the mind. The body reflects the mind-set of an individual; it is the mind's instrument, as it were, for sensually contacting reality and promoting mental intentions. The mind can gradually expand its directive control over every portion of the body and thus increase and improve its biological longevity. Physical health and emotional integration are within the mind's capacities.

This spiritual tradition disagrees with the current medical model of man's capacities. The body is viewed as being, in principle, completely under the sole direction of the mind. The implication here is that the unknown areas of the body and the subconscious mind can be integrated into spiritual awareness. The trained ability to bring the contents and force of the subconscious or unconsciousness reveals further the holistic nature of sapiential spirituality. The more the religious educator can enter into his inner life, the more his spirit reveals its treasures. Revelation here includes integration. The negative side of the person is rebalanced, purified, as this integration takes place.

Before this wondrous integration can occur, there are certain preliminaries that require fulfillment. The customary relationship of the body-mind complex is too slack in most people. The sensitivity of each level requires a basic toning. This general conditioning is aided by keeping the body clean and fit. Regular exercise as indicated and especially learning how to relax and reduce the stress of life are necessary.

Genuine spirituality induces a tranquil mind. Stressful living is a malfunction. The religious educator cannot expect integration to transpire unless he learns to cope with stress. The goal here is to eliminate the disorder of stress entirely from his person. This achievement is not unrealistic. Most stress arises from habits now rooted in the subconscious realm. Stressful habits of reacting to challenges can become automatic. The religious educator's developing art of meditation allows for the clearing of these habitual responses by witnessing to their reappearance in thought. By remaining calm and regulating the integration of mind and body through proper breathing and concentration, the religious educator slowly comes to recognize the inner predicament for what it is: self-made stress. The practice of meditation dissolves the attachment for these habits, freeing the energy of the subconscious for more positive judgments.

6. *The human being is a microcosm whose normal expansion is the cosmos.*

Physical sciences have established that the various elements, compounds, and energies of nature are part of the human constitution. There is nothing in the cosmos that is not also found in human nature. Sapiential spirituality further insists that there is nothing beyond the cosmos that is not also in human nature.

The religious educator must see himself as complete but unfinished. He inherently possesses the ingredients to reach his ultimate vocation. It is a growth process that passes through integrative stages. Optimal development and spiritual maturity for the religious educator consists in the discovery of the natural order within his nature through the actualizing of these natural powers. The natural powers are stratified at the physical, emotional, mental, and supramental levels. The principle of unity is his consciousness. At each level of his being, from the physical to the intuitional, the presence of consciousness asserts its power and enables him to undergo varying cognitive, unifying experiences. By knowing the expansion of his consciousness, man realizes the spiritual unity he has with the cosmos. He abuses this relationship at his own peril. The current ecological crisis is just such an illustration.

7. *The aim of life is the self-realization of the truth of happiness.*

According to yoga, human nature inherently possesses the requirements for finishing the purpose of life. It is a practical process that systematically leads one from gross levels of experience to subtler dimensions of awareness. In this process of spiritual ripening, the religious educator gains experiential knowledge of the fundamental laws of being. In exercising these laws, he goes through a transformation in consciousness that opens his soul to his inner awareness. The process of transformation is a dynamic expansion that revises his attitudes toward culture and nature. He loses his fear of life and discovers a strength of purpose and serenity that can see him through any and all catastrophes.

For the religious educator, it is the more healthy display of his lifestyle that convinces the skeptical reserve of his students of this wisdom. Throughout the way, the journey is a personal critique of the disciplines involved. A definite ordering of experience takes place that goes beyond the ordinary limits of reason, but yet remains intensely intelligible. He discovers in experience that spirituality is a science.

More than anything else the practice of meditation achieves the spiritual transformation. Spirituality is not primarily a matter of being actively involved with the frustrations of society. Nor is spirituality incompatible with developing a social consciousness. But intense activity in social improvement is not equivalent to renewing the spiritual life. This tendency in our age to assume spirituality in terms of public protest against human oppression is meritorious when not exaggerated. However, the height of spirituality is not political reform. The religious educator is interested in a life of wisdom. Wisdom is holiness. It is first a transformative vision that makes him aware of his divine identity. From that holy vision action results appropriately. From that vision, he sees life charged with meaning hitherto undisclosed.

In the expansion of his consciousness, man's body and mind are appreciated as profound instruments. His internal harmony in knowing the purpose of life shows itself in the way he goes about the life. United as he is to the source of life, he sees and treats others as himself. For the integration of all his levels of being expands this consciousness to include in its care the entire universe. In meditation, the religious educator lives in the atmosphere of immortality.

> There is a spirit which is pure and which is beyond old age and death, beyond hunger and thirst and sorrow. . . . This is the atman, the spirit in man. . . . He who has found and knows his spirit has found all the worlds, has achieved all his desires.[16]

---

16. Chandogya Upanishad 8.7 in Mascaro, *The Upanishads*, p. 121.

Profiles of Contributors

JAMES MICHAEL LEE is Professor of Education at the University of Alabama at Birmingham. He was born in Brooklyn, New York, and is a layman. He received his doctorate from Columbia University. Three of Professor Lee's many books are *The Shape of Religious Instruction* (Religious Education Press, 330 pp.), *The Flow of Religious Instruction* (Religious Education Press, 379 pp.), and *The Content of Religious Instruction* (Religious Education Press, 814 pp.). His articles have appeared in numerous journals including *Religious Education, Living Light,* and *Review for Religious.* Dr. Lee is listed in *Who's Who in the World, Who's Who in America,* and *Who's Who in Religion.*

LEON McKENZIE is Associate Professor of Education at the University of Indiana. He was born in Chicago and is a layman. He received his doctorate from Indiana Univeristy. Three of Dr. McKenzie's books are *The Religious Education of Adults* (Religious Education Press, 256 pp.), *Creative Learning for Adults* (Twenty-Third Publishers, 185 pp.), and *Adult Education and the Burden of the Future* (University Press of America, 96 pp.). His articles have appeared in many journals including *Adult Education, Living Light,* and *Lifelong Learning.*

RANDOLPH CRUMP MILLER is Horace Bushnell Professor Emeritus of Christian Education in the Divinity School of Yale University.

He was born in Fresno, California, and is a priest of the Protestant Episcopal Church. He received his doctorate from Yale University. Three of Professor Miller's numerous books are *The Theory of Religious Education Practice* (Religious Education Press, 312 pp.), *This We Can Believe* (Hawthorne Books, 200 pp.), and *The American Spirit in Theology* (United Church Press, 253 pp.). His articles have appeared in a wide variety of journals including *Religious Education, Anglican Theological Review,* and *Christian Century.* Dr. Miller is listed in *Who's Who in America* and in *Who's Who in the East.*

JOANMARIE SMITH is Associate Professor of Christian Education at the Methodist Theological School in Ohio. She was born in New York City and is a religious of the Congregation of Saint Joseph. She receive her doctorate from Fordham University. Three of Sister Smith's recent books are *Morality Made Simple But Not Easy* (Argus, 119 pp.), *Modeling God* (Paulist, 92 pp.) which she co-authored, and *(Aesthetic Dimensions of Religious Education* (Paulist, 235 pp.) which she co-edited. Her articles have appeared in such journals as *Who's Who in American Education, Directory of American Scholars,* and *Contemporary Authors.*

M. BASIL PENNINGTON is a member of St. Joseph's Abbey. He was born in Brooklyn, New York, and is a monk-priest of the Order of Cistercians of the Strict Observance (Trappists). He received licentiates from both the Pontifical University Gregorianum and the Pontifical University St. Thomas Aquinas. Three of his recent books include *Centering Prayer* (Doubleday, 222 pp.), *The Eucharist Yesterday and Today* (Crossroad, 140 pp.), and *Called: New Thinking on Christian Vocation* (Seabury, 107 pp.). Father Pennington's articles have appeared in a wide variety of journals including *Jurist, Cistercian Studies,* and *America.* He is listed in the *Academie Française de Reim, American Catholic Who's Who,* and *Contemporary Authors.*

WILLIAM E. REISER is Associate Professor of Religious Studies at the College of the Holy Cross. He was born in Hartford, Connecticut, and is a priest of the Society of Jesus. He received his doctorate from Vanderbilt University. Three of his recent books are *What Are They Saying About Dogma?* (Paulist, 86 pp.), *The Potter's Touch* (Paulist, 92 pp.), and *Into the Needle's Eye* (Ave Maria Press, 144 pp.). Among the journals in which Dr. Reiser's articles have appeared are *Spirituality Today, Heythrop Journal,* and *Thomist.*

ANDREW J. SOPKO is Assistant Professor of Theology at Loyola Univeristy of Chicago. He was born in Sewickley, Pennsylvania, and is a layman. He received his doctorate from the University of London. He is the author of the book *Gregory of Cyprus* (Center for Patristic Studies at Thessaloniki in Greece). Dr. Sopko's articles have appeared in *Greek Orthodox Theological Review* and in *St. Vladimir's Theological Quarterly.*

JUSTIN O'BRIEN is a senior faculty member at the Himalayan International Institute of Yoga Science and Philosophy. He was born in Chicago and is a layman. He received his doctorate from the University of Nijmegen. Three of his recent books are *Yoga and Christianity* (Himalayan Publishers, 105 pp.), *Running and Breathing* (CSA Press, 165 pp.), and *Toward a Theory of Religious Consciousness* (University of Nijmegen, 275 pp.). Dr. O'Brien's articles have appeared in such journals as *Dharma, Dawn,* and *Man and Development.*

Index of Names

Index of Subjects